Drive Around

Thomas
Cook

Dordogne

& Western France

YOUR GUIDE TO GREAT DRIVES

Titles in this series include:

- Andalucía and the Costa del Sol
- Australia
- Bavaria and the Austrian Tyrol
- Brittany and Normandy
- Burgundy and the Rhône Valley
- California
- Canadian Rockies
- Catalonia and the Spanish Pyrenees
- Dordogne and Western France
- England and Wales
- Florida
- Ireland
- Languedoc and Southwest France
- Loire Valley
- New England
- New Zealand
- Northern Italy & Italian Lakes
- Portugal
- Provence and the Côte d'Azur
- Scotland
- Tuscany and Umbria
- Vancouver and British Columbia
- Washington DC, Virginia, Maryland and Delaware

For further information about these and other Thomas Cook publications, write to Thomas Cook Publishing, PO Box 227, The Thomas Cook Business Park, 9 Coningsby Road, Peterborough PE3 8SB, United Kingdom.

Drive Around

Dordogne
& Western France

The best of the Dordogne's lofty
châteaux, fortified medieval towns
and green mountain slopes, plus
the vineyards of the Bordeaux
region and the beaches of Biarritz
and the Atlantic Coast

Eric and Ruth Bailey

Thomas Cook
Publishing
www.thomascookpublishing.com

Written by Eric and Ruth Bailey, updated by David Browne
Driving information by Michael Hafferty
Original photography by Image Select International/Chris Fairclough Colour Library

Published by Thomas Cook Publishing
A division of Thomas Cook Tour Operations Limited.
Company registration no. 1450464 England
The Thomas Cook Business Park, Unit 9, Coningsby Road,
Peterborough PE3 8SB, United Kingdom
E-mail: books@thomascook.com, Tel: + 44 (0) 1733 416477
www.thomascookpublishing.com

Produced by Cambridge Publishing Management Limited
Burr Elm Court, Main Street, Caldecote CB23 7NU

ISBN: 978-1-84848-014-8

© 2005, 2007 Thomas Cook Publishing
This third edition © 2009
Text © Thomas Cook Publishing
Road maps supplied and designed by Lovell Johns Ltd, OX8 8LH
Road maps generated from Collins Bartholomew Digital Database © Collins Bartholomew Ltd, 1999
City maps prepared by RJS Associates, © Thomas Cook Publishing

Series Editor: Adam Royal
Production/DTP: Steven Collins

Printed and bound in India by Replika Press Pvt Ltd

Cover photography: Front: © Fantuz Olimpio, 4Corners Images. Back: © Thomas Cook

About the authors

Eric and Ruth Bailey first met as trainee journalists on a provincial English newspaper. They went their separate professional ways until their paths converged some years later, when they married and formed a freelance travel-writing team that has so far produced 16 books and countless articles for magazines and newspapers. Their travels have taken them across Canada from coast to coast and along the Eastern seaboard of the United States from Maine to Florida. They have also travelled extensively in Ireland, Mexico and Southern Africa. They are inland waterway enthusiasts and are passionately interested in rural life and dogs.

Acknowledgements

The authors would like to thank Helena Aldis, the Comité Régionale de Tourisme d'Aquitaine, the French Government Tourist Office in London, Holiday Autos, London Stansted Airport, Ryanair, Geoff and Maureen Smith and the staff of tourism offices throughout the region who so readily assisted in the research for this guide.

Contents

About Drive Around Guides

Thomas Cook's Drive Around Guides are designed to provide you with a comprehensive but flexible reference source to guide you as you tour a country or region by car. This guide divides the Dordogne and Western France into touring areas – one per chapter. Major cultural centres or cities form chapters in their own right. Each chapter contains enough attractions to provide at least a day's worth of activities – often more.

Ratings

To make it easier for you to plan your time and decide what to see, every area is rated according to its attractions in categories such as Architecture, Entertainment and Children.

Chapter contents

Every chapter has an introduction summing up the main attractions of the area, and a ratings box, which will highlight the area's strengths and weaknesses – some areas may be more attractive to families, others to wine-lovers visiting vineyards, and others to people interested in finding castles, churches, nature reserves or good beaches.

Each chapter is then divided into an alphabetical gazetteer, and a suggested tour. You can select whether you just want to visit a particular sight or attraction, choosing from those described in the gazetteer, or whether you want to tour the area comprehensively. If the latter, you can construct your own itinerary, or follow the authors' suggested tour, which comes at the end of every area chapter.

The gazetteer

The gazetteer section describes all the major attractions in the area – the villages, towns, historic sites, nature reserves, parks or museums that you are most likely to want to see. Maps of the area highlight all the places mentioned in the text. Using this comprehensive overview of the area, you may choose just to visit one or two sights.

One way to use the guide is simply to find individual sights that interest you, using the index or overview map, and read what our authors have to say about them. This will help you decide whether to visit the sight. If you do, you will find plenty of practical information, such as the street address, the telephone number for enquiries and opening times.

Symbol Key

- ❶ Tourist Information Centre
- ❷ Advice on arriving or departing
- ❷ Parking locations
- ❷ Advice on getting around
- ❷ Directions
- ❶ Sights and attractions
- ❷ Accommodation
- ❶ Eating
- ❷ Shopping
- ❷ Sport
- ❷ Entertainment

Practical information

The practical information in the page margins, or sidebar, will help you locate the services you need as an independent traveller – including the tourist information centre, car parks and public transport facilities. You will also find the opening times of sights, museums, churches and other attractions, as well as useful tips on shopping, market days, cultural events, entertainment, festivals and sports facilities.

Alternatively, you can choose a hotel, perhaps with the help of the accommodation recommendations contained in this guide. You can then turn to the overall map on pages 10–11 to help you work out which chapters in the book describe those cities and regions that lie closest to your chosen touring base.

Driving tours

The suggested tour is just that – a suggestion, with plenty of optional detours and one or two ideas for making your own discoveries, under the heading *Also worth exploring*. The routes are designed to link the attractions described in the gazetteer section, and to cover outstandingly scenic coastal, mountain and rural landscapes. The total distance is given for each tour, as is the time it will take you to drive the complete route, but bear in mind that this indication is just for the driving time: you will need to add on extra time for visiting attractions along the way.

Many of the routes are circular, so that you can join them at any point. Where the nature of the terrain dictates that the route has to be linear, the route can either be followed out and back, or you can use it as a link route, to get from one area in the book to another.

As you follow the route descriptions, you will find names picked out in bold capital letters – this means that the place is described fully in the gazetteer. Other names picked out in bold indicate additional villages or attractions worth a brief stop along the route.

Accommodation and food

In every chapter you will find lodging and eating recommendations for individual towns, or for the area as a whole. These are designed to cover a range of price brackets and concentrate on more characterful small or individualistic hotels and restaurants. In addition, you will find information in the *Travel facts* chapter on chain hotels, with an address to which you can write for a guide, map or directory. The price indications used in the guide have the following meanings:

€   budget level
€€   typical/average prices
€€€   de luxe.

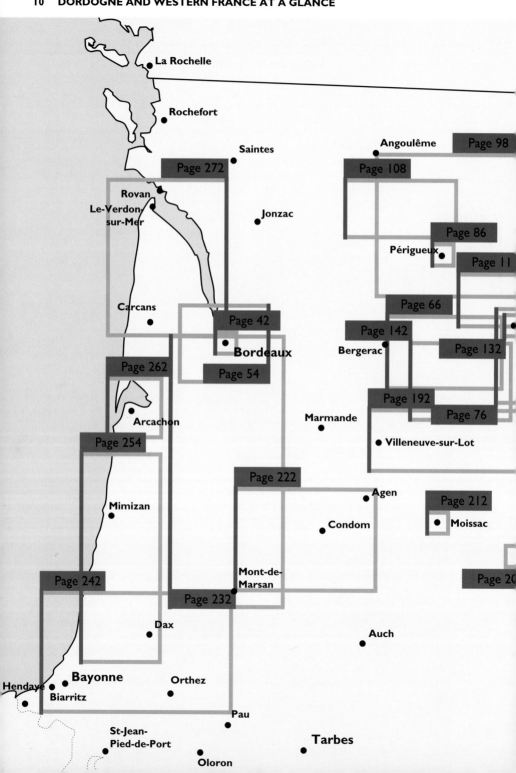

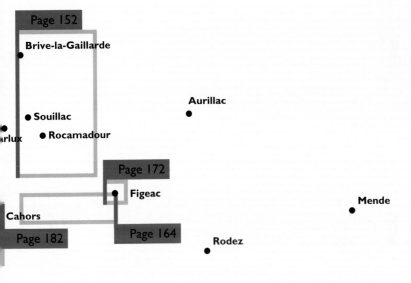
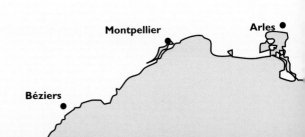

Limoges

Page 152

Brive-la-Gaillarde

Souillac

rlux   Rocamadour

Aurillac

Page 172

Figeac

Mende

Cahors

Page 182   Page 164

Rodez

uban

Albi

Nîmes

Castres

ulouse   Montpellier   Arles

Béziers

Introduction

A favoured region

Some of the best things in life are found in Western France. Gourmet foods, fine wines, well-preserved history, prehistoric cave paintings, lofty châteaux, fortified medieval towns and villages, miles of beaches, deep forests, river valleys, farmland and a mix of beautiful scenery from the pastoral to the steep green slopes of the Midi-Pyrénées.

All this and more is what can turn a casual first-time visitor into a dedicated lifelong Francophile.

Certainly there are many aspects of the Dordogne and the Bordeaux region that can be addictive. Those who like to keep their feet on the ground, however, will be aware of some of those idiosyncrasies that set France apart.

The Southwest is one of the country's most tourist-favoured regions. The resident population is comparatively low – under 50 to the square kilometre in places – but in high summer every hotel, *gîte, auberge, chambre d'hôte* and campground is fully booked. Narrow roads are jam-packed with holiday traffic.

And yet… While private individuals offer the warmest of welcomes, accommodations and places of interest, how seriously does the French government take its tourist industry?

Without a doubt the nation has a beautiful and fascinating product for visiting holidaymakers to enjoy – a product that sells itself. Perhaps that is the key to the situation. The climate in France is more temperate and predictable than that of its northerly neighbours in Europe. The weather starts to warm up in March and the sun usually shines well into the autumn, give or take the odd short spell of rain or wind. The tourist season could profitably be extended to seven months, taking the pressure off the peak months in the baking heat of July and August.

Some of the attractions and activities get into gear only in these two months.

In a May heatwave you may want to hire a canoe or rowing dinghy and spend an hour or two on the river, then find that boats can be hired only from mid-June to mid-September. It would be good to have more of what's available more of the time.

You may strike lucky and find some attractions and activities operating from May to October, or even from Easter, but this is not the norm.

The long French lunch break continues to rule. Hardly a museum or gallery or even a tourist office can be penetrated between noon and 2pm. However eager you are to complete a full itinerary you may just as well follow the French example and take a long, leisurely lunch break.

Of course this is exactly what appeals to many visitors, who go to the region with one specific aim: to relax. Campgrounds with amenities on site, somewhere to sunbathe and swim, a playground for the children and some music or entertainment at night provide a wonderful carefree holiday. It's the see-and-do visitor who is frustrated by restricted opening times.

Eating out in the West is a major delight. Duck appears on many a menu, the gizzard frequently getting star billing. *Foie gras* is popular among those without scruples about its origins; likewise veal. Rabbit, once a favourite in French eateries, is seen only occasionally in French restaurants, though it is still the basis of a good meal in the home, served with locally produced prunes.

The fixed-price menu is a boon, banishing the fear of the unintentionally daunting bill. You usually have a choice of three or four fixed-price menus. The higher-priced ones may include house wine – a consideration, as the days of ordering a carafe of wine for peanuts are long gone. Self-caterers, though, may find good low-cost wines on supermarket shelves.

If you plan to stay put in one place on holiday, which part of the Southwest offers the most? Impossible to say. There is great variety, scenic beauty, history and the alluring ambience and *je ne sais quoi* of France throughout the region. Just decide whether it's to be seaside or inland, town (Bordeaux? Biarritz?) or country, the gentle hills of the Tarn and Garonne, the forests and beaches of the Landes, the rural ambience of Gascony or the heights and valleys of the Dordogne and the Midi-Pyrénées. It's all enchanting.

Below
The seafront at Biarritz

Travel facts

Accommodation

In Southwest France you'll find a wide range of accommodation, in all price ranges, from campsites and converted farmhouses to luxury hotels and even châteaux. Bear in mind, however, that the main resorts are heavily booked at the height of the summer, especially during the French holiday season (mid-July to mid-August), and that in winter many hotels and campsites close – so be sure of getting what you want by booking in advance, especially if you're travelling with the family. Prices are generally higher along the Dordogne Valley, in the fashionable resorts, in towns and along the Côte d'Argent.

Chambres d'hôtes
A green-and-white sign denotes *chambres d'hôtes* – accommodation in a private home, which can range from a château to a farm cottage. Rooms can be booked through local tourist offices, the French Tourist Office or through **Château Accueil** *tel: 02 32 33 78 87;* **Bienvenue à la ferme** *tel: 01 53 57 11 44; www.bienvenue-a-la-ferme.com/en/accueil.htm* is a network of farmers who offer hospitality on their properties.

Bed and Breakfast
Thomas Cook Publishing, in co-operation with Bed & Breakfast (France), publish an annual directory, available from **Thomas Cook Publishing**, *PO Box 227, The Thomas Cook Business Park, 18 Coningsby Road, Peterborough PE3 8SB, UK; tel: 01733 416477.*

Bed & Breakfast (France) has a website at *www.bedbreak.com.* You can book your bed and breakfast on the website or by phone or e-mail using a credit card; *tel: 0871 781 0834; e-mail: bab@bedbreak.com*

Hotels

French hotels are graded from one to four stars and 'luxury'. Unstarred establishments are cheap but have few facilities – always inspect a room before taking it. Tariffs are posted in reception and in every bedroom. Prices are quoted for a double room with two people sharing (not including breakfast) – check whether the 15 per cent VAT is included in the price. Single rooms are thin on the ground, so expect to pay for a double even if you're travelling alone. Most rooms have showers (cheaper than baths) but in smaller hotels there may be only one bathroom per floor. Breakfast often works out quite expensive – you'll find it more economical to eat out in a local café.

Reservations should be made in writing (letter or fax); you'll have to pay a deposit (usually the equivalent of one night or 25 per cent). If you cancel your stay after paying the deposit, the hotel may require you to pay the total cost of the reservation. If you call in person, tourist offices will make reservations for the coming week (for a small fee).

You will be expected to arrive at the hotel before 1900 and no room will be held beyond 2200. If you're planning to arrive later, make sure you inform the hotel in advance.

One of the best-known and most reputable groups of hotels is the **Fédération Nationale des Logis de France** *tel: France 01 45 84 83 84; www.logis-de-france.fr.* These are inexpensive, family-run hotels, often in attractive surroundings out of town. The restaurants are equally good value and usually feature regional specialities. They are classified by 'fireplaces' (1–3).

There are dozens of hotel chains in France, offering a range of categories from four star to budget. The main chains are listed opposite.

Hotel chains

Accor (includes Ibis, Mercure, Novotel, Sofitel, Formule-1) *www.accorhotels.com. Central reservation number: UK tel: 020 8283 4500; USA tel: 800 515 5679.*

Best Western *www.bestwestern.com. UK tel: 0800 39 31 30; USA tel: 800 937 8376.*

Campanile *www.campanile.fr. Central Reservations tel: 01 64 62 46 46.*

Choice Hotels (includes Comfort and Quality Inns) *www.choicehotels.com. France tel: 0800 91 24 24; UK tel: 0800 44 44 44; US/Canada tel: 800 424 6423.*

Holiday Inn *www.sixcontinentshotels.com/ holiday-inn. UK tel: 0800 40 50 60; USA/Canada: 800–HOLIDAY (800 465 4329).*

Relais et Châteaux *www.relaischateaux.com. France tel: 01 45 72 90 00; USA tel: 800 735 2478; e-mail: info@relaischateaux. com. Central Reservations: 00800 2000 0002 (International freephone).*

Fédération Nationale des Logis de France *83 avenue d'Italie, 75013 Paris; tel: 01 45 84 70 00; reservations tel: 01 45 84 83 84; www.logis-de-france.fr; e-mail: info@logis-de-france.fr*

Gîtes

A *gîte* is self-catering accommodation, often in a converted farmhouse or country cottage. Lists of the *gîtes* in the government-run scheme are available in *The Gîtes de France Handbook* or from the internet – *www.gites-de-france.fr*

Lists are graded in 'ears of *Gîtes* wheat' (14). Traditionally they are booked by the week although some now offer weekends out of season. To book a *gîte*, contact the owner direct or go to the website of **Gîtes de France** (*www.gites-de-france.fr/eng/index.htm*). **Maison des Gîtes** *59 r. Saint-Lazare, Paris, tel: 01 49 70 75 75 (e-mail: info@gites-de-france.fr), is open Mon–Sat 1000–1830*. Many holiday and travel firms also offer *gîtes* as alternatives to hotels.

Campsites

Campsites are graded from one to four stars. All have clean water, a refuse collection and a telephone; many have swimming pools, restaurants, children's play areas, camp shops and fabulous outlooks, depending on the price. Most sites have fixed tents, caravans or holiday bungalows on offer as well as spaces for people bringing their own tent or caravan. Camping is very popular with the French, so book in advance. For more information, **Camping France**, *www.campingfrance.com/indexuk.htm*, handles online bookings for a range of owners covering more than 1100 campsites in Southwest France. **Mistercamp** operates a free telephone call-back service for information about campsites in France, *tel: 02 51 70 05 55; www.mistercamp.com/uk/index.htm; e-mail: info@mistercamp.com*. **ABC Camping** at *www.abccamping.com/aquitaineuk.htm* is an online directory of campsites in the region. Another is **Les Campings** at *www.les-campings.com/gb/index.html*

Camping Card International is a very useful item to carry on a camping tour. It is a small plastic card available from the AA or RAC and is accepted as an identity card at campsites in France, so it is not necessary to hand over your passport when registering on arrival. The CCI also entitles you to privileges on insurance and discounts on travel goods and services.

Climate

The climate in Southwest France is generally clement. Summertime can be capricious in the Dordogne, with heavy rain often following a period of hot, windy weather. In winter, snow is rare, but temperatures can drop to very low levels. The Atlantic coast enjoys more than 2000 hours of sunshine a year, with the brightest days between May and September. Rain is more frequent around Biarritz because of the mountains.

Airports

There are international airports at Bergerac, Biarritz, Bordeaux, Carcassonne and Toulouse. The airport at Périgueux is for internal flights. Angoulême is the gateway to the Dordogne for budget airlines.

Conversion tables

Distances

Metric	Imperial
1m	3ft 3in
5m	16ft 6in
10m	33ft
50m	164ft
100m	330ft
1km	0.75 mile
2km	1.5 miles
5km	3 miles
10km	6 miles
20km	12.5 miles
50km	31 miles
100km	62 miles

Weight

Kg	Lbs
1	2.2
2	4.5
5	11
10	22
20	45
50	110
75	165
100	220

Fluid measures

Litres	Imperial gallon
5	1.1
10	2.2
20	4.4
50	11

Area

1 hectare = 2.471 acres
1 acre = 0.4 hectares

Currency

The unit of currency, the euro (€), is divided into 100 cents. When sums are written, a comma rather than a decimal point is used to separate euros from cents.

Major credit cards are accepted (and sometimes preferred) by hotels, restaurants and petrol stations, but be aware that machines for automatic payment for services such as train tickets and motor fuel are often programmed to accept only French credit cards. They are gradually being adapted to accept cards issued by foreign banks. They can also be used in multilingual cash dispensers (ATMs) known in France as *distributeurs*, found outside most banks. Cash advances can also be drawn against credit cards in some banks. Traveller's cheques are no longer widely accepted for payment and only main bank branches offer encashment services.

Customs regulations

There are no restrictions on goods brought to and from EU countries, provided they are for personal use (try to adhere to official guidelines: 10 litres of spirits, 90 litres of wine, 110 litres of beer and 800 cigarettes maximum). For motorists returning to the UK on Eurotunnel trains, British Customs checks are made at the French station before you board the train. Goods purchased in duty-free shops are still subject to restrictions and visitors from outside Europe have to abide by stricter regulations – ask before you leave home. The import of weapons, drugs and pornography is prohibited. For prescription medicines, carry a copy of your doctor's note.

Drinking

Tap water is safe to drink, but many people prefer to drink mineral water, which is available under a wide range of product names at supermarkets and convenience stores. Wine is produced in many parts of the region, with those of the famous châteaux in the Bordeaux region heading the list. The area around Cahors produces a 'black' wine – deep red in colour and robust in flavour. From the vineyards of Bergerac come both red and white wines, with sweet Monbazillac taking pride of place – a wonderful wine to take at the start of a meal with *foie gras* or with the dessert. Gascony has never produced great wine, but the lip-pursing tingly output from the grapes there is put to good use by being distilled as Armagnac, believed by some people to be the world's finest brandy.

Selling or offering alcoholic drinks to children aged under 16 in bars (*cafés*), shops and other public places is banned, and you are not allowed to bring alcoholic drinks into establishments for fitness and sporting activities.

Eating out

Traditional mealtimes are 1200–1400 and 1900–2100. Restaurants are often pre-booked by French families for Sunday lunch, so be sure to reserve a table well in advance.

Bars and cafés sell snacks all day. It's often cheaper to stand at the counter and drink rather than sit on a terrace. *Salons de thé* are a more refined alternative if all you want is a light meal. *Crêperies* are everywhere but you'll find little on the menu besides pancakes and salads.

Restaurants and brasseries are comparable in terms of price and quality, but the latter stay open longer. Prices are generally posted outside and there is usually at least one fixed-price menu, often good value. *Service compris* means that a service charge of 15 per cent has been included.

Most towns in Southwest France have a produce market so you can stock up on picnic fare. In some you can buy such delicacies as truffles, *foie gras* and oysters. Delicatessens (*charcuteries*) also sell prepared dishes and salads. Other useful food outlets are bakers (*boulangeries*) and *pâtisseries* specialising in cakes and pastries.

Electricity

The electric current is 220 volts (50 MHz). Plugs should be circular with two round pins. Take an adaptor for non-continental appliances.

Emergency phone numbers

Police and ambulance *17*

Fire brigade *18*

Entry formalities

All visitors require a valid passport. EU citizens, US, Canadian and Japanese visitors do not need visas for stays of less than three months; Australian, New Zealand and South African nationals need a visa and should apply to the nearest French consulate before entering the country.

Food

So many excellent foods are reared or grown in Southwest France and its coastal waters that you could spend a couple of months touring in the region, living like a gourmet and gourmand combined and never have the same meal twice. Here the self-caterer may have the edge on the person who constantly eats out, because you can not only look avidly at the wonderful produce – poultry, fish, meats and cheeses in the markets and shops – you can also buy them and enjoy transforming them into really memorable meals in your holiday home. You can serve a breakfast of big fleshy *cèpes* (wild mushrooms) from the Dordogne with grilled sausages made from veal and lamb, or omelettes flavoured with black truffles from Périgord – truffles are very expensive but a little goes a long way in an omelette. You could have a light lunch of oysters from Arcachon, bought for absurdly low prices, or a supper of *lamproie* (lampreys) caught from the Garonne, the Gironde or the Dordogne rivers.

Insurance

Adequate insurance is essential. Most package holiday companies offer policies, but you can make your own arrangements if you prefer. Some house contents and health policies cover losses and accidents abroad, so check your existing policies.

Opposite
Squashes for sale at market

A restaurant meal can be a gastronomic treat. If you've promised yourself some high-fat holiday eating go for the *foie gras* or the duck conserve. The French do amazing things with goose gizzards, which are considered a delicacy. At a low cholesterol level you may prefer pheasant or woodpigeon, or maybe woodcock. The Landaise chickens that range freely in Europe's largest forest have a superb flavour. Lamb from Pauillac is delicious. Those who like eels will love the *piballes* from the Gironde. Basque country tuna and *koskera* cod are good choices.

One curious tendency in the classier restaurants seems to be to serve meat or fish artistically with sauce and garnish but with a minimum of vegetables. You may have slices of duck arranged with one or two asparagus spears, half a mushroom, a sprinkling of chopped herbs, a cherry and a couple of tiny potatoes. The posher the establishment the lower the vitamin C content, it seems, or perhaps it's just a passing phase among trendy chefs.

You can compensate with fresh fruit for dessert – big beautiful plums from around Agen or the Lot Valley, or some of the sweet golden grapes of Moissac.

The French have their cheese course before the dessert and the cheese board usually has some goat's or sheep's milk cheeses among the selection. Some may be bland but many are beautifully flavoursome.

And dessert? You couldn't do better than Armagnac pie. It's a pudding for grown-ups.

Eating out in France can be a problem for vegetarians. The French are great meat-eaters and few restaurants understand the concept of a meal comprising only vegetables. Mashed potato and quiche often come loaded with *lardons*, tiny pieces of chopped pork or ham. The term *vegan* is virtually unheard of, and you may be offered cheese or egg dishes or even fish as substitutes for meat. The Dordogne is renowned for *foie gras*, a great delicacy consisting of duck liver pâté, but this is particularly offensive to vegans because it is made by force-feeding the birds to enlarge their livers.

Health

You should obtain a European Health Insurance Card (EHIC) before leaving the UK. The EHIC is available free of charge through UK post offices or via *www.ehic.org.uk, tel: 0845 606 2030*. The leaflet *Health Advice for Travellers* has more information and an application form.

The EHIC is not a substitute for medical and travel insurance, but entitles you to emergency medical treatment on the same terms as French nationals. The card does not cover you for medical repatriation, ongoing medical treatment or treatment of a non-urgent nature.

American Express cardholders should apply to Global Assist *tel: (France) 01 47 77 70 00*, for any medical emergency. Pharmacies (marked with a green cross) will treat minor complaints. They will also direct you to a doctor or dentist.

There are no vaccinations specifically recommended for visitors to France, but rabies is prevalent in some areas and you are advised to avoid any contact with stray dogs.

Information

There are tourist offices (Syndicats d'Initiative or Offices de Tourisme) in most towns. English is usually spoken and there is a comprehensive range of information on accommodation, local attractions, restaurants and other facilities.

Regional tourist office *Comité Régional du Tourisme d'Aquitaine, 23 Parvis des Chartrons, Cité Mondiale Bordeaux; tel: (33) 05 56 01 70 00; e-mail: tourisme@crt.cr-aquitaine.fr; www.crt.cr-aquitaine.fr*

Regional tourist office *Comité Départemental du Tourisme de la Dordogne, 25 r. du Président Wilson, Périgueux; tel: 05 53 35 50 00; fax: 05 53 09 51 41; e-mail: dordogne.perigord.tourisme@wanadoo.fr; www.perigord.tm.fr/tourisme/cdt*

Regional tourist office *Comité Départemental du Tourisme de la Gironde, 21 cours de l'Intendance, Bordeaux; tel: 05 56 52 61 40; fax: 05 56 81 09 99; e-mail: tourisme@gironde.com; www.tourisme-gironde.fr*

Regional tourist office *Comité Départemental du Tourisme des Landes, 4 r. Aristide Briand, Mont-de-Marsan; tel: 05 58 06 89 89; fax: 05 58 06 90 90; e-mail: cdt.landes@wanadoo.fr; www.tourisme-landes.com*

Regional tourist office *Comité Départemental du Tourisme du Lot, 107 quai Cavaignac, Cahors; tel: 05 65 35 07 09; e-mail: info@ tourisme-lot.com; www.tourisme-lot.com*

Regional tourist office *Comité Départemental du Tourisme Béarn-Pays Basque, 4 allée des Platanes, Bayonne; tel: 0820 054 054, 05 59 46 52 52; fax: 05 59 46 52 46; e-mail: infos@tourisme64.com; www.bearn-basquecountry.com*

Magazine

The French tourist board, Maison de la France, publishes a quarterly English-language magazine, *Traveller in France*, which is packed with ideas, offers and background articles. Printed copies are available by phoning the France Information Line, *tel:* 09068 244 123 (UK) (60p/min), or it can be downloaded free from the website *http://uk.franceguide.com*

Nature parks

There are two regional nature parks in the area covered by this book: the Parc Ornithologique, where there are birdwatching and natural history activities on the edge of the Bassin d'Arcachon, and the Parc Régional des Landes, Europe's largest forest, which has an outdoor ecological museum, workshops and exhibitions, environmental studies and activity programmes including canoeing and cycling tours.

Opening times

As a general rule, food shops *open Mon–Sat 0800–2030*; other shops *open 0900–0930 and close 1900–1930*. Bakers (*boulangeries*) *open on Sun mornings too. Lunchtime closing is 1200–1400*, but supermarkets and shopping complexes stay open all day and sometimes later into the evening. Half-day closing is often Mon, but all these times are subject to seasonal variations.

Banks *open Mon–Fri 0900–1200, 1400–1600*. Some open Sat morning; some close Mon. They usually close early the day before a public holiday.

Maps

The best maps for drivers are the Michelin 1:200,000 maps of Aquitaine (No 234), Midi-Pyrénées (No 235) and Auvergne-Limousin (No 239). Town plans are issued free by French Tourist Information and vary in their quality and usefulness. Most offices also have maps showing local footpaths with suggested routes.

Museums

Opening times vary according to season – some museums close altogether in winter. Most have at least one *closing day per week (often Mon or Tue) and few are open all day; lunch usually falls from 1200–1400.* If in doubt, check at the local tourist office.

Packing

Shorts and a T-shirt will be perfectly adequate during the day in summertime, especially on the coast, but in the higher areas inland, where the weather is more variable and there can be sudden rainstorms, it would be wise to have a light raincoat or anorak and a cotton sweater handy. The sun's strength can be deceptive everywhere, so don't forget to pack or buy a high-factor protection lotion. Also, remember to bring insect repellent and any prescribed medicines.

Postal services

Post offices (*bureaux de poste*) are indicated by a yellow sign and the words *La Poste* in blue. They are generally *open Mon–Fri 0800–1700 (or 1900), Sat 0800–1200.* Smaller offices will *close for lunch (1200–1430).* Letters marked *poste restante* may be sent to any post office, to be collected on payment of a small fee (take your passport as proof of identity). Many post offices also have photocopying and fax facilities. Post boxes are yellow. Letters for abroad should be posted in the *départements étrangers* slot. Stamps (*timbres*) can be bought from post offices, and from shops and cafés displaying a red diamond (*tabacs*).

Public transport

Public transport is generally reliable and efficient. SNCF is the national rail system. Services are frequent and fares reasonable – InterRail Eurailpass, Flexipass and Saver Pass are all valid in France. SNCF also offers its own range of discounted tickets. Under-4s travel free on public transport, 4–11s travel half-price. For more information *tel: 020 7647 4900 or visit www.sncf.co.uk.* All train tickets must be validated with a date stamp in the orange automatic machines at the entrance to platforms. Rail maps and timetables are available at stations. TGV high-speed services between large towns require reservations, especially at peak times. You are not allowed to take a bicycle on TGV services, only local trains (if in doubt, look for the bike sign on timetables). Buses cover more towns than the train network and are a cheaper way of getting around. The central bus station is often next to the rail station; route maps and timetables can be picked up here and from tourist information. Bicycles may be taken on some bus services at the discretion of the driver.

Reading

Fiction
The Three Musketeers – Alexandre Dumas. Dashing d'Artagnan was a man from Gascony. *Bonjour Tristesse* – Françoise Sagan, the author, was born at Cajarc in the Lot Valley. *Beloved Enemy* – Ellen Jones. A novel based on the life of Eleanor of Aquitaine.

History
Eleanor of Aquitaine: the Mother Queen – Desmond Seward. The fascinating tale of the most powerful woman in medieval England and France. *The Hundred Years War* – Jonathan Sumption. Two volumes (so far!) on the complicated violence that rumbled on for more than a century, disturbing life across the whole of the region.

Wine
The Wines of Bordeaux – David Peppercorn. An authoritative survey by a top taster. *Enjoying Wine* – Don Hewitson. A handbook for

Post codes

Post codes (zip codes) in France are five figure numbers inserted in an address in front of the city name. The first two digits indicate the *département* or county. Dordogne post codes, for example, begin with 24, Gironde (which includes Bordeaux) 33, Lot-et-Garonne 47 and Paris 75. The post code is needed for letters sent in the mail, of course, but it is also very useful for locating an address on internet map sites, satellite navigation and hand-held devices.

Public holidays

New Year's Day
1 January
Easter Sunday
and Monday
Labour Day
1 May
VE Day – 8 May
Ascension Day
Whitsunday and
Monday
Bastille Day – 14 July
Assumption Day
5 August
All Saints' Day
1 November
Armistice Day
11 November
Christmas Day
25 December

aficionados of DIY (*drink* it yourself, that is). *The Winemasters* – Nicholas Faith. A look at 200 years of wine-making in Bordeaux.

Safety and security

Southwest France is a safe place to holiday, but groups of tourists will always attract the opportunist thieves. Beware pickpockets, especially on public transport and in crowds – keep your money in a belt or other secure place and don't leave valuables lying about where they can be seen. Never leave luggage unattended. It is a good idea to have photocopies of your passport and records of your credit cards, traveller's cheques and insurance policies stored separately from the items themselves. If you do lose something, report it to the police immediately.

Shopping

Ask a Frenchman or woman for advice on what to take home as a memento of your holiday and you'll never get them off the subject of food and drink. Certainly there are plenty of wonderful gastronomic treats that come from the Southwest and are canned or otherwise preserved in a way that makes them easy to carry and keep for a while. As for the wines...

But what of more permanent souvenirs and gifts?

Jewellery: Fine silver or gold chains and chunkier jewellery in the form of Celtic crosses.

Laguiole knives: This knife (pronounced lay-ole) is a true symbol of the plateau of Aveyron, used by shepherds and others.

Copperware: This has been made in the Montagne Noire region of the Midi-Pyrénées since the Middle Ages. Kitchenware – pots, pans and dishes – are still produced in local workshops. Ornamental beaten brass and copper items are also made.

Leatherware: Belts, purses, handbags and other leather goods can be found in distinctive designs. Specialised leatherware and glove-making by craftsmen in Millau, a small village at the foot of the Larzac plateau, is sought-after by fashion designers.

Earthenware: Items with hand-painted flower and bird designs are traditional products of Martres-Tolosane, 50km from Toulouse.

Combs: These, made from the horns of young bulls, are a speciality of the Hers valley (Ariège) craftspeople.

Back to food and drink. Any of the wines of Bordeaux, Bergerac, Cahors, Fronton – red, white or rosé – will give great pleasure, and don't forget Armagnac. *Foie gras* and duck *confit* are obvious ideas. An extensive choice and good prices are available to visitors to the Labeyrie company's recently opened Pavilion du Foie Gras at St-Georges-de-Maremme in the south of the Landes, 30km from Biarritz. Take home some tinned truffles and the aroma will instantly evoke memories of your holiday.

Smoking

Throughout France smoking is prohibited inside public places such as museums, monuments, theatres and cinemas and on all public transport. Since December 2007, smoking has been banned in public bars and restaurants.

Time

France is on Central European Time, I hour ahead of GMT; 6 hours ahead of US Eastern Standard Time; 9 hours ahead of Pacific Standard Time. French summertime begins on the last Sunday of March and ends on the last Sunday in September.

Tipping

Service charges (15 per cent) are automatically added to hotel and restaurant bills; it's at your discretion whether you leave an additional tip in restaurants (a couple of euros will suffice). Taxi drivers, doormen and petrol pump attendants, etc, may be tipped, again at your discretion.

Toilets

Public toilets can be found at shopping centres, petrol stations, etc. Standards vary; however, facilities in cafés, restaurants, hotels and museums are usually very good. *Messieurs* – men; *Dames* – women.

Sport

You'll find all the literature you need on sports and outdoor activities in tourist offices.

Golf – Aquitaine has around 50 high-quality courses, many of them laid out by the best international golf course designers. The variety of the region's terrain has enabled courses to be set up in woodlands, close to vineyards, among dunes on plains, and in valleys and mountains. The Aquitaine Golf Pass covers five green fees on courses in Gironde and Biarritz/Landes.

Watersports – sailing, surfing, windsurfing, sand-yachting, canoeing, kayaking, whitewater rafting, diving and rowing are all widely available.

Other outdoor activities include fishing, walking, cycling and horse riding. The guide to the long-distance footpaths marked by red-and-white posts *Sentiers de grande randonnée* (GR) can be bought from tourist information or from the **Fédération Française de la Randonnée Pédestre**, *14 rue Riquet, Paris; tel: 01 44 89 93 93; e-mail: info@ffrandonnee.fr; www.ffrp.asso.fr*

Telephones

The country code for dialling numbers in France is *33*. French numbers have ten digits and in this book are given as they are in France, so when dialling from outside France, add *33* but leave out the zero at the start of the number. When you ask French people for a phone number they will usually read it out in pairs of digits, so you will hear *05 56 59 24 24* as zero-five, fifty-six, fifty-nine, twenty-four, twenty-four.

Public call boxes are in plentiful supply except in remote countryside. You'll need a phone card (*télécarte*), available from post offices, railway stations and *tabacs* in 50 or 120 units. Calls from a restaurant or hotel are usually subject to a surcharge. Mobile phones (cell phones) work in France, but you must check with your service provider at home that your handset is programmed for international roaming. You will be charged when you receive calls in France from people calling your usual mobile number. French mobile numbers begin 06.

Travellers with disabilities

Facilities for travellers with disabilities have improved in recent years, particularly in the main resorts. However, it's a different story once you venture into rural areas. Local police may be sympathetic to the parking needs of people with limited mobility, and the Blue Disabled Badge is recognised, but the steep cobbled streets in some medieval towns may make life difficult. More information can be obtained from the **Association des Paralysés de France**, *17 bd Auguste Blanqui, Paris; tel: 01 40 78 69 00; fax: 01 45 89 40 57; www.apf.asso.fr*

Driver's guide

Automobile clubs

Members of UK motoring organisations (AA or RAC) can extend their accident insurance and breakdown services to France. Both organisations offer a wide range of information and advice as well as suggesting itineraries and routes. *www.theaa.com* offers a free, turn-by-turn route map of your journey. See also *www.rac.co.uk* *www.viamichelin.co.uk*

Autoroutes

Most of the French autoroutes are toll roads. The commonest system of charging (*péage*) involves taking a ticket from a machine at the start of the toll section, which raises an automatic barrier. On leaving the system, or at an intermediate tollbooth, the ticket is presented and the amount to pay is displayed on an illuminated sign. Payment may be made in euros or by credit card. On autoroutes speed is sometimes automatically computed from time of entry and distance covered on arrival at the tollbooth. If a speeding offence is disclosed you may be prosecuted.

ASFA, the federation of motorway toll operators, has a website in English (*www.autoroutes.fr/voyage/iti neraires.php?lng=2*) which will calculate the total cost of your planned journey, including an estimate of fuel consumed if you enter some details about the type of vehicle you drive.

Right
Scenic road

Accidents

You must STOP after any accident. You can be in serious trouble if you don't. Call 15, 17 or 18 to alert the Ambulance, Police or Fire Service as appropriate, or use the EU universal emergency number 112. On an autoroute or main road, use one of the bright-orange free SOS emergency roadside telephones located at frequent intervals.

Give whatever aid you are capable of to any person injured or in peril. It is an offence not to do this if it lies within your ability. This applies whether you are driver, passenger or witness. Safeguard against a secondary accident. Hazard lights – warning triangle – signal to other traffic. Exchange details of vehicles, driver's insurance etc. (French cars display insurance details on a windscreen sticker.) Complete a 'European Accident Statement' form – ask your insurers for this before you leave, the French driver will almost certainly have one. This forms a factual record. It is not an admission of fault. Note as many details as you can. Photographs? Witnesses? If someone has been injured, you must inform the police. If you have damaged someone else's vehicle or property and you are unable to give the owner your details, you must inform the police. The police will not usually take details where an accident involves material damage only, unless there is evidence of an offence such as dangerous or drink driving. Inform your insurers as soon as possible.

Documents

Members of EU countries and US citizens only need a valid national driving licence, but an international driving licence is essential for other nationals. Provisional licences are not valid and drivers must be over the age of 18. UK photo card licences are best. Paper licences are lawful but further proof of ID may be required. Registration papers (a logbook) and a letter of authorisation if the car is not registered in your name, insurance papers and Test Certificate (MoT) (originals – photocopies are not valid) and a nationality plate must be carried. The above documents must be produced at the time on request by police. An immediate fine may be imposed if they are not to hand. For UK drivers a 'Green Card' is not required in France for car insurance. Your certificate of insurance issued in Britain conforms to French legal needs. However, this is minimum legal cover. You should ask your insurers to extend your normal, full cover for use abroad for the period of your stay. Continental breakdown insurance is recommended. Should you visit the state of Andorra in the Pyrenees you will require a Green Card. Holders of US insurance must take out a European policy.

Breakdowns

If you are on an autoroute, stop your vehicle on the hard shoulder, getting it as far to the right as possible. On ordinary roads, consider using the verge but beware of roadside ditches. Hazard lights on. Place a warning triangle at least 30m from the scene, visible from 100m away. (Remember, it can be very dangerous to walk on the hard shoulder of any motorway.) You and your passengers are probably safer out of the vehicle and well up the verge away from the traffic.

If you need assistance on an autoroute you must use one of the free roadside telephones to connect you with the police. You cannot arrange recovery yourself, even if you are a member of a breakdown service. No garage will send a recovery vehicle onto an autoroute without police permission. There is a fixed scale of charges (€72 by day, €108 by night). You may not carry out a DIY tow on an autoroute and you may only do so on an ordinary road for 'a few metres' in an emergency. Makeshift towing is strongly discouraged and usually voids French car insurance.

Continental breakdown insurance is strongly recommended and one phone call is all it takes to hand the whole problem over to multi-lingual operators who are experts in sorting things out.

Caravans and camper vans (Trailers and RVs)

France is probably the most 'camping and caravanning friendly' country in Europe and there are numerous attractive campsites from economical to de luxe in the area covered by this guide. Booking ahead is really only necessary in the height of the season. The Alan Rogers' campsite guides are very useful. *Camping sauvage* ('wild' camping) is completely banned. Camping in State Forests or any wooded area is virtually always prohibited because of the serious risk of fire. Overnight parking of motorhomes is frequently permitted (and often free) in the central square of smaller towns and villages where water and toilet facilities are available. There are no formalities about bringing a caravan into France if your stay is for less than six months.

Motorhomes and cars towing trailers have to pay a higher toll on autoroutes. Some caravanners use the facilities of the autoroute *aires de repos* (rest areas) for an overnight stop. This is quite lawful, as your autoroute ticket lasts for at least 24 hours. If you do this, you are advised to use common sense and stop in a well-lit spot, in view of passers-by. Thefts and break-ins are, unfortunately, not unknown.

Speed limits for cars towing trailers or caravans are the same as solo vehicles. Occasionally, there may be a reduced speed limit for caravans on long declines. This is to reduce the danger of instability when the caravan is being neither pulled nor braked but is 'floating' behind the towing vehicle.

Drinking and driving

The French limit is 50mg of alcohol per 100ml of blood, and penalties increase sharply if an 80mg limit is exceeded. There is a determined campaign to reduce incidences of drinking and driving, and penalties are severe, with heavy fines and imprisonment. Random breath tests are common and you should not underestimate the powers of the police or the consequences of failing a test. A large fine may be demanded on the spot and your vehicle may be impounded until it is paid. Any disqualification is immediate. If you are the sole driver, you will be stranded and any 'get-you-home' insurance will be invalidated by reason of you having committed an illegal act.

Essentials

You *must* have a red warning triangle and hazard lights in case of accident, a headlight dip adjusted to the right, a first-aid kit and spare bulbs. You'll also need nationality (GB, IRL, etc.) plates (or a sticker, usually supplied with Channel crossing tickets), a torch, and a petrol container.

Petrol = *Essence*
Unleaded = *Sans plomb 95 and 98 octane*
4-star = *Super*
Diesel = *Gazole, Gasoil or Diesel*
LPG = *GPL*

If you intend driving in the Pyrenees or the Alps (and particularly if you are towing a trailer) you should remember that engine efficiency decreases with altitude, by about 10 per cent per 900m. This can mean that a heavily laden non-turbo car, just coping with the additional load at sea level, may not manage the incline as it climbs higher.

Driving in Dordogne

There are three classes of road – motorway (*autoroute* – A); main road (*route nationale* – RN or N); and secondary road (*route départementale* – D). Major roads also have an E number in green indicating that they are part of the European route network. The French Ministry of Transport is in the process of transferring responsibility for some N roads to *Départements* and these will be reclassified as D roads.

Autoroutes are of excellent quality with frequent rest and service areas, offering the fastest means of covering long distances by car. The exit slip roads tend to have very tight curves and should be negotiated at much reduced speed, especially if towing a trailer or caravan.

While the autoroutes generally offer the shortest distance between two points, the RN and D roads tend to meander as they follow the geography of the region, and are more scenic.

Driving rules

Traffic drives on the right in France. A fundamental driving rule is that traffic from the right has priority at junctions. In practice, priority from the right applies mostly in towns and on rural roads. Main roads are clearly signed as such by a yellow and white diamond sign which is repeated every 5km, or the conventional triangle showing a broad vertical black stripe with a narrow horizontal line crossing it (*see page 29*). Junctions marked with a simple X, or not marked at all, are governed by the 'Priority from the Right' rule. Any unmarked junction in a town or village must be treated as subject to this rule.

The rule applies to *junctions* and does not mean giving way to vehicles coming out of lay-bys, driveways, garages, parking spaces, etc. You should, however, give way to buses moving away from a bus stop.

Traffic on roundabouts has priority and drivers entering the system must wait for a safe opportunity. Unfortunately, French drivers are very haphazard about signalling their intentions on roundabouts and care is needed.

Pedestrians have right of way when on marked crossings, but the practice of stopping for a pedestrian waiting to use a crossing is unknown. If you decide to display such courtesy, remember that following drivers may not anticipate your action.

Fines

The police/*gendarmes* have wide powers to impose on-the-spot fines for a variety of motoring offences. Speed checks are frequent and merciless. Payment must be in cash, and should you not be able to pay there and then, for instance if the banks are closed and there is no ATM nearby, your vehicle and your passport may be impounded until you do. The fine is, in fact, a part payment (*amende forfaitaire*) and you may receive notification of a higher penalty later. At present such extra fines cannot be enforced abroad, but EU legislation is being contemplated to make this possible. Speed-trap detection devices are illegal, whether in use or not. The device is invariably seized and a heavy fine imposed. In practice, if you drive sensibly, you are no more likely to be stopped or prosecuted in France than any other country. It is the *consequences* of such a prosecution that should be considered, especially when you are on holiday.

'Inforoute'

If your car radio is equipped with RDS this will work in France, interrupting radio programmes with road news flashes (in French). You may also receive traffic news on 'Inforoute' on 107.7 MHz FM. These low-power transmitters cover the motorway routes and provide local up-to-date traffic reports, in French.

Fuel

Service stations are *open all day* but are normally *closed on Sundays and public holidays*. If a public holiday falls on, say, a Thursday, it is common practice to take the Friday off as well, rather than spoil a good weekend. This can mean that petrol stations are closed for four days, especially in the country. In rural areas petrol stations can be few and far between, especially on *départementale* roads.

Fuel is cheapest at big supermarkets in out-of-town retail parks (*Centre Commercial*) and, not surprisingly, most expensive on motorways. Keeping the fuel tank well filled is good practice.

Information

You should take an up-to-date map with you. Changes in road numbers and motorway interchanges can booby-trap old editions. The Michelin 1:200 000 'yellow' maps are ideal. Free *Bison Futé* (Crafty Bison) maps, showing alternative routes using secondary roads to avoid traffic problems, are available from the French Government Tourist Office or information offices in France. These routes are well signposted and make a pleasant change from main roads. If you want to be a 'Crafty Bison' yourself, you could try taking an early or late lunch and stay on the road between 1200 and 1400. The French drop everything for lunch and the roads become much quieter.

The RAC or AA can advise on special requirements for driving in France while further advice, in French, is available on a French government road safety website, *www.bison-fute.equipement.gouv.fr*. It has details of accident black spots, major roadworks and other traffic delays and adverse weather conditions affecting main roads, with an interactive map to pinpoint areas you are visiting.

Parking

There is some free parking in Disc Parking zones, where the bays are marked out in blue. Purchase a disc (*Disque de stationnement*) at petrol stations or supermarkets. Setting your arrival time on the disc automatically displays the expiry time in a cut-out window. Meter or ticket parking follows the usual pattern. Very often parking is free 1200–1400. These times are displayed on the ticket machine.

If parking in the street, you *must* park facing the direction of travel, i.e. on the right in two-way streets. It is, in any case, bad practice to park on the left, as you may drive off forgetting to move to the correct side of the road.

It is illegal to leave a vehicle parked in the same place for more than seven days, and a lesser time in some cities. Obstructive or illegal parking often results in the offending vehicle being uplifted and taken to a pound. Foreign number plates will not save you.

Lights

All traffic must use headlights in rain or poor visibility. Right-hand-drive cars must have their headlight beam modified to prevent dazzle. This can take the form of masking off part of the headlamps (which unfortunately reduces the light output) or stick-on optical beam deflectors which cause the headlight to dip to the right. Some vehicles which have quartz-iodine headlamps cannot be modified in these ways and you should check with the car dealer. Driving with defective lights can result in a fine. The fine is less likely if you can remedy the defect right away. It is a legal requirement to carry a spare set of bulbs. Motorcycles must display headlights at all times.

Mobile phones

The use of a hand-held phone when driving is specifically forbidden. The use of hands-free phones is strongly discouraged. The only safe and legal way for the driver to use a mobile is to stop and switch off the engine beforehand.

Seat belts

Wearing of seat belts for front and rear passengers is compulsory when the vehicle engine is running. Children under 10 must occupy the rear seats but an infant up to 9 months may travel in the front seat if secured in an approved rear-facing seat, *but not if a passenger air bag is fitted.*

Some parking zones work on the basis of parking on the odd-numbered side of the street for the first fortnight of a month (1st–15th) and on the even-numbered side for the second. A special sign indicates the entry to the zone. (*See page 29.*) Changeover time is between 2030 and 2100 on the last day of each fortnight.

Security

Sensible care should be taken, particularly where vehicles are left for long periods in vulnerable places such as tourist site car parks. Do not leave items on view inside the car, even if you know they are of little or no value – a potential thief does not.

In the large cities it is wise to keep car doors locked and windows up, if in slow-moving traffic or while stationary at traffic lights, as thieves on motorcycles occasionally reach inside to steal valuables. If hot weather means you must have the window open, be sure that handbags, wallets, cameras etc. are well out of sight and reach and, above all, never on a passenger's lap.

Should you have the misfortune to become a victim of crime, your insurers will require you to report the circumstances to the police and obtain a record that you have done so. In the country go to the *Gendarmerie* and in larger towns the *Commissariat de Police*.

E routes

In addition to the national classification of roads in France, motorways (*autoroutes*) and some major N roads form part of a network of cross-border European routes. They have their own numbering system and E route numbers are shown in green on road signs.

With the completion of the A28 autoroute sections between Rouen and Alençon and between Ecomoy and Tours, it is now possible to drive all the way from Calais to Bayonne and Biarritz by motorway, and without passing through Paris. This is an important western Europe route and is designated E402 on road signs in addition to the national autoroute A classification.

Speed limits

Autoroutes – 130kph (110kph in rain). If windscreen wipers are needed it's 'raining'.
Dual carriageways – 110kph (100kph in rain)
Other roads – 90kph (80kph in rain)
All built-up areas – 50kph on roads between the entrance sign to a town and departure sign (place name crossed with diagonal bar).
There's a 50kph limit on any road when visibility is less than 50m.
Drivers with less than two years' experience must not exceed the 'rain' speed limits even in fine weather.

Road signs

All major routes are clearly signed; even most minor roads have their destinations and route numbers marked. International European traffic signs are used throughout France.

accôtement non-stabilisé – soft verge
aire de repos – rest area
cédez le passage – give way
chaussée déformée – uneven surface
défense de stationner/stationnement interdit – no parking
dépassement interdit – no overtaking
déviation – diversion
gravillons – loose chippings
passage protégé – right of way
péage – toll
priorité à droite – priority to traffic from the right
priorité aux piétons – give way to pedestrians
ralentissez – slow down
rappel – reminder of previous restriction
renseignements – information
rives dangereuses – dangerous roadsides
route barrée – road closed
sens interdit – no entry
sens unique – one way
seulement riverains – residents only
sortie de camions – HGV exit
station d'essence – petrol station
stationnement gratuit – free parking
stationnement interdit – no parking
stationnement payant – paid parking
toutes directions – route for through traffic
un train peut en cacher un autre – one train may hide another
virage – bend
vous n'avez pas la priorité – you do not have priority

Right
Baynac-et-Cazenac

FRENCH ROAD SIGNS

Ⓐ
You have Priority at *all* junctions on this road.

Ⓑ*
You have Priority at *next* junction. (Note: important difference with A.)

Ⓒ*
Be prepared to *Give Way* to traffic from right at next junction.

End of Priority road.

CÉDEZ LE PASSAGE
'Give Way'.

*Signs B and C may indicate a junction from either side, not necessarily a full crossroads.

VOUS N'AVEZ PAS LA PRIORITE
You do not have Priority. *Give Way* at roundabout.

Signs attached to traffic lights are valid only if lights are OFF or yellow light is flashing.

Flashing yellow light = Proceed with caution. *Give Way* to traffic on right.

BERGERAC
The red border on a town sign *means start of 50kph limit*. If surmounted by 'Priority' sign (as here), you are on the Priority road through the town.

PARKING

Disc Parking.

Parking on payment at meter.

Entry to zone where Parking is allowed first fortnight on odd-numbered side of street – second fortnight on even-numbered side.

WARNINGS

RISQUE DE VERGLAS
Risk of black ice.

Snow chains obligatory.

ALLUMEZ VOS FEUX
Switch on Headlights.

70m
Minimum distance between vehicles.

Itinéraire Bis
Alternative Route.

Déviation
Diversion.

Frequently found at tunnels.

Getting to Dordogne and Western France

Eurostar *Tel: 08705 186 186; www.eurostar.com* – London St Pancras Intl to Paris (2 hrs 15 mins), also Lille Europe (1 hr 20 mins) for connecting trains to Bordeaux (Mon–Fri only).

Eurotunnel *Tel: 08705 35 35 35; www.eurotunnel. com* – drive-on trains from Folkestone to Calais Coquelles (35 mins). For more information contact **Rail Europe** *Tel: 08705 848 848* (UK); or **Eurotunnel** Direct reservations *tel: 08705 35 35* (UK).

Brittany Ferries *Tel: 08705 360 360; www.brittany-ferries.co.uk* – Portsmouth to St-Malo (11 hrs) and Caen (6 hrs); Poole to Cherbourg (5 hrs, high speed 2¼ hrs), Plymouth to St-Malo (7½ hrs) and Roscoff (6 hrs). Also Cork to Roscoff (13 hrs), summer only.

P&O Ferries *Tel: 08716 64 64 64; www.poferries. com* – Portsmouth to Cherbourg 2¾ hrs (fast ferry) or 4¾ hrs (ship), Portsmouth to Le Havre 5½ hrs, Dover to Calais 1½ hrs, Rosslare to Cherbourg 19 hrs.

SeaFrance *Tel: 08705 711 711; www.seafrance.com* – Dover to Calais 90 mins.

Flying

Southwest France is well served by a choice of airline services, including scheduled flights and low-cost no-frills services. Your travel agent will have information, and all airlines have online or phone booking facilities. There are scheduled flights from London to Toulouse, Bordeaux, Biarritz, Bergerac and Carcassonne, and internal flights with Air France from Paris. Contact **Ryanair** *tel: 0871 246 0016* (UK), *0818 30 30 50* (Ireland), *www.ryanair.com*; **Easyjet** *tel: 0871 7500 100* (UK), *www.easyjet.co.uk*; **Air France** *tel: 0845 359 1000* (UK) or *01 605 0383* (Ireland), *www.airfrance.com*; **British Airways** *tel: 0870 850 9850, www.britishairways.com*; **Flybe** *tel: 08705 676 676* (UK), *www.flybe.com*. Air France also flies from Dublin to Bordeaux, BA flies from Birmingham direct to Bordeaux, and British European has a direct service from Birmingham to Toulouse.

To get to Southwest France from the USA it is necessary to fly to Paris and change to an internal service or continue by train or car.

Ferries

The ferry is still a popular way to take a car to France, and there is a wide range of options. Booking ahead is strongly recommended, especially in high season. Cross-Channel car ferries leave from various points along the south coast of England, and also from Cork and Rosslare in Ireland. There's an equally good choice of arrival ports in Normandy and Brittany. Some ferry operators offer a high-speed crossing. All have online information and booking facilities.

Coaches

Coaches are more economical than taking the train, but journey times are longer. Coach reservations can be made at any **National Express** travel office (*tel: 08717 81 81 81, www.nationalexpress.com*). **Eurolines** (*tel: 08717 81 81 77*) operates a network of routes from London Victoria Coach Station, including a direct service to Tours (12 hours) with connections to Bordeaux, Brive, Cahors and Toulouse – *e-mail: welcome@eurolinesuk.com; www.eurolines.co.uk*. There are also direct coach services from Dublin Busaras to Paris.

Transmanche *Tel: 0800 917 1201 (UK), 0800 650 100 (France); www.transmancheferries.com* – Newhaven to Dieppe (3 hrs).

LD Lines *Tel: 0870 428 4335 (UK), 0825 304 304 (France); www.ldlines.co.uk* – Portsmouth to Le Havre (6 hrs).

Norfolk Line *Tel: 0870 870 10 20 (UK), 03 28 28 95 50 (France); www.norfolkline.com* – Dover to Dunkerque daily.

Speedferries *Tel: 0871 222 7456; www.speedferries.com* – Dover to Boulogne by large catamaran, 50 mins.

Condor Ferries *Tel: 0845 609 1024; www.condorferries.com* – Poole to St-Malo 5¹/₂ hrs; Portsmouth or Poole to Cherbourg 5 hrs (summer only).

Irish Ferries *Tel: 08705 171717 (GB), 0818 300 400 (Rep. of Ireland), www.irishferries.com* – Rosslare to Cherbourg 19¹/₂ hrs, Rosslare to Roscoff 17 hrs (summer only).

French Motorail *Tel: 08702 415 415; e-mail: motorail@raileurope.co.uk; www.raileurope.co.uk* – car-carrying train services operate in summer from Calais to Brive and Toulouse.

For up-to-date details of long-distance bus, ferry and rail services, consult the *Thomas Cook European Rail Timetable*, published monthly.

Rail services

Eurostar trains link London with Paris and Lille Europe via the Channel Tunnel. The major railheads in Southwest France are Bordeaux, Brive and Toulouse, and there are connecting services from Lille Europe to avoid crossing Paris to Montparnasse or Austerlitz stations which serve the Southwest from the French capital. There are 15 TGV trips a day in each direction between Bordeaux and Paris (3 hours), and there are up to six direct trains a day between Bordeaux and Lille Europe. SNCF operates an overnight Motorail service from Calais to Brive (and onwards to Toulouse) on Friday nights with additional trains on Wednesday and Sunday in August. Sleeping accommodation is couchette style (4-berth and 6-berth compartments) and breakfast is provided on the train. For enquiries and reservations from the UK contact RailEurope, *tel: 08702 415 415 (UK); e-mail: motorail@raileurope.co.uk; www.raileurope.co.uk/french motorail/timetable.htm*

Rail Europe and Eurostar offer a through-ticket service. Contact main station travel centres or high-street travel agents for more details. Discounted tickets are available for students and young people under 26 and for InterRail pass-holders.

If you are planning to take your car through the Channel Tunnel, the entrance is off the M20 at junction 11A just outside Folkestone. After driving on to the Eurotunnel train the journey time is 35 minutes to Calais Coquelles and the terminal gives direct access to the A16 autoroute and the rest of the French motorway network. LPG or dual-fuel vehicles may not use the Tunnel.

Driving

If you are taking your own car, the autoroute system (mostly toll roads) is an excellent means of getting to your destination. Using the A16 from Calais to Paris and the A10 from Paris means it is possible to drive all the way from the Channel Tunnel to Bordeaux by motorway. The A10 and A20 provide an all-motorway route from Paris to Bordeaux and Brive. If you are taking your car through the Channel Tunnel, you join the French motorway network as soon as you drive off the train and out of the tunnel at Calais Coquelles.

You can avoid long-distance driving in France by using the French Motorail (*www.raileurope.co.uk*) which will transport your car to your destination overnight, April to October, in a purpose-built train. Services are from Calais to Bordeaux, Brive and Biarritz.

Car hire is expensive in France; it is normally cheaper to arrange before you leave, or consider a fly-drive. You must be over 21 and have held a licence for at least one year. All the usual main car hire firms have offices in France, and often at airports, main railway stations and ferry ports. It is wise to book ahead for peak holiday periods.

Above
St-Céré fountain

Setting the scene

Landscapes

Anyone touring the entire area covered in this book will experience diverse types of landscape. Farmland with great acreages of sunflowers, vines, orchards, walnut groves, tobacco and many other fruit, vegetable and cereal crops. Rugged rocky hills, deep ravines, wide rivers, cliff-hanging villages, rolling hills – it's all to be found in the Southwest. There's also a long Atlantic coastline with sandy beaches and exhilarating surfing.

It is amazing, considering the long and terrible wars suffered by the French, how many buildings – indeed whole villages – have survived from the Middle Ages and earlier. The sculptured Romanesque capitals of the 11th-century cloisters at Moissac, with their biblical scenes and animal, bird and plant carvings, are worth crossing continents to see.

Prehistory also plays a major part in the enjoyment of the region. Some of the best-preserved examples of cave art in the world are in the foothills of the Pyrenees and the Dordogne, some dating from the last Ice Age. Limestone caverns thick with grotesque shapes and colourful 'curtains', pillars, stalagmites and stalactites can be visited in the Dordogne Valley. The gorges and *causses* (limestone plateaux) of the Aveyron are between the Dordogne and the Cévennes. The wide open contours are punctuated with villages of character from the Lot to the Tarn gorges.

The Dordogne

The Dordogne is one of the great hands-on holiday destinations in which people can hike, cycle, go on horseback or reach by car to stroll around châteaux and historic villages and sites of interest. Some take to the water, hiring canoes or kayaks either by the hour or for long-distance trips, or taking a more leisurely cruise by trip boat.

Until the late 18th century what we know as the Dordogne was called Périgord. In 1790 the French *départements* were formed, most taking the name of the most important river in the *département*. Geographically the *département* divides conveniently into four areas with the chief town, Périgueux, more or less in the middle. These areas are called Périgord Vert, Blanc, Noir and Pourpre (Green, White, Black and Purple).

Périgord Vert is the wide crescent in the north, crossed by the Dronne, Bandiat and Auvézère rivers, with lush valleys, woodlands and streams much loved by landscape painters. Périgord Blanc takes its name from the chalky limestone outcrops. Périgueux is here, and the village of Sorges, known for its 'black gold' (the truffle) and its Truffle Museum. The lower section of this area is shared by Périgord Noir to the east, dotted with châteaux and with the Vézère and Dordogne rivers following historic courses, and Périgord Pourpre to the west contains the scenic wine-growing area around Bergerac. Here the Dordogne grows wider.

The Midi-Pyrénées is one of France's most varied regions, ranging from warm limestone plateaux in the north to the snowy peaks 270km south in the Pyrenees. Rolling farmland dotted with dovecotes is a feature of the area, with medieval towns and *bastides* (fortified towns) in its crests and valleys. *Foie gras*, Armagnac and the 'black' Cahors wines are some of the products of the Midi-Pyrénées.

The Bordeaux wine-growing area of the Gironde sustains many tiny villages. The great metropolis, Bordeaux city, is at the heart of the *département*. An hour's drive east takes you to the lovely up-market seaside resort of Arcachon, a yachting base and fishing harbour, with oyster beds, pine woods and the biggest sand dune in Europe.

South of Arcachon is the Landes *département*, with another superlative – Europe's biggest forest. Much of Landes is a great natural park, providing an opportunity for wildlife watching, rambling, fishing and canoeing along remote streams.

Gascony, in the Landes, has one of the lowest populations in France. Most of it is farmland and it is known for the great quantities of garlic grown there. Geese, ducks and other poultry, marketed in various forms, contribute to the local economy. Being so dependent on the land, the farmers of the Gers are adept at sticking up for their rights and defending their way of life. Local government offices and politicians have often been at the receiving end of a trailer-load of dumped cow dung or a well-aimed egg.

The ever-popular city of Biarritz, with its many golf courses and world-class surfing, is in the southernmost part of the region, in the *département* of Pyrénées-Atlantique. People come here for therapeutic seawater treatments and, inland, on the borders of Landes and Pyrénées-Atlantiques, mud and hot springs provide the basis for curative spa treatments.

Tarn et Garonne

East of Gironde and south of Dordogne is the Tarn et Garonne *département*, bisected by the Garonne river. In spring much of the countryside explodes into massed white and pale pink blossom as the orchards of many varieties of fruit promise a good harvest to come. Montauban, the county town, with its lovely ancient bridge over the Tarn, draws visitors to its Ingres Museum. Paintings by Montauban-born painter Ingres and other artists with local connections are exhibited on five floors of a historic building in which the Black Prince had a room.

Moissac, with its abbey, cloisters and exquisitely carved south doorway from the 11th century, is worth a night or two's visit. The Canal Latéral à la Garonne goes through the town, with attractive moorings, and the River Garonne, on which boat trips are available, is nearby.

A drive east in this *département* takes you to the Aveyron Gorges, providing exciting landscapes. Medieval villages cling to cliff sides. The Causse de Quercy overlooks the gorges, and the daring will enjoy the challenge of potholing, climbing and hang-gliding. Canoeing, cycling and horse riding are also popular pastimes here. One of the old villages in the vicinity is Bruniquel, hanging down the southern slopes of an 80m cliff overlooking the Aveyron and Vere rivers. This area has an interesting prehistoric site rich in cave dwellings and rock shelters. The 12th-century castle sitting at the top of the cliff has been a classified Historic Monument since 1840.

Throughout the Southwest, towns and villages present a cheerful aspect of stone buildings with red crinkly-tiled roofs. Narrow side-streets and alleys paved in brick, with central runnels or gutters, reflect medieval charm.

The beginnings

Archaeologists and cave explorers have produced evidence that there were human beings in Southwest France as far back as 450,000 years ago. The earliest known settlers, *Homo erectus*, shaped pebbles of quartz, flint, jasper and other minerals into chopping and scraping tools. Neanderthal man, who appeared on the scene around 200,000 BC, had learned how to make and use fire.

The caves of the Dordogne and Lot valleys – sites such as Lascaux and Pech Merle – especially reveal how Cro-Magnon man, who replaced the Neanderthals in about 35,000 BC, soon learned to produce sophisticated works of art. Findings in the village of Les Eyzies-de-Tayac, in the Vézère Valley, indicate continuous habitation of the caves there from the Stone Age to the 1950s.

No one knows for certain whether the paintings and etchings created on the walls of the caves were ceremonial, linguistic or purely artistic – but there is no questioning the skill and dynamism of the work.

The Romans

Aquitaine was conquered by Julius Caesar's forces in 56 BC, though not without a struggle. The inhabitants of today's Périgord and Quercy put up a ferocious fight, but their neighbours to the south, around the Tarn and Aveyron rivers, were more acquiescent and at last the region fell to the Roman raiders. Under the new rulers, however, trade flourished, and Cahors and Périgueux became very prosperous.

Above
Les Eyzies-de-Tayac

Visigoths and Franks

The good life under the Romans was shaken during the 3rd century AD by successive raids by Germanic tribes from the north and the Visigoths swept through Southwest France on their way to Spain. As the Roman Empire crumbled, the Visigoths were able to establish a semi-Romanised kingdom, continuing the Latin culture and Roman law in the 5th century. Their rule did not last long. In 507 Clovis, king of the Franks, defeated the Visigoths in the Battle of Vouillé and took control of much of the Southwest. But there was further instability as Saracens invaded from the east and a succession of wars broke out among Clovis's successors.

Emperor Charlemagne

By the time he was crowned Holy Roman Emperor in 800, Charlemagne had already created the Kingdom of Aquitaine and he soon brought a fragmented France together, maintaining control by placing his most trusty supporters in positions of power. The counts of Toulouse and the dukes of Aquitaine emerged during this time as powerful barons.

Charlemagne's rule over Southwest France was soon to fail, destabilised by Viking raiders, who rampaged through the Dordogne and Isle valleys, and the increasing power of the barons. By the year 1000, the Count of Toulouse ruled over most of Quercy, while a smaller consortium of barons, including the Count of Périgord, was at least nominally part of Aquitaine.

Eleanor of Aquitaine

In 1137 Eleanor, only daughter of William of Aquitaine, married Louis, the Dauphin of France. She was aged 15 and her marriage took with it a dowry, which included the duchies of Aquitaine, Gascony and Périgord. Within a year her husband was crowned Louis VII, but theirs was not to be a lasting romance. In 1152 the marriage was annulled on grounds of consanguinity (related by blood), and Eleanor retained all the lands in her dowry. In the same year Eleanor, a wily and powerful woman, married Henry Plantagenet, Duke of Normandy and Anjou, and between them the couple ruled over land extending from the English Channel to the Pyrenees, a territory as vast as that of the French crown's. Relations between France and England began to be strained, and when Henry was crowned Henry II of England in 1154 the delicate thread holding the two countries together snapped,

Above
La Roque-Gageac

resulting in a struggle that was to continue off and on for the next three centuries.

Eleanor could not resist plotting. After separating from Henry she set up court in Poitiers and began a series of intrigues. When she encouraged her son Richard the Lionheart in the fight against his father, Henry had her imprisoned in London and she was not released until 15 years later – in 1189 – when her husband died.

The Hundred Years War

Under the Treaty of Paris of 1259 the Plantagenets agreed to pay homage to the French king for their lands in Aquitaine, and in the following years *bastides* (fortified towns) were established as the French and English marked out their newly agreed territories. But there were too many complications for the fragile treaty, and Aquitaine changed hands repeatedly.

Edward III, who was crowned king of England in 1327, had a strong claim to the French throne because he was a grandson on his mother's side of Philip IV of France. In 1340 Edward put forward his claim and formally styled himself king of France. The stage was set for the Hundred Years War.

The war started in 1345 in Brittany and Normandy and ended in 1453 when the English were defeated at the Battle of Castillon in the Dordogne Valley. The intervening 108 years saw much bloodshed and plunder and towns and territories changed hands repeatedly. Aquitaine, and especially the Dordogne, saw much violence.

The Wars of Religion

The next serious outbreak of violence came in 1562 with the outbreak of the Wars of Religion – a series of bloody conflicts that was to last for 37 years. It all came about as a result of the spread of Lutheran and Calvinist doctrines, and by the middle of the 16th centuries Southwest France was split. Cahors and Périgueux were Catholic, while much of the old lands of the Count of Toulouse, including Montauban and Toulouse, were Protestant. Périgueux was taken by the Protestants in 1575. Cahors fell in 1578 after a siege that lasted three days.

As strife raked back and forth across the land, the old castles and fortified churches that had given the people some protection during the Hundred Years War were brought into use again, but as before it was the villages and smallest towns that suffered most.

Castles and caves

Day 1: **Bergerac** – visit the châteaux of Lanquais and Monbazillac, where you can also try the wine (*see pages 71–2*).

Day 2: **St-Cyprien** – ideally placed for visits to Josephine Baker's Les Milandes château, Castelnaud and the pretty village of Beynac-et-Cazenac (*see pages 69–70*).

Day 3: **Sarlat-la-Canéda** – châteaux galore and the Dordogne river are within easy reach of this lively town (*see pages 132–4*).

Days 4–5: **Les Eyzies-de-Tayac** – so much to see around this attractive village, including the Musée National de la Préhistoire and troglodyte caves (*see pages 120–3*).

Days 6–7: **Montignac** – leave plenty of time to visit Lascaux II, the ultimate painted cave experience (*see page 123–4*).

Below
Terrasson-la-Villedieu

Top 10

Bergerac – lovely riverside town with an attractive medieval quarter (*see pages 66–8*).

Ecomusée de la Grande Lande – extensive open-air folk museum (*see page 234*).

Les Eyzies-de-Tayac – a cliff on one side, a river on the other (*see pages 120–3*).

Lascaux II – a superb reproduction of the most famous painted cave in France (*see page 123*).

Moissac – stunning cloisters, nearly 1000 years old (*see pages 212–21*).

Musée de Plein Air de Quercy – entertaining and informative open-air museum (*see page 167*).

Pont Valentré – remarkable 14th-century bridge (*see page 187*).

Rocamadour – the famed pilgrimage centre (*see pages 157–8*).

St-Cirq-Lapopie – a fairy-tale village hanging steeply over the River Lot (*see pages 168–9*).

St-Emilion – charming hillside town of narrow twisting streets (*see page 61*).

Bordeaux

Ratings

Architecture	●●●●●
Museums	●●●●●
Art	●●●●○
Food and drink	●●●●○
Restaurants	●●●●○
Shopping	●●●●○
Entertainment	●●●○○
Historical sights	●●●○○

B ordeaux wears its history with pride. It was known as Burdigala before the Romans came and has played a major part in European, especially Anglo-French, politics and trade for more than a thousand years. Eleanor of Aquitaine and Henry Plantagenet, England's King Henry II, were married here, and from here the Black Prince set forth on his missions of terror. The city's wine industry has flourished since Roman times and the Plantagenets' penchant for 'claret', as they called the region's red wine, cemented a special relationship between the city and English consumers which has flourished over the centuries. Today, Britain is the leading customer for Bordeaux's wines. France's eighth-largest city, Bordeaux is an architectural treasure house, with whole streets standing as monuments to its lively past. The old part of the city has been designated a UNESCO World Heritage Site (the largest urban area to be so honoured), covering the outer boulevards to the banks of the Garonne River, where historic façades have been renovated. But it is also a modern city with high-tech industries that keep its mind very much on the future.

Getting there and getting around

ⓘ **Town Centre** *12 cours du XXX Juillet; tel: 05 56 00 66 00; fax: 05 56 00 6601; e-mail: otb@bordeaux-tourisme.com; www.bordeaux-tourisme.com. Open daily, all year. Closing times vary according to season. Information office also at Bordeaux-Mérignac airport and at Bordeaux St-Jean railway station, tel: 05 56 91 64 70.*

Arriving and departing

The Bordeaux-Mérignac International Airport *(tel: 05 56 34 50 50; e-mail: info@bordeaux.aeroport.fr)* is 12km out of town. A shuttle bus operates to the city centre and the railway station (45 mins).

Bordeaux has good road links in all directions. From the north the A10 brings traffic from Paris, Orléans, Tours and Poitiers. From the southeast, the A62 and A61 form the Autoroute de Deux Mers, linking the Mediterranean with the Atlantic. The A63 is the main link from Northwest Spain, Biarritz and Bayonne. *Information about tolls is available from Autoroutes du Sud de la France, www.asf.fr*

Trains run from the Gare Bordeaux-St-Jean, r. Charles Domercq.

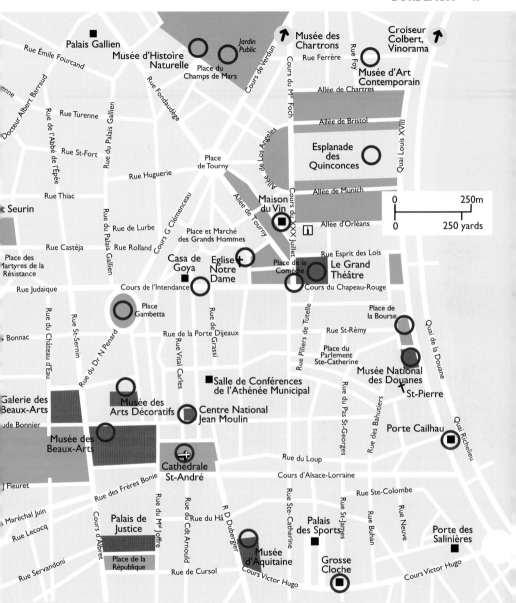

Getting around

You can enjoy guided tours of the city on foot, bicycle, horse-drawn carriage, vintage bus, tour coach, river boat, taxi, limousine and even helicopter: details of these are available from the tourist offices.

There are about 20 car parks in the city centre. The largest are at pl. de Tourny, the Mériadeck Shopping Centre on r. Claude Bonnier and

Cité Mondiale, quai des Chartrons. Best thing for visitors is to leave the car at the hotel, if possible.

CGFTE operates bus and tram services within the city (*tel: 05 57 57 88 88*). The nearest terminus to the tourist office is pl. Jean Jaurès. Bus and tram tickets cost €1.30 single (valid 1 hr) and €4 all day. One- and three-day bus passes are available. Out-of-town routes are covered by Transgironde (*tel: 05 56 43 68 43*); the nearest terminus to the tourist office is allées de Chartres.

There are 24-hour taxi ranks at r. Esprits des Lois (*tel: 05 56 81 99 15*), and cours G. Clémenceau (*tel: 05 56 81 99 05*). Both are close to the tourist office.

Below
Grosse Cloche (Great Bell Gate), Bordeaux

The Gare St-Jean, r. Charles Domercq (*tel: 05 56 91 64 70*), is *open daily 0430–midnight*. The free Carte Bordeaux Découverte allows entry to museums, monuments and other places of interest at discount prices.

Sights

Bordeaux is a fascinating city full of interesting streets and squares and historic buildings and sites. Here are some of the must-see locations.

Cathédrale St-André

Cathédrale St-André Pl. Pey Berland; tel: 05 56 52 68 10. Open daily. Guided tours Wed 0730–1130, 1400–1800; for information tel: 05 56 87 17 18.

A smidgin smaller than the Cathédrale Notre-Dame in Paris, the major and most imposing religious building in Bordeaux took more than 400 years to build – from the 11th to the 15th centuries. The many buttresses and flying buttresses were added to stave off imminent collapses during the years of construction. The Port Royale entrance, dating from the 13th century, is adorned with remarkable sculptures, including the Gothic *Last Judgement* on the tympanum.

Centre National Jean Moulin

Centre National Jean Moulin Pl. Jean Moulin; tel: 05 56 79 66 00; e-mail: cnjm@mairie-bordeaux.fr. Open Tue–Fri 1100–1800, Sat and Sun 1400–1800. Closed Mon and public holidays. Free entry.

Named in honour of the most famous of the French Resistance heroes, who was captured by the Gestapo, tortured and executed in 1943, the museum is devoted to World War II, the Resistance movement and the activities of the Free French Forces. Among the three floors of displays of illicit radio equipment, underground newspapers and photographs is a reconstruction of Jean Moulin's hidden office.

Cours du Chapeau-Rouge

Croiseur Colbert €€ Port de la Lune, Quai des Chartrons; tel: 05 56 44 96 11; e-mail: colbert.croiseur@ free.fr; http://colbert.croiseur. free.fr. Open Apr–Sep daily 1000–1800, Oct–Mar 1300–1800 weekdays and public hols only.

Running from pl. de la Comédie to the river front, this wide elegant street owes its name to a tavern that stood here in the 15th century. In the 1600s it was a fashionable residential area.

Cours de l'Intendance

A continuation of cours du Chapeau-Rouge, travelling away from the river, this is the city's gold-card shopping street – the place for high-fashion clothes and very expensive accessories.

Croiseur *Colbert*

Eglise Notre-Dame Pl. du Chapelet; tel 05 56 10 21 83. Open Mon 1430–1800, Tue–Sun 0800–1200, 1430–1800.

Launched in 1959, the *Colbert* is to Bordeaux what HMS *Belfast* is to London. Designed as an anti-aircraft warship, the cruiser was converted into a missile-launcher. Among her more newsworthy missions were the rescue of Agadir earthquake missions in 1960 and Général de Gaulle's trips to South America (1964) and Quebec (1967). The Admiral's cabin, officers' and ratings' quarters, weapons and engine rooms and other parts of the ship are open to visitors.

Eglise Notre-Dame

Jardin Botanique Pl. Bardineau, 33000 Bordeaux; information centre r. Gustave Card; tel: 05 56 52 18 77; e-mail: j.botanique@mairie-bordeaux.fr. Open 0830–1730. Collection of exotic plants and medicinal herbs from all over the world. A modern display area is open to the public.

Completed in 1707, the church has a wealth of stonework both outside and in. Its baroque-style exterior is decorated with a frieze of leaves, and carved ornamentation covers other surfaces. The interior contains barrel-and-groin vaulting, and elegant balconies flank the organ loft.

Esplanade des Quinconces

Open space on a grand scale (when it isn't overrun by fairground rides and stalls selling *crêpes* and sticky sweetstuffs), the 12-hectare esplanade was laid out in the early 19th century. Its focal point is the massive Monument aux Girondins, 50m high, 65m long and 44m wide, a cornucopia of allegory with the Spirit of Liberty breaking free from the chains of oppression on top of a column surrounded by gushing fountains filled with statues. It honours the Bordeaux *députés* who went to the guillotine during the Revolution. There are also huge statues of the writers Montaigne and Montesquieu. At the riverside end of the esplanade two monuments in the shape of ships' figureheads symbolise Commerce and Navigation.

Le Grand Théâtre

The name says it all. This imposing building, adorned with Corinthian columns and statues representing the Muses and goddesses, was completed in 1780 and echoes the high regard for culture in 18th-century France. The interior is superbly overblown, with lots of marble, carved wood, gilt and more statues. The auditorium has a magnificent frescoed ceiling from which hangs a huge chandelier with 14,000 glittering crystals.

Jardin Public

Created in 1746 to link the suburbs of St-Seurin and Chartrons, the 10-hectare gardens were laid out in the English style in 1856 by the landscape artists Fisher and Escarpit. A collection of some 3000 plant species is housed in the Botanical Garden.

Maison du Vin

The history of the maritime wine trade is outlined in the home of an early 18th-century Irish wine merchant. Among the collections on show are lithographed wine labels from the mid-19th century and wine bottles dating from the 17th century.

Musée d'Aquitaine

This excellently planned museum gives a very clear insight into the region's history from humankind's very beginnings. Exhibits range from Stone Age relics, through tools and jewellery from the Bronze and Iron Ages, Roman coins and glassware and early Christian religious artefacts to sections on Bordeaux in the 18th and 19th centuries.

Musée d'Art Contemporain

The museum is imaginatively housed in a converted early 19th-century quayside warehouse, which was rescued from demolition in the 1980s. It serves as a home for all forms of modern art and has a bookshop, library, restaurant and café.

Above
The old and the new in Bordeaux

Musée des Beaux-Arts €€ *Jardin de la Mairie, 20 cours d'Albret, Bordeaux; tel: 05 56 10 20 56; www.culture. fr/culture/bordeaux; e-mail: musbxa@mairie-bordeaux.fr. Open 1100–1800. Closed Tue and public holidays. Free entry first Sun of the month.*

Musée National des Douanes € *1 quai de la Douane; tel: 05 56 48 82 85; e-mail: communication. mnd@gmail.com. Open daily 1000–1800, closed Mon, 25 Dec, 1 Jan.*

Musée d'Histoire Naturelle € *Hôtel de Lisleferme, 5 pl. Bardineau; tel: 05 56 48 26 37; e-mail: museum@mairie-bordeaux.fr. Open 1100–1800 (1400–1800 Sat and Sun). Closed Tue and public holidays. Free entry to permanent collection.*

Musée des Arts Décoratifs

Collections of furniture, ceramics, glassware, gold plate and wrought ironwork are housed in a fine Louis XVI-style mansion designed for the Marquis de Lalande by the Bordeaux architect Etienne Laclotte in 1779. Examples of furniture, locksmithery, weapons, china and miniature paintings on ivory and paper are displayed in the lofts. There is also a restaurant and a tearoom.

Musée des Beaux-Arts

Created in 1801, the Fine Arts Museum houses the tenth largest collection of paintings in France as well as drawings and sculptures. Among the most prestigious works on show are Titian's *Tarquin and Lucretia*, Brueghel's *Wedding Dance*, *Greece Expiring on the Ruins of Missolonghi* by Delacroix, *Martyrdom of St George* and *Jupiter Carrying Away Gannymede* by Rubens, and Ter Brugghen's *The Lute Player*. Three major Bordeaux painters are also represented: André Lothe, Albert Marquet and Odilon Redon.

Musée National des Douanes

The clearance warehouse of the old royal customs hall is an appropriate setting for this museum, which tells the story of the French Customs Department through the ages. Documents, uniforms, weapons, models and equipment – including the latest computer technology – are displayed. A special section shows how aspects of the service have been portrayed in different media: film, literature, comic strips – and in Claude Monet's painting *The Customs Inspectors' Hut*.

Musée d'Histoire Naturelle

A wide range of specimens from the flora, fauna, minerals and fossils of the world's continents and oceans illustrates the evolution

Vinorama de Bordeaux €€ *12 cours du Médoc; tel: 05 56 39 39 20. Open Tue–Sat 1030–1230, 1430–1830 (Sun pm only). Closed Sun from Oct to May. Visit includes a tasting.*

of planet Earth. There are temporary exhibitions on a wide range of themes.

Place de la Bourse

This magnificent square flanked by the Garonne is the former Place Royale, designed by the architects Jacques and Jacques-Ange Gabriel and constructed 1731–55. The Stock Exchange, which gives it its present name, stands on the north side of the square, facing the former Hôtel des Fermes, the Customs Hall, which now houses the Musée des Douanes. The Fountain of the Three Graces was erected in place of a statue of Louis XV, which was removed during the Revolution.

Place Gambetta

Completed in 1747, when it was known as Place Dauphine, the square has a collection of pleasing façades surrounding an English-style garden that was the site of the guillotine during the Revolution.

Porte Cailhau

Standing at the river end of Place du Palais, this splendid tower, with its coned roofs and parapets, was completed in 1496 as one of the city's main gates. It was used as the entrance for visiting royalty. The history of Bordeaux is traced in exhibits on three floors inside the tower.

Porte de la Grosse Cloche

The 15th-century gate, built on the site of one dating from the 13th century, has become an unofficial emblem of the city, thanks to the huge bell hanging in an arch beneath the tower's conical roofs. The bell was cast in 1775 and the clock underneath it was made in 1772. Another clock inside the building dates from 1592.

Vinorama de Bordeaux

The history of Bordeaux wine from Gallo-Roman times to the present day is told by 75 costumed wax figures and a commentary in French, English, German and Japanese. The tour ends with a wine tasting.

Accommodation and food

Café des Arts € *138 cours Victor Hugo and 184 r. Ste-Catherine; tel: 05 56 91 78 46. Open daily 0830–0200. Closed 25 Dec, 1 Jan.* Large and lively establishments serving simple but well-cooked dishes. Wine by the glass. Terrace dining available. Jazz concerts and traditional *chansons françaises* staged in the evenings.

Baud et Millet €€ *19 r. Huguerie; tel: 05 56 79 05 77. Closed Sun.* Themed dinners are a speciality in this 80-seat air-conditioned restaurant, which boasts a stock of 200 different cheeses and a cellar of 950 bottles of wine from many parts of the world.

Opposite
The Cathédrale St-André

🚌 The city's main shopping street – where you can buy almost anything you're likely to need – is r. Ste-Catherine, running through the heart of the old quarter from pl. de la Victoire to pl. de la Comédie, a distance of about 2km free of motor traffic. The department stores Galeries Lafayette and Galeries Bordelaises are a few moments' walk from pl. de la Comédie. Another major shopping centre is in r. Claude Bonnier in the Mériadeck district. Traditional street markets are held on Sat in pl. Canteloup and pl. Maynard. Pl. St-Pierre is the scene of a market for organic produce on Thur and there's a flea market Sun–Fri in pl. Canteloup.

Le Bistrot des Quinconces €€ *4 pl. des Quinconces; tel: 05 56 52 84 56. Open daily 0730–0200. Closed Sun 1900, 25 Dec.* Good food – including wonderful salmon and veal dishes – is served 364 days a year in this centrally located bistro.

Le Brocéliande €€ *15 pl. des Martyres de la Résistance; tel: 05 56 96 38 93. Open Tue–Sun 1200–1415 and 1930–2230. Closed Sat lunchtime.* A good selection of wines is available by the glass. The chef's specialities include *escalope de foie gras* with apples and Calvados.

Château de Lantic €€ *10 route de Lartigue, Martillac; tel: 05 56 72 58 68; e-mail: contact@chateau-de-lantic.com; www.chateau-de-lantic.com. Open all year.* Rooms in a restored 18th-century manor house in a village south of Bordeaux, off the A62 autoroute.

Chez Brunet €€ *9 r. de Condé; tel: 05 56 51 35 50. Open Mon–Sat 1100–1430 and 1830–2230. Closed public holidays and weekends in Jul and Aug.* All types of oyster served every which way. Wines by the glass.

Citotel Le Chantry €€ *153 r. Georges Bonnac; tel: 05 56 24 08 88; e-mail: contact@chantry-bordeaux.com; www.chantry-bordeaux.com.* In a quiet part of the Mériadeck district, this modern hotel has 40 rooms, half with air conditioning, and all with en-suite facilities, TV and direct-dial telephones; there is also secure rooftop parking. No restaurant, but breakfast available.

Connemara €€ *18 cours d'Albert, Bordeaux; tel: 05 56 52 82 57; www.connemara-pub.com. Closed Sun.* Bordeaux's most popular Irish pub serves bar snacks, fish and chips, Guinness® pie and apple crumble. The upstairs restaurant is predictably green and there is free live music most nights.

Didier Gélineau €€ *26 r. du Pas St-Georges, Bordeaux; tel: 05 56 52 84 25. Closed Sat lunch and Sun.* An elegant dining room offering regional dishes at reasonable prices, including *foie gras*, lobster, pigeon and truffles.

L'Estaquade €€ *Quai des Queyries; tel: 05 57 54 02 50. Open daily 1200–1430 and 2000–2400.* Located on the east bank of the Garonne, in the city's La Bastide quarter, L'Estaquade is modern and deservedly fashionable, specialising in seafood dishes, especially those originating in Morocco and Mediterranean France.

Hôtel Alton €€ *107 r. de la Pelouse de Douet, Bordeaux; tel: 05 56 99 55 55; e-mail: hotel-alton@wanadoo.fr; www.hotel-alton.com.* Conveniently located in a quiet suburb at the end of a tram line, the Alton has 170 en-suite rooms, a restaurant and a pleasant enclosed garden.

Hôtel Bristol €€ *Pl. Gambetta; tel: 05 56 81 85 01; e-mail: Bristol@hotel-bordeaux.com; www.hotel-bordeaux.com.* Right in the thick of things, with 19 en-suite rooms. No restaurant; breakfast available.

Above
The Esplanade des Quinconces

Hôtel Clémenceau €€ *4 cours Georges Clémenceau; tel: 05 56 52 98 98; e-mail: hotel.clemenceau@orange.fr; www.hotel-bordeaux.com.* Just off the pl. Gambetta with almost everything Bordeaux has to offer near at hand. Each of the 44 rooms has en-suite facilities. No restaurant, but breakfast available.

Hôtel de Sèze €€ *23 allée de Tourny; tel: 05 56 52 65 54; e-mail: hotel.seze. medoc@wanadoo.fr; www. hotelsezemedoc.com.* As close to the centre of things as you could want. Twenty-four en-suite rooms. No restaurant, but breakfast available. The same owners also run **Royal Médoc Hotel €€** *3–5 r. de Sèze, Bordeaux; tel: 05 56 81 72 42.* Forty-five modern guest rooms in an 18th-century building.

Chez Philippe €€–€€€ *1 pl. du Parlement; tel: 05 56 81 83 15. Open Tue–Sat 1200–1400 and 1930–2300. Closed 1 Jan, 1 May, the whole of Aug and 25 Dec.* In the pleasant heart of the city's old quarter, this is a well-established and well-respected restaurant. Specialities include *fruits de mer* and grilled turbot. Wines by the glass.

Hôtel de Normandie €€–€€€ *7 cours du XXX Juillet; tel: 05 56 52 16 80.* Close to the tourist office, with views over Esplanade des Quinconces and the River Garonne. Ninety-eight en-suite rooms with TV and direct-dial telephones. No restaurant, but breakfast available.

Hôtel des Quatre Soeurs €€–€€€ *6 cours du XXX Juillet; tel: 05 56 81 19 20; e-mail: 4soeurs@mailcity.com.* Similar location and facilities but cheaper and smaller than the Normandie, with 34 en-suite rooms. No restaurant, but breakfast available. Run in partnership with **Hôtel de l'Opera** *35 r. Esprit des Lois, Bordeaux; tel 05 56 81 41 27; e-mail: hotel.opera.bx@wanadoo.fr*

La Tupiña €€–€€€ *6–8 r. Porte de la Monnaie; tel: 05 56 91 56 37; e-mail: latupina@latupina.com; www.latupina.com.* Authentic traditional cuisine, with the emphasis on specialities of the Southwest: The owner, Jean-Pierre Xiradakis, is probably Bordeaux's best-known chef.

Nightlife

Bordeaux is not one of the world's most swinging cities, but many late-night bars can be found around quai de Paludate, pl. de la Victoire and along r. des Pilliers de la Tutelle, off pl. de la Comédie. Many restaurants and bistros offer soirées of jazz, traditional *chansons* or – mon Dieu! – karaoke. **L'Avant Scène** (*r. de la Borie; tel: 05 57 87 55 88*) is a simple bar where they dispense traditional jazz – and beer from a piano. For those with more highbrow tastes, there's a continuous programme of theatre, opera and classical concerts. Check the tourist office for the latest information. **Bar de l'Hôtel de Ville (BHV)** €€ *4 r. de l'Hôtel de Ville, Bordeaux; tel: 05 56 44 05 08. Open daily.* A centrally located gay café-bar that gets crowded late at night.

Hôtel Burdigala €€€ *115 r. Georges Bonnac; tel: 05 56 90 16 16; e-mail: burdigala@burdigala.com; www.burdigala.com.* Quietly situated, yet within walking distance of pl. Gambetta and major attractions, the four-star establishment has 83 en-suite rooms with television and telephones, garage parking and a restaurant (€€€).

Suggested walk

Total distance: About 4km, but because it's a circular route it can be shortened or terminated at any point.

Time: Allow 3 leisurely hours.

Route: Start at pl. de la Comédie, which is dominated by the colonnaded bulk of **LE GRAND THEATRE ❶**. Cross to **COURS DE L'INTENDANCE ❷** and within 150m turn right into Passage Sarget and follow it into pl. Chapelet. This gets its name from the bas-relief above the main entrance to **EGLISE NOTRE-DAME ❸**, which shows the Virgin handing a rosary (*chapelet*) to St Dominic.

After a tour of the church, retrace your steps to pl. de la Comédie and turn right into r. Ste-Catherine, a long pedestrianised street lined with shops large and small and with a warren of fascinating lanes and alleys leading from each side. This is the district known as Vieux Bordeaux.

Continue to cours d'Alsace Lorraine, where a right turn leads to pl. Pey-Berland. Here, the Tour Pey-Berland, a 15th-century tower, stands apart from the main body of **CATHEDRALE ST-ANDRE ❹**, scene of the wedding in 1152 of Eleanor of Aquitaine and Henry Plantagenet, soon to become King Henry II of England. Opposite the tower, follow r. D. Dubergier into cours Pasteur and at the **MUSEE D'AQUITAINE ❺** bear left into cours Victor Hugo. Cross r. Ste-Catherine and opposite la **GROSSE CLOCHE ❻** take r. du Mirail, remarkable for its grand houses from the 17th and 18th centuries.

Next, turn left into r. St-François, which has a fine collection of 18th-century buildings. This leads to pl. Canteloup and **Basilique St-Michel ❼**. This impressive church took two centuries to complete from the start of construction in 1350, and has the second highest spire in France – a 15th-century structure 114m tall.

From the riverside end of the church, in pl. Duburg, follow r. de la Fusterie, where the Porte de Bourgogne, a triumphal archway built in 1755, stands on the site of a medieval city gate. Cross cours Victor Hugo and continue along r. de la Rousselle, where the family home of the 16th-century essayist Michel de Montaigne stands at Nos 23–25.

At the end of r. de la Rousselle, turn right and from r. Ausone cross cours d'Alsace Lorraine into r. Chai des Farines, which leads into pl. du Palais, where you can visit **PORTE CAILHAU ❽**. Follow r. des

Agentiers, then r. du Parlement St-Pierre into pl. du Parlement, once a royal marketplace, now a pleasing cobblestoned square surrounded by Louis XV buildings. From here bear right along r. F. Philippart to **PL. DE LA BOURSE ⑨**. Facing the river, turn left and a short walk along the quayside brings you to **COURS DU CHAPEAU-ROUGE ⑩**. Another left turn here returns you to pl. de la Comédie.

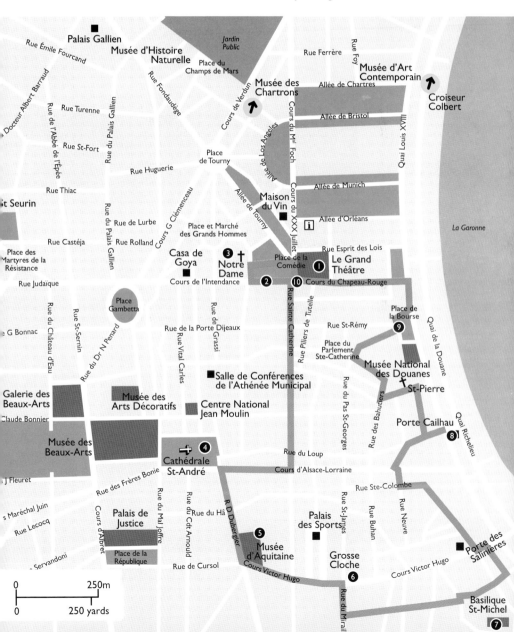

Bordeaux vineyards

Ratings

Cellar tours and tasting	●●●●●
Château vineyards	●●●●●
Architecture	●●●●
Food and drink	●●●●
Heritage	●●●●
Markets	●●●●
Scenery	●●●●
Walking	●●●

Even if your interest in wine has been restricted to its taste and its effect, a visit to Bordeaux, one of the great wine-growing regions of France, is almost sure to kindle a desire to learn more about one of nature's most delectable products. This is easy to arrange. Bordeaux has at least 5000 wine châteaux, many of which offer highly informative guided tours of their cellars, and a tasting. The Bordeaux region, in which the Garonne and Dordogne rivers flow, has up to 121,400 hectares of vineyards, with 57 appellations and six main families of Bordeaux wine. Villages of pale stone houses with crinkly-tiled red roofs punctuate the miles of farmland and the straight rows of vines. Visitors in winter and spring will see great spheres of mistletoe decorating leafless trees – sometimes half a dozen clumps of the parasite in one tree.

Wine tasting

Tourist Office *12 cours du XXX Juillet, 33080 Bordeaux; tel: 05 56 00 66 00; e-mail: otb@bordeaux-tourisme.com; www.bordeaux-tourisme.com. Open daily May–Aug 0900– 1930 (Sun 0930–1830), rest of year closes at 1830.*

The Bordeaux wine region is divided into five main areas, Médoc, The Graves and Sauternais, Entre-Deux-Mers, Saint-Emilion and the Libournais, and the Côtes de Blaye and de Bourg. Each one has a range of facilities for visitors including distinctive museums and suppliers, besides the numerous wine-producing châteaux and vineyards. Wine producers welcome visits to their châteaux and some can arrange a tour and tasting if you drop in, but most prefer that you phone ahead and make an appointment.

How can a person interested in wine become a knowledgeable connoisseur in less than a week? The tourist office in Bordeaux city centre is a good place to start. They can arrange tours of vineyards and *caves* (wine cellars) throughout the region. The tourist office offers its

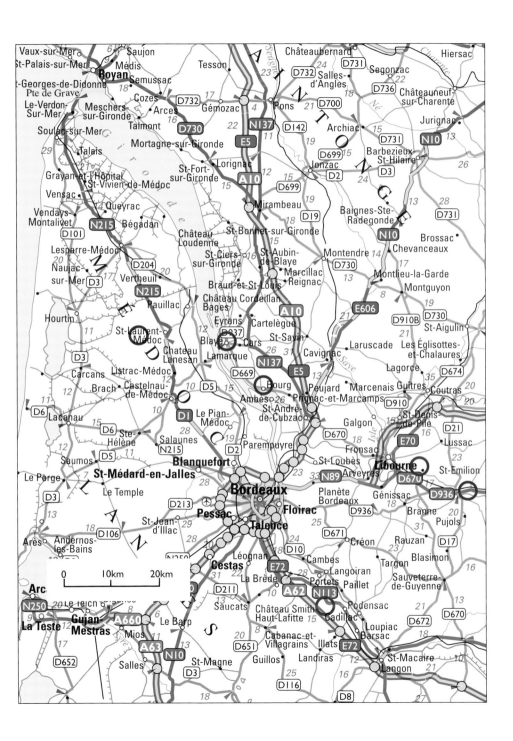

Yellow rose

The yellow roses between the vine rows are not purely for decoration. Highly susceptible to vine diseases, the roses give early warning of any such problems affecting the vines.

Right
Where it all begins …

ℹ️ **Ecole du Vin de Bordeaux €€–€€€**
1 cours du XXX Juillet, Bordeaux; tel: 05 56 00 22 85; e-mail: ecole@vins-bordeaux.fr; www.ecole.vins-bordeaux.fr/anglais/index.asp

Planète Bordeaux €€
Maison des Bordeaux et Bordeaux Supérieurs, on the N89 towards Libourne, Beychac-et-Caillau; tel: 05 57 97 19 36; e-mail: contact@maisondesbordeaux.com; www.planete-bordeaux.net. Open Mon–Fri 0930–1730, Sat 1000–1800.

Ecole du Bordeaux €€€ *7 r. du Château Trompette, Bordeaux; tel: 05 56 90 91 92; e-mail: contact@ecoledubordeaux.com; www.ecoledubordeaux.com*

own twice-weekly (Thur and Sat) introduction to wine tasting which includes a selection of wines and a cheese platter, and a fun try-out of smells from essence samples, to train your nose to recognise subtle aromas in the wines.

For a more advanced experience, the **Ecole du Vin de Bordeaux**, located opposite the tourist office, offers a range of courses and has opened a wine bar on the premises. You will get an introduction to the techniques and vocabulary used in tasting fine Bordeaux wines with the help of wine industry professionals. Courses are at various levels, from two-hour introductory courses, Saturday School and wine weekends to more intensive courses with visits to vineyards and wine producers.

Another good place to start exploring Bordeaux wines is **Planète Bordeaux** located in the Pauillac in the Médoc area. The centre is equipped with multi-media facilities to tell the story of wine production in the Bordeaux region, a huge wine cellar and shop. For groups, there are fun speed-dating style tasting sessions.

Jean-Michel Cazes, owner of Château Lynch-Bages at Pauillac, has opened a wine school in Bordeaux, **Ecole du Bordeaux**, offering initiation courses and three-day seminars.

The Médoc

The Médoc is a strip of land about 80km long and up to 5km wide on the left bank of the Gironde estuary, north of Bordeaux city. It is home to some world-renowned châteaux. The main road N215 runs its length but it is the D2 that makes the best wine route, as it passes through important wine-making towns such as Margaux, St-Estèphe and Pauillac. The Médoc produces mostly red wine, but a few estates make white wine from Sauvignon and Sémillon grapes.

Château d'Arsac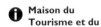
€€ Tel: 05 56 58 83
90; www.chateau-arsac.com

Château Lanessan €€
Domaines Bouleller, Cussac
Fort-Médoc; tel: 05 56 58
94 80; e-mail:
bouteiller@bouteiller.com;
www.bouteiller.com.
Open all year. Visits daily
0900–1200, 1400–1800.

Château Loudenne €
St-Yzans-de-Médoc; tel: 05
56 73 17 97; e-mail:
visites@lafragette.com;
www.lafragette.com

Château Lynch-Bages
€€ Tel: 05 56 73 24 00;
www.lynchbages.com

**Château Mouton-
Rothschild** Tel: 05 56 73
21 29; e-mail: visites@
bphr.com

Château d'Arsac
Guided tour of the cellars by appointment. Château d'Arsac is well-known for its collection of modern art related to wine production.

Château Lanessan
Guided tours of the grounds, gardens and the Dutch greenhouse are provided in this late 19th-century, Tudor-style château in the Médoc. An additional point of interest is the display of horse-drawn carriages from the early 1900s, tack room, stables and other items. The narration is in French and English.

Château Loudenne
Located in St-Yzans-de-Médoc beside the Gironde, Château Loudenne has gardens, a museum and exhibition of wine making through the centuries. Visit by appointment.

Château Lynch-Bages
The 19th-century fermenting room is still in its original state, but wine-making facilities are modern and you can see how technology has developed. Visits by appointment.

Château Mouton-Rothschild
One of the most prestigious wine-producing châteaux. Located in Pauillac and includes a fine museum of wine in art, a collection of valuable items gathered by Baron Philippe de Rothschild.

PAUILLAC

**ⓘ Maison du
Tourisme et du
Vin de Médoc** La Verrerie,
33250 Pauillac; tel: 05 56
59 03 08, e-mail: mtvp@
wanadoo.fr; www.pauillac-
medoc.com, offers a free
video presentation on the
local vineyard scene.
Vineyard visits and tastings
are organised mid-Jul–mid-
Sep. Open daily 0930–1930;
Sun and public holidays
1000–1800.

A major centre of the wine trade in one of the Médoc's most prestigious wine-growing areas, Pauillac is on the Gironde river. It was once a busy port, with transatlantic steamers tying up at its quays. Today it attracts private yachts, cruisers and other pleasure craft. Famous châteaux (Premiere Grand Cru Classe) in the vicinity include **Château Lafite-Rothschild** (tel: 05 56 59 26 83; e-mail: visites@lafite.com. Open for individual visits 1400 and 1530 with free guided tour and tasting by appointment with two weeks' notice. Closed public holidays and during grape harvest from Aug to end Oct), **Château Mouton-Rothschild** and **Château Margaux**. Free one-hour guides of the Château Margaux wine stores are available: book at least two weeks ahead. As well as the wine stores you will see various apparatus used in wine making and a collection of wine bottles from past ages.

Probably the most fascinating of these to visit from the tourist's point of view is the **Château Mouton-Rothschild** €€ (Pouyalet, 33250 Pauillac; tel: 05 56 73 21 29. Book two weeks ahead. Mon–Thur 0930–1215 and 1400–1700, Fri 0930–1100 and 1400–1500. Also weekends Jun–Oct. Open all year except 1 May and between Christmas and New Year). Baron Philip de Rothschild, who died in 1988, was

Château Filhot
Tel: 05 56 76 61 09;
e-mail: filhot@filhot.com;
www.filhot.com

Château Haut-Brion
Tel: 05 56 00 29 30;
e-mail: visit@haut-brion.com;
www.haut-brion.com

Château Latour-Martillac Tel: 05 57 97 71 11; e-mail: latourmartillac@latourmartillac.com;
www.latour-martillac.com

Château Smith-Haut-Lafitte €€ Martillac;
Tel: 05 57 83 11 22;
e-mail: smith-haut-lafitte@smith-haut-lafitte.com;
www.smith-haut-lafitte.com

Château d'Yquem
Tel: 05 57 98 07 07;
www.yquem.fr

Maison des Vins de Graves 61 Cours du Maréchal Foch, Podensac;
tel: 05 56 27 09 25;
www.vins-graves.com

passionate about wine. He built his 'Great Cellar' in 1926 as a young man and went on to develop a museum of wine in art. The museum covers many centuries through paintings, tapestries, glassware and other exhibits from all over the world.

The Graves and the Sauternais

Supposedly the birthplace of the Bordeaux wine industry, the Graves gets its name from the gravel soil in which vines thrive. The A62 autoroute runs through the area but it is the N113 that takes you through the main wine villages, running southeast from Bordeaux city along the river Garonne. Graves wines are both red and white, while the Sauternes produces rich sweet white wine.

Château Filhot
Set in an English-style park with a lake and terraces adorned with Médici vases. Visits and wine tasting *Mon–Fri 0900–1800* and by appointment at weekends.

Château Haut-Brion
Located in Pessac just outside Bordeaux. Visits during the week by appointment.

Château Latour-Martillac
Visits by appointment on weekdays. This château is proud that its wine was served at Buckingham in 1936 for the coronation of King George VI.

Château Smith-Haut-Lafitte
Visits and tasting daily by appointment. Located in Martillac, adjacent to the vinotherapy centre, Les Sources de Caudalie.

Château d'Yquem
The premier producer of Sauternes sweet white wine, this château has been owned by the same family for over 400 years. It is said that each vine plant produces only one glass of wine. Visits *Mon–Fri 1400–1530*, but you must make a written request at least three weeks in advance.

Also worth visiting is **Maison des Vins de Graves**, the base of the Graves wine-making union. A video describes the stages of wine making and the centre updates a list of châteaux open for visits without appointment.

Entre-Deux-Mers

Literally between two seas, but in reality the land lies between the two great rivers of the region, the Garonne and the Dordogne, east of

⊕ Château de Fontenille *La Sauve Majeure; tel: 05 56 23 03 26; e-mail: contact@ chateau-fontenille.com; www.chateau-fontenille.com*

Château de Grand Branet *Capian; tel: 05 56 72 17 30; e-mail: d.mainvielle@free.fr; http://chateaugrandbranetuk. free.fr; www.entredeuxmers. com/chateaugrandbranet*

Château La France *Tel: 05 57 55 24 10; e-mail: contact@ chateaulafrance.com; www.chateaulafrance.com*

Château Langoiran *Le Pied du Château, Langoiran; tel: 05 56 57 08 55; e-mail: infos@ chateaulangoiran.com; www.chateaulangoiran.com*

Maison Ginestet *19 avenue de Fontenille, Carignan de Bordeaux; tel: 05 56 20 90 74. Open Mon–Sat 1000, 1400 & 1600.*

Planète Bordeaux *Tel: 05 57 97 19 35; www.planete-bordeaux.net*

Bordeaux city. The main roads through the area are the D10, D671 and D936. Steep slopes overlook the river valleys and catch the sun. The area produces dry white and red wines, and also medium-sweet whites. Tourist offices have a map of the wine route and some winegrowers are organised for weekend visits.

Château de Fontenille

Located on a ridge in the village of La Sauve Majeure with a fermentation room dating back to the 15th century. *Visits and tasting daily by appointment.*

Château de Grand Branet

Visits and tasting *daily 1000–1800* and bed and breakfast accommodation is available in this renovated 19th-century château.

Château La France

Open for visits *daily during the summer and Mon–Fri the rest of the year*, and there is a children's area. Located in Beychac-et-Caillau off the A89 autoroute.

Château Langoiran

A 19th-century family house with underground wine cellars housing the ageing barrels. Visit and tasting by appointment.

Also worth visiting are the cellars of the wine merchant **Maison Ginestet** in Carignan-de-Bordeaux and **Planète Bordeaux** in Beychac-et-Caillau. Located off the N89 (exit 5), the centre offers an enthralling presentation of wine making from the landscape, the vines, the seasons and the work of the vinegrower. A visit is completed with a wine tasting of the *Caves des 1001 Châteaux*.

Right
Château Margaux, Bordeaux

Right
A range of wines

St-Emilion and the Libournais

Château Angélus
Tel: 05 57 24 71 39;
e-mail: chateau-angelus@
chateau-angelus.com;
www.chateau-angelus.com
and www.angelus.com

Château de Carbonneau *Tel: 05 57 47 46 46; e-mail: carbonneau@wanadoo.fr; www.chateau-carbonneau. com*

Château Figeac *St-Emilion; tel: 05 57 24 72 26; e-mail: chateau-figeac@chateau-figeac.com; www.chateau-figeac.com*

Château de la Rivière *Tel: 05 57 55 56 51; e-mail: reception@vignobles-gregoire.com; www. chateau-de-la-riviere.com*

This is an area bordered by the rivers Dordogne and Isle, to the east of Bordeaux city around Libourne. The N89 main road and A89 autoroute pass through. The main towns are Fronsac, Pomerol, St-Emilion, Libourne and Lussac. The wine-making landscape of St-Emilion was the first vineyard to be listed as a UNESCO World Heritage Site.

Château Angélus
Visits and tasting *Mon–Fri* by appointment at least one week in advance.

Château de Carbonneau
Visits *daily by appointment* and bed and breakfast offered in six rooms. Located in Pessac-sur-Dordogne.

Château Figeac
Eighteenth-century architecture combined with impressive underground cellars housing oak barrels and modern stainless-steel containers. Visits and tasting *Mon–Fri by appointment. Closed Aug.*

Château de la Rivière
Located in Fronsac and dating back to 1553 but restored in the 19th century. There are 3 hectares of underground cellars. Visits and tasting *daily by appointment.*

St-Emilion

St-Emilion *Pl. des Créneaux; tel: 05 57 55 28 28; e-mail: st-emilion.tourisme@ wanadoo.fr; www.saint-emilion-tourisme.com. Open year round. Guided tours €€.*

Fancy a change of pace? From Langon, southeast of Bordeaux, a barge carries up to 80 passengers for trips along the Garonne river. *For information and reservations contact L'Escapade, 43 bis, r. des Salières, Langon; tel: 05 56 63 06 45.*

It doesn't take long to realise why St-Emilion is such a favourite with visitors to the region. Sprawled over the slopes of two hills, it's a small but lively town of narrow, steep streets and ancient buildings, and its people are as proud of its history as they are of the renowned vineyards in the surrounding countryside. The town owes its name to an 8th-century hermit monk who settled in a grotto, which exists to this day.

The major attraction is the **Eglise Monolithe**, the largest troglodyte church in France. Carved out of solid rock between the 8th and 12th centuries, the huge structure contains three aisles and impressive vaulting and square pillars. Nearby, the **Chapelle de la Trinité** is a small 13th-century sanctuary built by Benedictine monks. Below the chapel is the **grotto** used by St Emilion, a small cell containing a natural spring and the hermit's chair, carved from rock. **Catacombs** opening off a cliff facing the Chapelle de la Trinité connect with the troglodyte church. Guided tours of the chapel, catacombs and church can be arranged through the tourist office.

Savour the flavour

For nearly 1000 years the extensive Bordeaux vineyards have been producing fine wines in a variety of landscapes. The region is midway between the North Pole and the Equator.

Placed between the Atlantic Ocean and the estuary formed by the Garonne and Dordogne rivers, it has a steady temperate climate and state of humidity. Europe's largest forest, the Landes Forest (11,000 sq km, or one-third the size of Belgium), forming a triangle between Bordeaux, Bayonne and Nérac, protects the wine region from the wind.

Experienced growers know which soil types and which grape varieties are the most appropriate, resulting in a whole range of flavours, each distinctively Bordeaux.

If it's a first-time experience, a visit to a château will open your eyes to the intricacies of wine production. Some people become so intrigued that they visit several wineries – all different in character – and are launched into a lifetime interest.

To ensure reliable quality, wine growers must adhere to strict rules relating to such considerations as a limit on the number of vines per hectare, maximum permissible yields, pruning methods and percentage of alcohol. It is forbidden to irrigate the vineyard.

Rich soil is not necessarily a plus factor in the growing of wine. The poor, gravelly soil that produces the greatest Graves wines (hence the name) encourages the vines to push their roots deep to reach water and the elements of the subsoil, bringing richness into the grape. Vine roots can penetrate underground for nearly 2m.

The huge cellars on the wine estates are an impressive site. The vat house or vat room contains great stainless-steel vats in which the tannin is slowly extracted. Some vineyards have installed superbly made wooden vats.

The barrel room is even more memorable: hundreds of oak barrels mounted on their sides in straight rows. Each barrel contains 225 litres of wine.

At the end of the tour comes the tasting, bringing the eyes and nose into action as well as the taste buds.

Right
Wine and other gifts

Côtes de Blaye and de Bourg

🅑 Château Fougas
Lansac; tel: 05 57 68 42 15; e-mail: info@chateau-fougas.com; www.fougas.com

Château Mercier *Tel: 05 57 42 66 99; e-mail: info@chateau-mercier.fr; www.chateau-mercier.fr*

Château Mille-Secousses *Bourg-sur-Gironde; tel: 05 57 68 34 95; e-mail: info@ mille-secousses.com; www.mille-secousses.com*

Château Moncoseil *Plassac; tel: 05 57 42 16 61; www.chateaumoncoseil.com*

Château Tayac *Bourg-sur-Gironde; tel: 05 57 68 40 60; www.chateau-tayac.fr*

Maison du Vin des Côtes de Bourg *1 pl. de l'Eperon, Bourg; tel: 05 57 94 80 20; e-mail: info@cotes-de-bourg.com; www.cotes-de-bourg.com*

Maison du Vin des Premières Côtes de Blaye *Blaye; tel: 05 57 42 91 19; e-mail: contact@ boutique-vin-blaye.com; www.boutique-vin-blaye.com*

This area lies 30km north of Bordeaux on the right bank of the Gironde and stretches over a vast plateau with sloping sides that are covered with vineyards bearing both red and white grapes. Three lines of hill slopes run parallel with the Dordogne river. The A10 passes through and N10 and N137 are the main roads that lead to the wine-producing villages.

Château Fougas
Originally part of a monastery. Visit and tasting *Mon–Fri 0900–1200 and 1400–1800, and Sat by appointment.*

Château Mercier
A family enterprise for 13 generations. Visit *Mon–Fri 0800–1200 and 1400–1800 and by appointment at weekends.*

Château Mille-Secousses
Visits *Mon–Fri 0830–1200 and 1400–1800.* The large wine-tasting room has arched openings and old ploughing implements are displayed alongside oak barrels.

Château Moncoseil
Steeped in history, it is said Charlemagne held council here. *Open for visits Mon–Fri 0800–1200 and 1400–1800, Sat 0900–1230, Sat afternoon and Sun by appointment.* Located in Plassac.

Château Tayac
Renaissance-style château built in 1827 on the site of a much earlier property in a superb location where the Dordogne and Gironde rivers meet. *Visit by appointment.*

Also worth visiting are the area's wine centres, **Maison du Vin des Côtes de Bourg**, which is *open daily mid-Jun to mid-Sep and Mon–Sat the rest of the year*, and **Maison du Vin des Premières Côtes de Blaye**, which is *open Mon–Sat all year.*

Accommodation and food

Castillon-la-Bataille *Pl. Marcel Paul; tel: 05 57 40 27 58; e-mail: otcastillonpujols@wanadoo.fr. Open all year. Mon–Sat 0930–1800.*

Hostellerie St-Pierre €€ *Verdelais; tel: 05 56 62 02 03*, is a good place for lunch or an overnight stop. One of its walls bears a sketch by Toulouse-Lautrec.

Clos Carré € *14 chemin de Carré, Libourne; tel: 05 57 51 53 01*, is an attractive old house with two double guest rooms and a family room, each with private facilities.

Le Médiéval €–€€ *Pl. de la Porte Bouqueyre, St-Emilion; tel: 05 57 24 72 37; e-mail: lemedieval@free.fr.* Everybody's idea of the small-town French bar-restaurant: good food and service and an attractive setting with outdoor tables where you can watch the world go by.

Hôtel de France et d'Angleterre €€ *3 quai Albert Pichou, Pauillac; tel: 05 56 59 01 20; e-mail: contact@hoteldefrance-angleterre.com; www.hoteldefrance-angleterre.com.* The hotel has 29 en-suite rooms and a restaurant.

Restaurant La Maison du Douanier €€ *2 route de By, St-Christoly-Médoc; tel: 05 56 41 35 25; e-mail: maisondudouanier@wanadoo.fr; www.maisondudouanier.com. Closed Tue.* On the Gironde north of Pauillac, this restaurant, open all year, serves locally produced food and has a good wine list. English is spoken.

Château Cordeillan-Bages €€€ *Pauillac; tel: 05 56 59 24 24, e-mail: cordeillan@relaischateaux.com; www.cordeillanbages.com*, has 25 individually furnished rooms available to the general public as well as those attending wine courses. Facilities include a babysitting service. A 10,000-bottle wine cellar supplies the restaurant.

La Grande Vigne €€€ *Chemin de Smith-Haut-Lafitte, Martillac; tel: 05 57 83 83 83; e-mail: sources@sourcescaudalie.com.* Run by Didier Banyol,

Côtes wines

Côtes wines – Côtes de Bourg, Premières Côtes de Bordeaux, Premières Côtes de Blaye, Côtes de Castillon and others – come from a vast area stretching from the edge of the Charentes in the northwest to the Périgord region in the east. This is a more hilly area than the Médoc and the vines are grown on wide slopes, some on clay soils which absorb sunlight. The Merlot grape is the basis of these wines from the right banks of the Garonne, Dordogne and Gironde rivers.

The vineyards producing Premières Côtes de Bordeaux are seen along a 60km-long, 5km-wide stretch along the right bank of the Garonne.

To the east, St-Emilion, heartland of the Merlot grape, is known as 'the hill with a thousand châteaux'. It certainly seems like it as you explore the narrow roads, punctuated by stone crosses, and pass château after château amid sloping vineyards around the ancient town.

Sweet and semi-sweet white wines, among them Barsac and Sauternes, are grown in the southern parts of the Bordeaux wine region. These wines spend two or three years in the cellar before bottling. Great vintages go on improving for several decades, developing concentration and power unequalled by other wines.

and awarded two Michelin stars, this new gourmet restaurant is at the four-star hotel on the Château Smith-Haut-Lafitte estate. M. Banyol also runs the country-style **Le Table du Lavoir €€** brasserie, where the décor is based on the place where grape pickers traditionally washed their clothes. In the hotel's tower is a cigar room, where guests can enjoy an aromatic cigar and a glass of cognac.

Les Sources de Caudalie, Vinotherapy Spa €€€ *Chemin de Smith Haut-Lafitte, Bordeaux-Martillac; tel: 05 57 83 83 83; e-mail: sources@sources-caudalie.com; www.sources-caudalie.com.* Offers vinotherapy in the setting of a luxury hotel, with spa treatments for relaxation, anti-ageing, improved circulation and skin conditioning, using materials made from grape seeds and local spring water.

Suggested tour

Maison du Vin de Barsac *Pl. de l'Eglise; tel: 05 56 27 15 44; e-mail: contact@maisondebarsac.fr; www.maisondebarsac.fr. Open daily year round.*

Maison du Vin de Castillon-la-Bataille *6 allée de la République; tel: 05 57 40 00 88; e-mail: contact@cote-de-castillon.com; www.cotes-de-castillon.com. Open daily 0830–1230, 1530–1900 (summer); 0830–1230 (winter).*

Maison du Sauternes *14 pl. de la Mairie, Sauternes; tel: 05 56 76 69 83; e-mail: maisondusauternes@tiscali.fr; www.maisondusauternes.com/default.htm. Open Mon–Fri 0900–1900, Sat and Sun 1000–1900.*

To get maximum benefit from the clear air of the vineyards around St-Emilion, you can hire a bicycle from the town's tourist office, pl. des Crénaux (signposted); tel: 05 57 55 28 29; e-mail: st-emilion.tourisme@wanadoo.fr

Total distance: The main route covers a total of 145km. The detour adds 31km.

Time: Comfortable driving time for the main route is about 3 hours, with an extra hour for the detour. Set aside a full day to allow for sightseeing.

Links: From Langon the A62 continues south towards Agen, Moissac and Montauban. If you prefer not to drive on the autoroute, a toll road, take the N113, which follows much the same course – that of the River Garonne, in fact – as far as Moissac.

Route: From central Bordeaux join the Rocade ring road (this can be accessed at the riverfront about 1km downstream of Pont d'Arcins) and follow signs for the A62 – the Autoroute des Deux-Mers – to Toulouse. After 12km (toll-free section) leave the autoroute at Exit 1 and follow signs to **La Brède ❶**, where the moated château was the birthplace in 1689 of the writer–philosopher Baron de Montesquieu. Take the D109 north for 4km to Martillac, home of the **Château Smith-Haut-Lafitte ❷** vineyard, then head east for 3km, turning right on to the N113.

Continue south for 25km to **Barsac ❸**, where half a dozen manor châteaux welcome visitors. From Barsac follow the D114 south for 10km to Budos then turn left on to the D125 to reach **Sauternes ❹** in 3km. Famous for its sweet white wines, the area around Sauternes also has a number of châteaux open to visitors. The D8 skirts the eastern edge of Sauternes and after 5km reaches the commercial town of Langon, where the N113 crosses the Garonne to the medieval village of St-Macaire.

Detour: From St-Macaire take the D19 north for 4km to the village of **Verdelais ❺**, where the painter Henri Toulouse-Lautrec died in 1901 at the age of 37. He lies in the local cemetery. Follow the D117 west for 3km to Ste-Croix-du-Mont, where there are extensive views across the river towards the far-off Pyrenees. Turn right here on to the D10 and continue for 5km to **Cadillac** 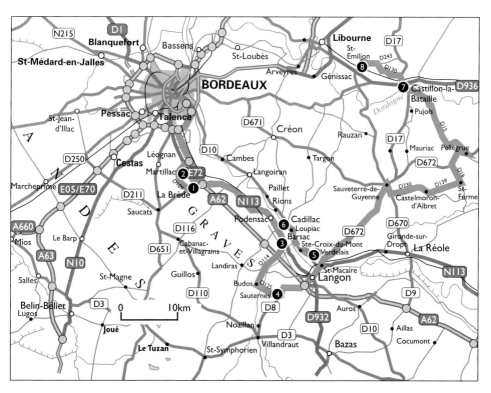, a riverside *bastide* founded in 1280, where the large château was completed in 1620, ruined during the French Revolution and later restored.

From St-Macaire take the D672 northeast for 21km to Sauveterre-de-Guyenne, a 13th-century *bastide* surrounded by châteaux in the heart of the Entre-deux-Mers region. A 7km drive east along the D230 takes you to Castelmoron-d'Albret, distinguished as France's smallest municipality. It covers an area of 4 hectares and has a population of 64. Next, follow the D139 east for 6km to **St-Ferme**, where there is an interesting fortified church dating from the 11th century.

From St Ferme take the D16 north for 4km, turn right on to the D672 for 3km to Pellegrue, then head north on the D15 to reach **Castillon-la-Bataille** ❼ in 19km. Located on the north bank of the River Dordogne, Castillon-la-Bataille is honoured in history as the place where the Hundred Years War ended in 1453. To reach **ST-EMILION** ❽ take the D130 northwest from Castillon-la-Bataille for 9km, then turn left on to the D243 for a further 4km.

Bergerac–Castelnaud

Ratings

Castles	●●●●●
Historical sites	●●●●●
Architecture	●●●●○
Food and drink	●●●●○
Scenery	●●●●○
Vineyards	●●●●○
Museums	●●●○○
Children	●●○○○

The River Dordogne, upstream from Bergerac to the ancient fortress of Castelnaud, offers a good range of touring experiences and contrasts. Bergerac, where the river is wider and quieter than in its upper reaches, manages to be both a modern commercial centre and a labyrinthine medieval city, where you can walk safely through narrow, traffic-free streets. The area is noted for its wines and at least a dozen appellations provide subtle variations. Growers on the designated Route des Vins welcome visitors and are eager to offer tastings. Upstream, the countryside becomes more rugged, the river a little wilder and history, it seems, rather closer. The châteaux here were built to repel raiders rather than satisfy fashion. The character of the river changes with every turn – flowing serenely through meadows, plunging over foaming rapids, looping back on itself as it meanders grandly between soaring walls of rock.

BERGERAC

ℹ️ **Bergerac** *97 R. Neuve d'Argenson; tel: 05 53 57 03 11; e-mail: tourisme-bergerac@aquinet.tm.fr; www.bergerac-tourisme.com. Open all year, but closed Sun mid-Sep–mid-Jun.*

🚢 **Périgord Gabarres** *€€ Quai Salvette, Bergerac; tel: 05 53 24 58 80; e-mail: perigord-gabarre@ wanadoo.fr. Open daily Apr–Oct. Free car parking.*

Capital of the Périgord Pourpre region, whose name derives from the rich, purple-hued wines of the area, historic Bergerac is surrounded by vineyards and farms where the principal crops are tobacco and cereals. The River Dordogne, an important trade route in the past, flows through the heart of the city, but the Ancien Port, where river craft loaded and unloaded their cargoes in the past, is now less picturesquely used as a car park. The old quarter is a labyrinth of medieval stone and half-timbered buildings, most of it mercifully barred to traffic.

Périgord Gabarres offers one-hour river trips aboard a replica traditional Dordogne craft. The story of the river's influence on Bergerac's social and economic development and the history of the region's wine trade are highlighted at **Le Musée du Vin et de la**

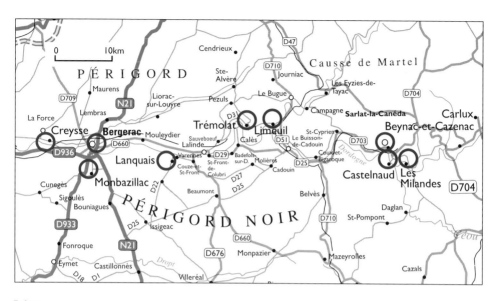

Below
Bergerac

Le Musée du Vin et de la Batellerie €€
5 r. des Conférences, Bergerac; tel: 05 53 57 80 92. Open mid-Mar–mid-Nov Tue–Fri 1000–1200, 1400–1730, Sat 1000–1200, Sun 1430–1830.

La Maison des Vins €€
1 r. des Récollets; tel: 05 53 63 57 57; e-mail: contact@vins-bergerac.fr; www.vins-bergerac.fr/gb/index1024gb.htm (English). Open daily Easter–Oct 1000–1900.

Le Musée d'Intérêt National du Tabac €€
Pl. du Feu; tel: 05 53 63 04 13; www.france-tabac.com/musee.htm. Open Tue–Sat 1000–1200, 1400–1800 (1700 Sat), Sun 1430–1830. Closed public holidays.

Camping Municipal de la Pelouse R. J-J Rousseau; tel: 05 53 57 06 67. Open all year. The site is on the south bank of the Dordogne, facing the Ile Pelouse. 70 pitches.

Opposite
Beynac-et-Cazenac

Batellerie. To learn about the modern wine industry and taste some of its products visit **La Maison des Vins**. Headquarters of the regional wine council, it is entered through the tranquil Cloître des Récollets, part of a monastery dating from the 12th century. The city's association with tobacco is reflected at **Le Musée d'Intérêt National du Tabac**, which houses a unique collection of art and artefacts associated with smoking.

Accommodation and food in Bergerac

Le Family € 3 R. du Dragon; tel: 05 53 57 80 90. This small (only eight rooms) but atmospheric hotel stands at the heart of the old quarter. Rooms are equipped with television, direct-line telephones and double-glazed windows. There is a terrace bar and a garage for guests' cars. **Le Jardin d'Epicure €€**, the hotel's restaurant, specialises in Périgord cuisine (www.lepetitjardin.biz).

La Flambée €€ 153 av. Pasteur, Bergerac; tel: 05 53 57 52 33; e-mail: laflambee@laflambee.com; www.laflambee.com. Twenty-one rooms. Open all year.

Hôtel de France €€ 18 Pl. Gambetta; tel: 05 53 57 11 61; e-mail: contact@hoteldefrance-bergerac.com; www.hoteldefrance-bergerac.com. Adjoining the pedestrianised streets of the old quarter, this modern but quiet hotel has 20 rooms equipped with satellite TV, double glazing and direct-line telephones. Amenities include a swimming pool and garage parking.

Hôtel Verotel €€ Route d'Agen, Bergerac; tel: 05 53 24 89 76; e-mail: hotel-verotel@wanadoo.fr; www.hotelverotel.fr. On the city's southern outskirts, the hotel has 50 air-conditioned rooms with full amenities, a restaurant, sauna, garden, terrace and a bar.

Le Nautic €€ 12 promenade Pierre Loti; tel: 05 53 57 03 27; e-mail: nautic 24100@aol.com. Closed eves Sun–Tue. With shady terraces overlooking the river, the restaurant specialises in fish and regional dishes.

Manoir du Grand Vignoble €€€ St-Julien-de-Crempse; tel: 05 53 24 23 18; e-mail: info@manoirdugrandvignoble.com; www.manoirdugrand vignoble.com. Forty-four rooms. Open all year.

The vanishing nose

Bergerac's most famous citizen, the long-nosed Cyrano, never existed. He was created in 1897 by the playwright Edmond Rostand, who named his character after the real Cyrano de Bergerac, an eccentric 18th-century philosopher who had no connections with the city. A statue of the fictional Cyrano, flamboyantly standing in pl. de la Myrpe, frequently loses its nose to souvenir hunters.

Beynac-et-Cazenac

❶ Beynac-et-Cazenac
*La Balme, Beynac; tel:
05 53 29 43 08; e-mail:
ot.beynac@perigord.tm.fr;
http://ot.beynac.free.fr.
Open all year.*

**❿ Le Musée de la
Protohistoire and
Parc Archéologique €€**
*La Tour du Couvent; tel: 05
53 29 51 28; e-mail:
parc.beynac@wanadoo.fr.
Open daily Jul–Sep.*

Château de Beynac €€
*Tel: 05 53 29 50 40;
www.sigoules.com/visiter/
chateaux/beynac.htm
(French). Open all year;
guided tours mid-Mar–mid-
Nov 1000–1200,
1400–1830.*

Rising steeply from the north bank of the Dordogne, Beynac-et-Cazenac is a pretty village of houses dating from the 15th century. Barge trips are available and canoes and kayaks may be rented. A combined ticket provides access to **Le Musée de la Protohistoire** and **Parc Archéologique**. The museum houses a collection of original and facsimile artefacts, including agricultural implements and iron-working tools dating from 2000 BC. The park contains reconstructed dwellings from as far back as the Neolithic period.

About 3km west of the village, at the top of a 150m cliff, is the **Château de Beynac**. Standing on the site of a much older fortress, the castle dates from the 13th century and was a focal point of exchanges between French and English armies during the Hundred Years War.

Accommodation and food

Hostellerie Maleville €–€€ *Le Bourg, Beynac-et-Cazenac; tel: 05 53 29 50 06; e-mail: hostellerie.maleville@wanadoo.fr. Closed Jan.* Direct-line telephones and TV are installed in each of the 13 rooms in this delightful hotel overlooking the Dordogne. Home-made dishes are served in the riverside restaurant (**€–€€**).

CASTELNAUD

Château de Castelnaud €€
Tel: 05 53 31 30 00; e-mail: chateau@castelnaud.com; www.castelnaud.com. Open daily all year. Jul and Aug 0900–2000; May–Sep 1000–1900; Oct–mid-Nov 1000–1800; mid-Nov–Feb 1400–1700; Mar and Apr 1000–1800.

An English stronghold during much of the Hundred Years War, the **Château de Castelnaud** presents a belligerent face to the castle that was mainly held by the French at Beynac on the opposite side of the Dordogne. Today, you can enjoy one of the most stunning views of the Dordogne Valley from its terrace.

Abandoned at the beginning of the 18th century, but restored in recent years, Castelnaud now houses an imaginatively designed museum of medieval warfare. Audio-visual presentations outline the castle's colourful history and demonstrate the development of fortifications and battle tactics in the Middle Ages. Sound-and-light pageants highlighting historical events at the castle are staged *Jul–Aug*.

CREYSSE

Creysse Syndicat d'Initiative, Bella Riva, Creysse; tel: 05 53 23 20 45; e-mail: port-de-creysse@wanadoo.fr; http://perigord.tm.fr/servtourisme/otsi/creysse. Open all year.

Creysse Musée-Aquarium € 2bis
Impasse Bella Riva, Creysse; tel: 05 53 23 34 97. Open all year 1000–1800 (1900 Jul–Aug). Guided tours in the afternoon.

This small community fronting the Dordogne river 8km east of Bergerac is worth a stop or an out-of-town trip. Surrounded by the Pécharmant vineyards, the oldest in the region, the village has a centrally located information centre, museum and a jetty for river barge trips – all on a compact site, Bella Riva, near the town hall.

The **Creysse Musée-Aquarium** displays fish belonging to 33 species which live in the Dordogne River including migratory fish such as salmon, sturgeon, trout and lamprey. In the cellars, an exhibition recounts the history of fishing from prehistoric times to the present day and there are exhibits of local, Stone Age flint tools. From the jetty outside the Aquarium, you can take a river cruise on a traditional Dordogne sailing barge, a *gabarre*.

LANQUAIS

Château de Lanquais €€ Tel: 05 53 61 24 24. Open Jul and Aug daily 1000–1900; rest of year closed Tue; open pm only Mar, Apr, Oct, Nov.

Standing on a wooded hillside 15km east of Bergerac, the **Château de Lanquais** provides glimpses of the lives of its past inhabitants. The main part of the château, dating from the 14th century, has towers, machicolations and covered watchways for guards and served as a powerful fortress during the Hundred Years War. A magnificent Renaissance palace was added by the same architect and craftsmen who built the Louvre in Paris. There are grandly furnished apartments, some with huge, superbly carved and decorated fireplaces.

LIMEUIL

Office de Tourisme Limeuil, tel: 05 53 22 06 09; e-mail: ot.buissoncadoin@perigord.tm.fr

Jardin-Musée, Limeuil €€ signposted; tel: 05 53 63 32 06; Open Jul–mid-Sep daily. Closed Mon mornings.

An ancient fortified village and barge port, Limeuil is poised in picturesque tiers at the confluence of the Dordogne and Vézère rivers, each of which is spanned by a bridge from the town. The history of horticulture from prehistoric times to the present day is depicted in six gardens at the **Jardin-Musée**. Re-created by Michel and Véronique Guignard, the gardens contain flowers, vegetables and herbs grown as they were in the past and the appropriate tools for each age are displayed.

Accommodation and food in Limeuil

Hôtel Domaine de la Vitrolle €€ *Tel: 05 53 61 58 58; e-mail: contact@la-vitrolle.fr; www.la-vitrolle.fr.* A small manor house at the centre of a large estate has been transformed into a stylish hotel/restaurant with spacious rooms.

LES MILANDES

Château des Milandes €€€ Les Milandes; tel: 05 53 59 31 21; e-mail: josephin-les-milandes@wanadoo.fr; www.milandes.com. Open May, Jun & Sep. Falconry shows daily at 1100, 1500 & 1630.

On the south bank of the Dordogne, about 4km northeast of Castelnaud, the hamlet owes its fame to the late 15th-century **château** that became the home of the black American singer Josephine Baker (1906–75), who took the Parisian cabaret scene by storm in the years before World War II.

Star of the Folies Bergères, she became a French citizen in 1937 and during the war served with the Free French forces and the Résistance, work that earned her the Croix de Guerre. After the war she created a 'world village' at the château, providing a home and education for children of different nationalities and ethnic and religious backgrounds. Her story, and that of the château, is told through furnishings, photographs, a film and recordings of her songs.

A 7-hectare park surrounding the château contains 80 varieties of shrubs and there are demonstrations of falconry.

Opposite
Château de Castelnaud

MONBAZILLAC

🄷 Château de Monbazillac €€
Tel: 05 53 63 65 00 (Mon–Fri), 05 53 61 52 52 (Sat–Sun); e-mail: monbazillac@chateau-monbazillac.com; www. chateau-monbazillac.com. Open daily Apr 1000–1800; May, Oct 1000–1700; Jun–Sep 1000–1900; Nov–Mar 1000–1700. Closed Jan; lunch 1230–1400 except Jun–Sep.

Only 5km south of Bergerac, the 16th-century **Château de Monbazillac** stands on a hilltop grandly overlooking the vineyards that produce the Bergerac region's most famous wines. Monbazillac is a fine sweet white wine, which connoisseurs say goes perfectly with *foie gras*, blue cheeses, white meat and desserts. The wine is made only from grapes affected by *botrytis cinerea* – the 'noble mould'.

The château is a fortified Renaissance home surrounded by a moat, now drained. An imposing round tower with conical roof stands at each corner of the building. Highlights of the interior are the Great Hall – with its painted ceiling, massive Renaissance fireplace and beautiful Flemish tapestries – and the bedchamber of the Viscountess Monbazillac, furnished in Louis XIII style. Other rooms display rustic regional furniture.

Accommodation and food in Monbazillac

La Tour des Vents €€ *Moulin de Malfourat; tel: 05 53 58 30 10; e-mail: moulin.malfourat@wanadoo.fr; www.tourdesvents.com. Closed Jan. Closed Sun eve; Mon & Tue lunchtime.* At the highest point of the Monbazillac hills, the restaurant offers panoramic views of the Bergerac valley. The menu regularly features such regional specialities as *foie gras, cèpe* mushrooms, truffles and stuffed pigeon.

TREMOLAT

🄸 Syndicat d'Initiative *Ilot St-Nicolas Bourg, Tremolat; tel: 05 53 22 89 33; e-mail: mairietremolat@wanadoo.fr; www.pays-de-bergerac.com/ mairie/tremolat*

The attractive village of Trémolat is at the centre of what is almost an island where the Dordogne river sweeps in a majestic meander, a spectacle that may be viewed from a clifftop vantage point (signposted 'Route du Cingle de Trémolat'). From here you can see the entire loop. The main attraction in the village is the fortified church with high walls, a massive bell tower, four domes and a huge chamber where the entire population could seek refuge during an attack.

Suggested tour

Total distance: The main route, hugging the River Dordogne for much of the way, covers a little over 80km. The detour adds 35km.

Time: Driving time for the main route is about 1½ hours. Allow 2½ with the detour. If you decide to take in Eymet and Castillonès as a detour, picking up the main route again at Issigeac, the total driving time will be around 3½ hours. To take in all the sights allow a full day for the trip.

Above
Château de Monbazillac

Links: From Port-de-Couze, just west of Lalinde, the D660 heads south across the river, passing through the *bastide* towns of Beaumont (*see page 142*) and Monpazier (*see page 147*). Limeuil marks the start of a trip through the Valley of Caves – a picturesque and absorbing

Couze-et-St-Front has been a famous paper-making centre since the 16th century. At one time 13 paper mills operated in the Couze Valley – now only two are still working.

Le Moulin de la Rouzique €€ *Route de Varennes, 24150 Couze-et-St-Front; tel: 05 53 24 36 16; e-mail: sappac@ wanadoo.fr; www.cyrano. online.fr/moulin.html. Open daily Jul–Aug 1000–1900, Apr–Oct Mon–Sat 1400–1830. Museum of paper-making.*

journey through prehistory (*see pages 118–131*). From Limeuil the D31 heads north to Le Bugue from where a series of minor roads successively traces the winding Vézère river along the valley.

Route: From **BERGERAC ①** take the D13 south for 5km to **MONBAZILLAC ②**. Less than 1km north of the château, turn left on the D14 to join the N21 (the main route to Agen). Head south for 4km then bear left on the D14 and continue for 8km to **Issigeac**, a quaint medieval village of stone and timber houses, many of them occupied by English expatriates. With its Bishop's Palace, Provost's House and quiet streets, Issigeac is a pleasant place to stop off for a stroll.

Leave the village on the D25 east and after 2km turn left on to the D22 to reach **LANQUAIS ③** in 13km. At Varennes, 1km further on, turn right on to the D37. **Couze-et-St-Front**, where you can cross the Dordogne to Lalinde, comes after 2.5km.

Detour: From Couze-et-St-Front head south on the D660 for 6km, looking out for the remains of old paper mills on the river banks, then take the D27 east for 11km to **Molières** and a further 4km to **Cadouin**,

Moulin de Larroque €€

Couze-et-St-Front; tel: 05 53 61 01 75; e-mail: moulindelarroque@free.fr; www.moulindelarroque.com. Open Mon–Fri 0900–1200, 1400–1700, Sat 1800. Handmade paper workshop and gallery.

St-Front-de-Colubri

A magnificent view of the Dordogne Valley may be enjoyed from a 12th-century chapel built on a clifftop above this village. The chapel was meant to protect the crews of vessels negotiating the Saut de la Gratusse rapids, which can be seen from the viewpoint.

Opposite
Bergerac

two *bastides* (*see pages 144 and 146*). At Cadouin turn north on to the scenic D28 for 7.5km, through Calès, then head west on the D29 for 2km to Badefols-sur-Dordogne, where the castle, now in ruins, was once the hide-out of a pirate gang who raided barges on the river. Continue west to **St-Front-de-Colubri**, where you can cross the river to Lalinde.

From Lalinde, once an English *bastide* but now a workaday industrial town, head east on the D703 for 3km to the village of Sauvebœuf, where the D31 links up with the Route Cingle de Trémolat for spectacular views of the Dordogne. Continue to **TRÉMOLAT ❹**, where the D31 continues to **LIMEUIL ❺**, 7km away. The D51 follows the river upstream from Limeuil, reaching Coux-et-Bigaroque in 10km, and from here the D703 takes you upstream again to St-Cyprien (10km) and **BEYNAC-ET-CAZENAC ❻** (another 10km). **CASTELNAUD ❼** is 2km away on the opposite bank of the river.

Also worth exploring

From Bergerac take the D933 (Marmande route) to Eymet, 28km south, for a look at the vineyards and rolling countryside and at the *bastide* founded in 1271 and now renowned for *pâté de foie gras*, galantines and *charcuterie* products. Next, take the D18 and D111 to Lauzun then head east on the D1 to Castillonnès, another *bastide*. Then you can head north on the N21 to return to Bergerac, or join the D25 after 7km to reach Issigeac and follow the main route.

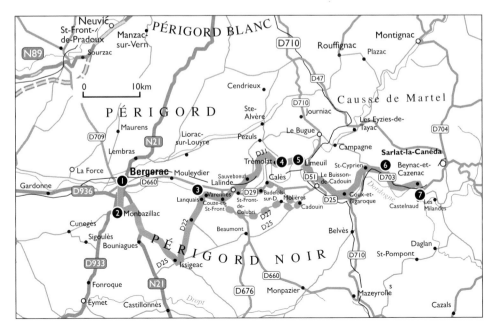

Ratings

Historical sites	●●●●●
Scenery	●●●●●
Architecture	●●●●○
Castles	●●●●○
Caves	●●●●○
Food	●●●●○
Children	●●●○○
Outdoor activities	●●○○○

Castelnaud–Carlux

The area of the Dordogne Valley between Castelnaud and Carlux is great for those who love exploring old churches. There are half a dozen of them listed in this chapter, offering *aficionados* a wealth of architectural and artistic styles to enthuse over. There are also châteaux – some no more than romantic ruins – caves and two ancient towns to explore. Above all, there is splendid scenery to enjoy. Most of the places listed are close to the River Dordogne, meandering grandly through dramatic gorges and passing attractive villages, one of them officially named as the prettiest in France. In contrast, there's a sneak preview of the craggy Lot *département* during a visit to the hilltop town of Gourdon. Some of the riverside communities – especially Domme and La Roque-Gageac – can be rather crowded at times in summer, but there are many charming hideaways waiting to be discovered.

CARLUX

ℹ **Maison du Tourisme** *Rouffillac, Carlux; tel: 05 53 59 10 70; e-mail: maison-du-tourisme-carlux@wanadoo.fr*

Carlux has nothing in the way of formal attractions and consequently does not draw the high-season crowds seen elsewhere in the Dordogne Valley. It is, nevertheless, a worthwhile stop for those who enjoy tranquillity and the magic of unrestored ancient ruins. The village is strategically placed, overlooking the valley, and some old houses and a small indoor market grace its pleasant streets. Its castle, burned out during the Hundred Years War and now reduced to a couple of crumbling towers and a piece of wall, once belonged to the Vicomte de Turenne. A gorgeous view can be enjoyed from the old terrace. In the past, the nearby river crossing was guarded by the Château de Rouffillac, now also in ruins.

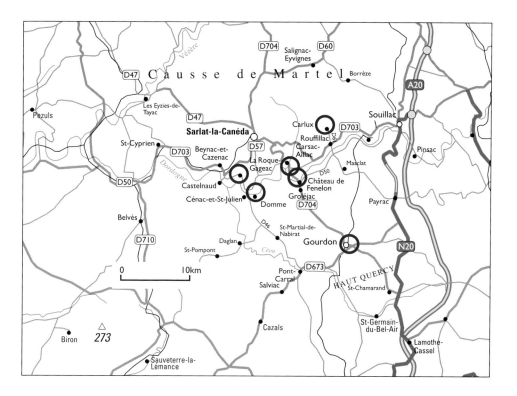

CARSAC-AILLAC

Barely 1km from the River Dordogne's north bank, the little community of Carsac-Aillac is easy to overlook as your eye scans the road map, but it is worth considering as an overnight stop. It has a couple of reasonable hotel/restaurants and three campgrounds and is handy for the best-known of the river's spectacular meanders, the Cingle de Montfort. The view of a perfect semicircle of water flowing between towering cliffs is made all the more stunning by the dramatic appearance of the Château de Montfort, seemingly clinging to the cliff edge. The château is not open to the public.

The château has had a lively history. Originally a Cathar stronghold, it was seized and razed to the ground in 1214 by Simon de Montfort. During violent times in the following centuries it was rebuilt and destroyed again no less than three times. Its present appearance owes much to restoration work carried out in the 19th century. Carsac-Aillac itself has the charming l'Eglise St-Caprais, dating from the 12th century. In contrast to some superb medieval stonework and 16th-century vaulting, there are dramatic, modern stained-glass windows depicting the Stations of the Cross.

DOMME

ⓘ **Domme** *Maison des Gouverneurs, pl. de la Halle, Domme; tel: 05 53 31 71 00; e-mail: domme-tourisme@wanadoo.fr; www.ot-domme.com. Open all year (except Jan) 1000–1800.*

Les Jardins de Marqueyssac €€ *Vézac, located between Domme and Castelnaud; tel: 05 53 31 36 36; e-mail: jardins@marqueyssac.com; www.marqueyssac.com. Open Jul and Aug 0900–2000 with candlelit evenings on Thur to midnight; Apr–Jun and Sep 1000–1900; Feb, Mar & Oct 1000–1800; Nov–Jan 1400–1700. Children welcome and offered nature hunt activities.*

Standing majestically atop sheer cliffs, affording some of the most stupendous views in the entire valley, Domme is dubbed 'the Acropolis of the Dordogne' and like its Athenian counterpart it suffers at times from overcrowding – especially at weekends during the height of summer. The best times to visit the town, therefore, are early in the morning, in the evening, or out of season.

Founded in 1283, it differs from the traditional *bastide* because its location on a triangular site made it difficult for planners to follow strictly the usual gridiron pattern, though they did their geometric best. Nevertheless, its streets are a joy to explore and it's easy to see why the American writer Henry Miller thought that in Domme he'd found the closest thing to an earthly paradise.

Les Jardins de Marqueyssac are magnificent gardens set in 22 hectares of parkland, offering some of the best views over the valley of the Dordogne. Marqueyssac is the most visited garden in the Périgord region and has 6km of green paths among fine topiary hedges and shrubs. Four terraces are laid out in the style of formal Italian gardens.

There are three superb viewpoints on the river side of the town: the Jardin Public du Jubilé, on the site of the camp installed by Simon de

The captain's cunning

Domme's founders chose well when they decided to build their new *bastide* on a sloping triangular site high above the River Dordogne – a place that must have seemed impregnable, especially when its south side was protected by enclosing walls, towers, strong gatehouses and a moat.

Its commanding position made it the focus of attention in any conflict, and although it changed hands a number of times during the Hundred Years War it suffered little damage. Then came the Wars of Religion and a cunning soldier who showed that complacency can be the greatest weakness in defending even the strongest fortress.

In 1588 Domme was an island of Catholicism in a sea swept by a Huguenot storm. Many places in Périgord had succumbed to the Protestants, but Domme, its back protected by those rocky cliffs, seemed secure – so secure that the defenders had not bothered to guard the river side of the town. That proved to be their Achilles' heel. Led by the Protestant Captain Geoffroi de Vivans, a party of 30 men scaled the precipitous la Barre cliff, created a noisy diversion and opened the town gates to their army outside.

Vivans burned down the church and priory, established Protestantism and occupied Domme for the next four years. In 1592 he saw that the tide was turning in the Catholics' favour – and again he had the last laugh. He offered to sell Domme back to the Catholics, took their money, then reduced the place to ruins before he left.

Domme caves €€
*Pl. de la Halle, Domme;
tel: 05 53 31 71 00; e-mail:
domme-tourisme@
wanadoo.fr. Open daily
0900–1900 (Jul and Aug);
0930–1200, 1400–1800
(Apr–Jun and Sep);
1400–1700 (mid-Feb–Mar
and Oct).*

**Musée des Arts et
Traditions populaires**
*€€ Pl. de la Halle; tel: 05
53 31 71 00. Open daily
1000–1230, 1400–1800
(Apr–Sep).*

Below
Domme

Montfort after defeating the Cathars in 1214; the Promenade des
Falaises, a cliff-side walk overlooking the river; and Belvédère de la
Barre, an attractive esplanade where you will find a bust
commemorating Jacques de Maleville (1741–1824), who helped to
draw up the Napoleonic Code.

On the south side you can take a walk along the Promenade des
Ramparts and through the well-preserved 13th-century Porte des Tours, a
defensive gateway once protected by a double portcullis and flanked by
two stone circular towers. Between these two parts lies a network of
attractive streets, including Grand'Rue, the main shopping thoroughfare.
In pl. de la Halle, the main square, is the 16th-century Maison des
Gouverneurs, housing the tourist information centre, and a 17th-century
covered market, which provides access to the **Domme caves**, some 450m
of galleries and low passages – some with stalagmites and stalactites and
the bones of prehistoric animals – in which the population sought refuge
during conflicts in the Hundred Years War and the Wars of Religion.
Views of everyday life at different stages of the town's past are presented
in the **Musée des Arts et Traditions populaires**.

Chateau de Fenelon

Château de Fénelon €€ *Ste-Mondane; tel: 05 53 29 81 45. Open Jun–Sep daily 0930–1900; rest of year daily 1000–1200, 1400–1800 (1700 Nov–Feb). Closed Dec–Jan.*

Just off the D50, close to the village of Ste-Mondane on the south bank of the Dordogne, the Château de Fénelon has three lines of fortified walls and dates from the 15th century, although considerable changes were made in the 17th century. Overlooking the river, the château was the birthplace in 1651 of François de Fénelon, author and tutor to the Duke of Burgundy, Dauphin of France. His tract *Télémaque*, addressed to the student duke and critical of Louis XIV, has become a classic of French literature. The author's bedroom, the château's chapel, a kitchen carved from solid rock and a military museum are open to the public.

Gourdon

Gourdon *24 r. du Majou; tel: 05 65 27 52 50. Open all year 1100–1800; Sun Jun–Sep only.*

Eglise des Cordeliers €€ *Av. Gambetta. Guided tours organised by the tourist office.*

Grottes de Cougnac €€ *D70 road, 3km north; tel: 05 65 41 47 54. Guided tours Jul and Aug daily 1000–1800; Jun and Sep daily 0930–1100, 1400–1700.*

Chapelle de Notre-Dame-des-Neiges € *Off D704 1½km southeast; tel: 05 65 41 32 77. Visits by arrangement with the presbytery in Gourdon.*

Gothic church € *Le Vigan; tel: 05 65 41 12 90. Open Jul–Aug Mon–Sat 1000–1200, 1400–1900; rest of year contact Gourdon presbytery.*

Musée Henri Giron €€ *Le Vigan; tel: 05 65 41 33 78. Open Jul and Aug Tue–Sun 1000–1800; May, Jun, Sep & Oct 1000–noon, 1500–1800.*

Spilling around the summit of a rocky conical hill on the borders of Périgord and Quercy, Gourdon is a medieval market town serving a forested region known as Bouriane. Its old streets – including one appropriately named rue Zig-Zag – follow the lines of the old fortified town walls. Steeper, narrower lanes, such as rue du Majou and its ancient houses with overhanging upper storeys, head uncompromisingly for the summit. Here panting visitors may enjoy a superb view of the surrounding countryside from the site of the old castle, which was demolished in the 17th century.

Immediately below the summit, dominating a small cobbled square, is the 14th-century Eglise St-Pierre, whose huge buttresses and machicolations echo its beginnings as a fortified church. Its elegant west door is flanked by tall twin towers. Inside, there are carved and painted wooden panels dating from the 17th century.

Nearby, the Hôtel de Ville, built as a consulate in the 13th century, has arcades that serve as a covered market. Further down the hill, on the southern side of the town, is the **Eglise des Cordeliers**, also from the 13th century, although the bulky belfry porch was added in the 19th century without regard to the slender Gothic lines of the original building.

Just north of the town, **Grottes de Cougnac** are twin caverns connected by a network of galleries and containing a treasure house of superb rock formations and outstanding prehistoric paintings of animals and human figures. Unlike some other caverns in the Dordogne region, these are rarely overrun with visitors.

Less than 2km to the southeast, **Chapelle de Notre-Dame-des-Neiges** is a 14th-century pilgrimage centre with a spring said to have miraculous qualities flowing through its chancel. At Le Vigan, 5km east of Gourdon, is a **Gothic church**, all that remains of a prosperous 11th-century abbey that was sacked by the English during the Hundred Years War. The **Musée Henri Giron**, also at Le Vigan, houses a collection of works by the contemporary Belgian painter.

Above
La Roque-Gageac

LA ROQUE-GAGEAC

Gabarres Caminades €€
Tel: 05 53 29 40 95;
e-mail: bestofperigord@
perigord.com. One-hour boat
trips with commentary depart
daily 0930–1800 (mid-
Mar–Oct).

Gabarres Norberts €€
Le Bourg, La Roque-Gageac;
tel: 05 53 29 40 44; e-mail:
gabarres-norbert@
norbert.fr; www.gabarres.com/
us/intro.htm or www.norbert.fr.
One-hour boat trips with
commentary depart 1030–
1800; Apr, Sep & Oct 1400
and 1500.

People argue over which is the most attractive village in France: La Roque-Gageac or St-Cirq-Lapopie in the Lot Valley. Well, officially the title goes to the village on the Dordogne and there seems to be no argument over its popularity. After Brittany's Mont-St-Michel and nearby Rocamadour, La Roque-Gageac is the country's third most-visited sight. In the summer, therefore, you're unlikely to take a photograph with no one in it.

It's easy to see what draws the crowds. The village is set tightly between the river and the craggy face of a sheer cliff and its picturesque streets are a pot-pourri of houses humble and grand. Until recently, it was a busy port for river barges carrying iron, salt, timber and wine. It was never ruled by an overlord and never taken in battle. Today, it earns its living from tourism and the main river traffic is canoes, which may be hired in the village. Two companies – **Gabarres Caminades** and **Gabarres Norberts** – operate trips on traditional river boats.

Accommodation and food

Camping Aqua Viva € *Carsac-Aillac; central bookings tel: 04 99 57 21 21; e-mail: aquaviva@perigord.com; www.village-center.com. Open mid-Apr–Sep.* As well as 160 pitches, the site has chalets and motor homes for hire. Amenities include restaurant, takeaway food, grocery store, bar and launderette. Swimming, tennis and golf available.

Camping Beaurivage € *La Roque-Gageac; tel: 05 53 28 32 05; e-mail: camping.beau.rivage@wanadoo.fr; www.camping-beau-rivage.com.* 200 pitches, with tents, chalets and mobile homes for hire. Full range of amenities, including hook-up facilities for motor homes.

Hôtel Delpeyrat €–€€ *La Tavernerie, Carsac-Aillac; tel: 05 53 28 10 43; e-mail: hotel.rest.delpeyrat@wanadoo.fr. Open mid-Nov–Sep.* Terrace dining and a garden are features of this quiet 13-room hotel/restaurant, which is located 1km from the River Dordogne. Private parking.

Le Nouvel Hôtel €–€€ *r. Malleville et Grand'Rue, Domme; tel: 05 53 28 38 67; e-mail: contact@domme-nouvel-hotel.com; www.domme-nouvel-hotel.com. Open Apr–Oct.* The proprietor/chef of this 15-room hotel–restaurant specialises in regional dishes. There is terrace dining and the restaurant is air-conditioned. Rooms have en-suite facilities and direct-dial telephones.

Les Prés Gaillardou €–€€ *La Roque-Gageac; tel: 05 53 59 67 89; www.lespresgaillardou.com.* The surroundings are rustic but comfortable and the cuisine inventive in this splendid little restaurant.

La Belle Etoile €€ *La Roque-Gageac; tel: 05 53 29 51 44; e-mail: hotel.belle-etoile@wanadoo.fr. Open late Mar–Oct.* Right at the water's edge and offering a superb view of the Dordogne river, this 15-room hotel has a shady terrace for dining or cocktails and the menu features traditional cuisine.

Domaine du Berthiol €€ *D704, 1km east of Gourdon; tel: 05 65 41 33 33; e-mail: domaine-du-berthiol@wanadoo.fr. Open Apr–Oct.* Swimming and tennis are available at this 27-room hotel–restaurant, which stands in a rural setting with extensive views. The restaurant is air-conditioned and the rooms have TV and direct-dial telephones.

Hostellerie de la Bouriane €€ *Pl. Foirail, Gourdon; tel: 05 65 41 16 37; www.hotellabouriane.fr. Closed mid-Jan–mid-Mar.* Each of the 20 rooms

Camping les Ombrages de la Dordogne € *Carlux; tel: 05 53 28 62 17; e-mail: ombrages@perigord.com; www.ombrages.fr/engels. Open Jun–Oct.* The site has 80 pitches and offers tents for hire. Takeaway food is available and there is a bar and a launderette. Swimming and tennis available.

Camping Le Pech de Caumont € *La Burague, Cénac; tel: 05 53 28 21 63; e-mail: info@pech-de-caumont.com; www.pech-de-caumont.com. Open Apr–Sep.* 100 pitches. Tents and chalets for hire. Takeaway food, bar, grocery store, launderette. Swimming.

Camping le Perpetuum € *Domme; tel: 05 53 28 35 18; e-mail: luc.parsy@wanadoo.fr; www.campingleperpetuum.com.* 120 pitches. Tents, chalets, mobile homes for hire. Restaurant, takeaway food, bar, groceries, disco, launderette. Swimming.

is equipped with TV and direct-dial telephones and the restaurant is air-conditioned. There is a garden.

Hôtel le Périgord €€ *Port de Domme, La Roque-Gageac; tel: 05 53 28 36 55; e-mail: bienvenue@hotelleperigord.eu; www.hotelleperigord.eu.* Standing in 2 hectares of parkland, the hotel has a restaurant and its 40 rooms are equipped with TV and telephones. Swimming and tennis are available and there is ample parking for guests and diners.

Les Quatre Vents €€ *Domme; tel: 05 53 31 57 57.* In a wooded setting with panoramic views, the hotel–restaurant has 26 rooms with TV and telephones. There are two swimming pools and a shady terrace. Canoeing, golf, tennis and horse riding are available.

Relais du Touron €€ *Route de Sarlat, Carsac-Aillac; tel: 05 53 28 16 70. Open Apr–mid-Nov. Restaurant closed Tue and lunchtime daily except Jul–Aug.* This simple hotel–restaurant has 12 rooms, a dining terrace, swimming pool and guest parking.

Hôtel l'Esplanade €€–€€€ *Le Bourg, Domme; tel: 05 53 28 31 41; e-mail: esplanade.domme@wanadoo.fr. Open mid-Feb–Oct. Closed mid-Nov–Feb.* The 20 rooms in this comfortable hotel in the heart of the medieval city are equipped with telephones and television, and there is dining outdoors as well as in the restaurant, which is open to the public. The cellar features Bergerac and Pécharmant wines.

Suggested tour

Total distance: The route covers only 75km, but it offers spectacular views of the River Dordogne and a trip through craggy countryside for a foray into the Lot *département*.

Time: Non-stop, you can cover the route in less than 2 hours, but allow at least half a day for sightseeing – more if you want to make the most of Domme and Gourdon.

Links: From La Roque-Gageac you can follow the D46 north for 5km to reach Sarlat-la-Canéda, start of the route to Souillac (*see pages 134–6*). At Gourdon you are only 37km from Cahors (*see pages 182–91*), focal point of the Lot and Célé valleys: travel south on D704 for 12km, then on the N20 for 25km.

Route: From Castelnaud (*see page 70*) cross the bridge over the Dordogne, turn right and follow the D703 for 5km to the pretty riverside village of **LA ROQUE-GAGEAC** ❶, where you cross the river again on the D46 to **DOMME** ❷. The road also passes through Cénac, an interesting place for a short break.

In the 11th century Cénac was important enough for a large priory to be built there. Today, all that remains of those heady days is the **Eglise de**

Eglise de Cénac €
*Open Jun–Sep daily
1000–1800; rest of year by
appointment.*

Cénac, a small Romanesque church, once part of the priory, and even that suffered damage at the hands of the Protestants in 1589 during the Wars of Religion, which swept back and forth across the Dordogne region in the 16th and 17th centuries. Much of the church was rebuilt during the 19th century, but the east end, which was undamaged in the conflict, is in its original state. A good view of this part of the building, with its splendid stone roof, can be enjoyed from the churchyard. Inside, there are fine carved capitals decorated with biblical scenes, including Jonah and the Whale and Daniel in the Lions' Den.

Continue south for 16km, then turn left at the village of Pont-Carral on to the D673 to reach **GOURDON** ❸ in a further 9km for a brief introduction to the Lot *département*. Heading north from Gourdon on the D704 provides an opportunity to stop off after 3km for a visit to the impressive **Grottes de Cougnac**. Continue north for a further 11km to **GROLEJAC** ❹. From here you can turn right on to the D50 and travel 6km to visit **Château de Fenelon**. Continuing north from Groléjac on the D704 will take you to **CARSAC-AILLAC** ❺, 2km away on the opposite side of the Dordogne and handy for a superb view of the **Cingle de Montfort**. From here you can turn right on to the D703, following the river upstream for 8km to Rouffillac, where a left turn on to the D61 will take you to **CARLUX** ❻ in under 3km.

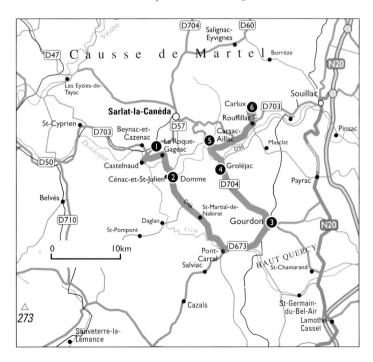

Périgueux

Ratings

Food	●●●●●
History	●●●●●
Architecture	●●●●○
Art	●●●●○
Markets	●●●●○
Museums	●●●●○
Scenery	●●●○○
Children	●○○○○

Well named the City of Art and History, Périgueux is the compact little capital of the province of Périgord. The Musée du Périgord takes you back through prehistory. You can see the shell of a round tower of the Gallo-Roman era from the 1st century AD. You can wander through the medieval city and touch stonework that generates a feeling of affinity with people from centuries past who touched the same stonework: or perhaps that is fanciful. Périgueux, with its 12th-century cathedral, its lingering remnant of the medieval walls and its ancient courtyards and archways, hones the imagination and you feel assured that nothing will change in the next 1000 years. Back to earth! Périgueux is a market town with world-famous delights spread out before you. Truffles and *foie gras* from November to March, *charcuterie* and cheeses, pâté and pies all year.

History

ⓘ *Périgueux 26 Pl. Fencheville, Périgueux; tel: 05 53 53 10 63; e-mail: tourisme@perigueux.fr; www.tourisme-perigueux.fr/ default.asp. Open in summer season Mon–Sat 0900–1900, Sun 1000–1800; rest of the year Mon–Sat 0900–1800. Closed Sun.*

Two thousand years ago the Gauls, living in the hills, got together with the Romans and built Vésunna, or Vésune. The city had public baths, temples, an amphitheatre accommodating 20,000 people and smart villas decorated with frescoes and mosaics. Traces of Vésune can still be seen in Périgueux. The Musée de Périgord exhibits items from the Gallo-Roman period found locally. It also has exhibits from many thousands of years before that period: its prehistory department is one of the largest in France.

The Cathédrale St-Front, dating from the 12th century, with 19th-century reconstruction work and embellishments, is one of the largest in France. Périgueux is rich in medieval and Renaissance architecture; careful restoration work has been going on since 1971. Much of the town's charm lies in its beauty, providing the sort of sightseeing that is mainly free. You stroll around encountering narrow medieval alleyways, nail-studded doors, archways, courtyards and corners. Guided walks of varying themes are worthwhile.

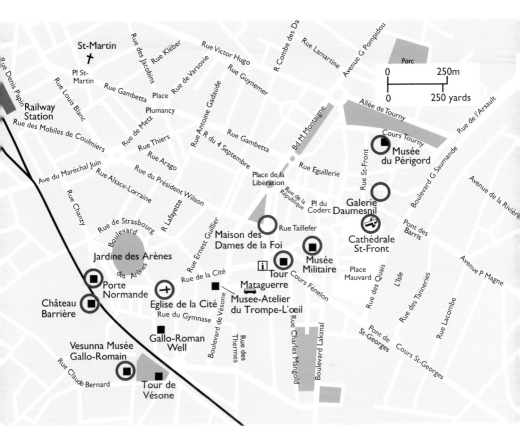

Pâté Pie

Pâté pie is an unusual gastronomic treat created in Périgueux, where it is better known as *pâté en croûte*. It is simply a pie made by enclosing pâté in crisp pastry. You can taste and buy this local speciality from **Espace du Sixième Sens** (6 pl. Saint-Silain; tel: 05 53 09 24 29); **Pierrot Gourmet** (6 r. de l'Hôtel de Ville; tel: 05 53 53 35 32); **Daniel Mazières** (9 r. des Chaînes; tel: 05 53 53 47 04).

Surrounded by agricultural terrain, Périgueux is renowned for its gastronomic attractions. You can buy tins of Pâté de Périgord made from pork meat, goose or duck liver and a modicum of the precious truffle. Walnut cake is another enticing speciality.

Sights

Cathédrale St-Front

The 12th-century cathedral, built in the Roman-Byzantine style, replaced a mid-11th-century church that burned down. Dedicated to St-Front, a former Bishop of Périgueux, the building forms a combination of a Latin cross and a Greek cross, separated by a tower. Its domes are more than 36m high and 24m wide. Substantial reconstruction and adaptation work was carried out from 1850 by Paul Abadie, who went on to design the basilica of the Sacré-Cœur in Paris. It was the latest of several restorations – work that some people feel

Cathédrale St-Front *Pl. de la Clautre; tel: 05 53 53 23 62. Open 0800–1900 (in winter closes at dusk). Free entry but donations are welcome.*

Château Barrière € *R. de Turenne. Freely accessible.*

La Tour de Vésone €€ *Guided tour from the tourist office Jul and Aug Mon–Fri 1030. Variable times during the rest of the year, mainly in school holidays.*

Jardin des Arènes *Public garden built on the site of a Roman amphitheatre. Open daily May–Aug 0730–2100, Sep–Apr 0800–1800. Free entry.*

Below
Cathédrale St-Front

considerably altered the cathedral's appearance, and not for the better. The domes and pinnacles were added at this time.

The semi-Roman, semi-Gothic cloisters, dating from the 13th to 16th centuries, remain in their original state. However, the cathedral is splendidly floodlit at night. In the Middle Ages the Cathédrale St-Front was an important resting place for pilgrims making the long trek through France to Compostela in Spain to pay homage at the shrine of St James.

Château Barrière

Named after the family who owned it in medieval times, the Gallo-Roman castle, with a 12th-century keep, caught fire in 1575 during the Wars of Religion and was never rebuilt. The ruin stands formidably against the skyline. The sculpted door to the stair tower, added in the Renaissance period, is in a well-preserved state.

La Cité

This is the site of the Gallo-Roman city of Vésone, built 20 centuries ago, prospering for many years, but declining in the 3rd century after suffering barbarian invasions. The **Tour de Vésone** (Vésone Tower) is an impressive sight. Although a chunk of the cylindrical building has gone, the major part of the tower remains, and is 27m high and 20m in diameter. Its walls were covered in marble plates fastened by iron hooks which can still be seen.

Vesunna Musée Gallo-Romain *Parc de Vésone; tel: 05 53 53 00 92; e-mail: vesunna@ perigueux.fr; www.vesunna.fr. Open daily except Mon 1000–1800, (closes 1900 Jul and Aug).*

Nearby, the **Jardin des Arènes** (*r. de l'Amphithéâtre, freely accessible*) is a public garden on the site of the huge amphitheatre where up to 20,000 citizens watched sporting events. Although demolition of the amphitheatre began in the 3rd century – it was turned into a fortification when Vésune came under attack – it is still recognisable as an arena.

Porte Normande (*r. Chanzy, freely accessible*), or the Normandy Gate, was built from enormous stones taken from tombs, temples and other sources. Its exact date of origin is not known, but it is thought to be from the 3rd century. The Vikings set fire to it in the 9th century.

Vesunna Musée Gallo-Romain €€ (*Parc de Vésone, between r. de Turenne and r. Claude Bernard*) is a modern glass building that encloses and preserves the remains of a villa dating from the 1st to 4th centuries. Its remains were discovered in 1959. It had living rooms and a bath: its heating system, by which hot air was carried through pipes, is well preserved. The villa would have been occupied by the wealthy and powerful Pompeius family.

Eglise de la Cité (€, *donations welcome, pl. de la Cité; tel: 05 53 53 21 35. Open daily 0830–1830, except Sun and public holidays*). Built in the 11th century in the Romanesque style, the church is dedicated to St Etienne. During the Wars of Religion it was partially destroyed, losing its belfry.

Galerie Daumesnil
Corner of r.
Limegeanne and r. de la
Miséricorde. Freely
accessible.

Tour Mataguerre €€
R. de la Bride, Périgueux.
The tower is outside the
Périgueux tourist office,
which organises discovery
visits to it in Jul and Aug
Mon–Fri 1030, enabling you
to see the view from the top.

Musée Militaire €€ 28
R. des Farges, Périgueux; tel:
05 53 53 47 36. Open
Apr–Sep Mon–Sat
1000–1200, 1400–1800;
Oct–Mar Mon–Sat
1400–1800. Closed Sun and
public holidays. 90-minute
guided tours available.

Musée du Périgord €€
22 cours de Tourny,
Périgueux; tel: 05 53 06 40
70; e-mail: contact@ville-
perigueux.fr; http://musee-
perigord.museum.com. Open
weekdays except Tue
1000–1700, Sat, Sun
1300–1800. Closed public
holidays. Free entry
1200–1400 on weekdays
mid-Sep–mid-Jun.

Opposite
Rue des Farges

Galerie Daumesnil

This is an example of restoration work in the old part of Périgueux. It involved demolishing some centuries-old houses, but it has resulted in a series of shady courtyards and attractive little squares. Façades from the 1400s to 1600s have been revealed. Walk through r. Limegeanne, a picturesque narrow street with some interesting shops.

Maison des Dames de la Foi (€ 4–6 r. des Farges)

This 13th-century house is said to be among the oldest in Périgueux. It was named after the Ladies of the Faith when it became a convent in the 17th century.

Tour Mataguerre

The walls that fortified Puy St-Front, the medieval predecessor to Périgueux, had 28 towers, and the Mataguerre Tower is the last remaining one. The round tower has been rebuilt several times, the last occasion being in the 1470s, when the fleur-de-lys of the king of France added ornamentation.

Musée Militaire

Exhibits here, in France's most important military museum, take you from the Middle Ages to World War II. Weapons, gun carriages, uniforms and many aspects of warfare and defence through the ages make for an interesting visit. One section deals with the work of the Resistance Movement in Southwest France in World War II.

Musée du Périgord

Allow plenty of time to browse in all the departments of the museum. Périgord has yielded an enormous wealth of archaeological finds and relics of the past, and the museum's remarkable prehistoric section is one of the most important in France. Here you find yourself in the company of a well-preserved fossilised Neanderthal skeleton from 70,000 years ago. It is in the foetal position and was found at Montignac, in the Vézère Valley, in the 1950s. There is a skeleton from the palaeolithic period, about 12,000 years old, found at Chancelade. A casting of a 27,000-year-old skeleton, found at St-Avit-Sénieur, is also displayed. Mammoths' tusks, engraved bones, and cutting and polishing stone tools are shown.

An incredible array of exhibits from the Gallo-Roman era in Périgueux and the department of Périgord makes fascinating viewing. They include an oak pump found in 1975 in La Maison Gallo-Romaine (see page 89), frescoes and mosaics, earthenware and jewellery, domestic items in terracotta and ivory, bone and bronze objects. An altar with a sculpture of a bull's head, used for the sacrifice of bulls, is one of the larger exhibits.

During his alterations to the Cathédrale St-Front in the 19th century, Abadie removed carvings of the medieval Romanesque façade, and these are displayed in the museum's arcaded gallery. Also

Musée Atelier du Trompe-L'œil €€
5 r. Emile Combes, Périgueux; tel: 05 53 09 84 40; e-mail: amc@ museedutrompeloeil.com; www.museedutrompeloeil. com. Open daily except Mon and public holidays 1030–1830 in summer, 1400–1730 in winter. Unique in Europe, a museum, gallery and workshop devoted to creating trick-of-the-eye decorative art. A guided tour presents examples of three-dimensional illusions in works of art from prehistoric times to present-day paintings and interior decorating.

Below
Old houses in Périgueux

in the Middle Ages collections is the diptych of Rabastens – the rare 13th-century illuminated manuscripts on parchment.

The Fine Arts sections include paintings by French, Spanish, Italian and Flemish artists from the 15th to the 19th centuries. Among these is Canaletto's *Le Grand Canal et le Pont Rialto*, *La Pierre de Folie* of Pieter Huys and *Port de Honfleur* by Othon Friesz. Enamels, carved furniture, portraits and popular arts are in the former chapel, representing periods from the 13th century onwards. Don't miss the cloisters, with sculptures, a 12th-century altarpiece, Renaissance exhibits, Gallo-Roman relics and pieces from miscellaneous periods in history.

Périgord Gabarres €€ *quai de l'isle Périgueux; tel: 05 53 53 10 63; e-mail: perigord.gabarre@worldonline. Open Easter–Oct daily 1000–1800.* Boat trips where visitors can get an introduction to the city and 2000 years of its history by taking a narrated cruise on the River Isle aboard the *Vesuna*: departures from the town-centre quay.

Themed walks

You can choose from more than a dozen guided walks organised by the Office of Tourism. They last from 45 minutes to two hours, with guides provided by the Ministry of Culture. Themes include the Gallo-Roman, medieval and Renaissance periods, the Cathédrale St-Front, l'Eglise de St-Etienne-de-la-Cité and a gastronomic tour, with or without a tasting.

Accommodation and food

B&B Le Ponteix € *Rond-Point Agora, Boulazac; tel: 08 92 78 80 78.* Rooms sleeping two, three or four people, all at very modest prices. Breakfast is similarly inexpensively priced: English breakfast of cereals, eggs and sausages is available. Rooms have TV and direct-dial telephones. The B&B is about 4km from Périgueux centre.

Restaurant de Clos St-Front € *5 r. de la Vertu, Périgueux (access through r. St-Front); tel: 05 53 46 78 58; e-mail: contact@leclossaintfront.com; www.leclossaintfront.com.* Near the Musée du Périgord, the restaurant has a shady terrace for outdoor eating.

Auberge Notre-Dame €–€€ *56 av. Jean et Léonce, Route de Vergt, Notre-Dame-de-Sanilhac; tel: 05 53 07 60 69. Open daily in summer, closed Sat rest of year.* Set in the countryside 8km from Périgueux, the seven-room *auberge* has an extensive terrace for outdoor dining, and private parking. Horse riding and tennis are available.

Brasserie Café de Bordeaux €–€€ *3 r. du Président Wilson, Périgueux; tel: 05 53 53 41 72. The brasserie is open daily 0800–2400.* The air-conditioned restaurant, run by the third generation of the same family, serves Périgord specialities.

⦿ **Antonne-et-Trigonant €** *La Pradelle, Antonne; tel: 05 53 06 17 88; e-mail: aufildel.eau@wanadoo.fr. Open mid-Jun–mid-Sep.* Just east of Périgueux by the River Isle, the two-star campground has 50 pitches for tents and caravans, a food store, bar and launderette.

Le Grand Dague €–€€ *Atur, Périgueux; tel: 05 53 04 21 01; e-mail: info@legranddague.fr; www.legranddague.fr/gb/present.htm (English).* South of Périgueux on the RN89, the campground is *open Apr–Sep* with 93 places for tents, mobile homes and chalets.

Markets You can find market stalls in one or other of the city's various squares every day. The main market at pl. de St-Louis is especially busy on Wed and Sat. The truffles and *foie gras* offered Nov–Mar attract people from many kilometres away. Stalls sell meat, poultry, cheeses, flowers and fresh produce, household goods, clothes and other goods.

Hostellerie de l'Ecluse €€ *Route de Limoges, Antonne; tel: 05 53 06 00 04; e-mail: contact@ecluse-perigord.com; www.ecluse-perigord.com.* Beside a lock on the River Isle to the east of Périgueux, this 45-room, 3-star property is in parkland. Its 2-star restaurant (**€€**) is known for its regional cuisine.

Hôtel Bristol €€ *37–39 r. A. Gadaud, Périgueux; tel: 05 53 08 75 90; e-mail: hotel@bristolfrance.com; www.bristolfrance.com/index_gb.htm.* The 3-star, town-centre property has 29 spacious air-conditioned en-suite rooms. English and German are spoken. Private parking.

Le Rocher de l'Arsault €€–€€€ *15 r. de l'Arsault, Périgueux; tel: 05 53 53 54 06; e-mail: rocher.arsault@wanadoo.fr. Closed for second half of Jul.* The air-conditioned restaurant with Louis XIII décor is run by a mother and daughter, Marie and Valerie, who take pride in serving fresh products from the land and sea.

Périgueux boasts an
eccentric collection of
highly decorated
roundabouts on the roads
around the city. The
tradition began as a
competition to enliven the
environment for motorists,
and the citizens of
Périgueux took it to heart.
Colourful floral displays,
sculptures made with
shrubs and a huge circular
mosaic are among the
many styles of decoration
to catch the eye of locals
and visitors as they
negotiate their way
around.

From April to
September visitors
can tour some of the
sights of Périgueux by a
jolly little tourist train. The
ride, with a commentary,
takes about 35 minutes.
*For information tel: 05 53
04 33 39.*

Opposite
Place Bugeaud

Hôtel Château des Reynats €€€ *Av. des Reynats, Chancelade; tel: 05 53
03 53 59; e-mail: contact@chateau-hotel-perigord.com; www.chateau-hotel-
perigord.com. Open all year.* Near the Abbey of Chancelade, less than
3km from the centre of Périgueux, the fully renovated 19th-century
castle is a 4-star hotel with 13 guest rooms in the castle and 24 in the
Orangery building. It has a heated pool, tennis and a restaurant
(**€€–€€€**).

Suggested tour

Total distance: The main route covers 65km. The detour adds 40km.

Time: In theory you should be able to cover the distance comfortably
in well under 2 hours, but much of the route is on winding rural roads
through some very scenic countryside, so allow for 3 hours' driving
time, plus another hour if you follow the detour.

Links: On the main route, from Thenon you can take the N89 east for
49km to Brive-la-Gaillarde (*see pages 152–3*), a major motorail terminus
with important road links in all directions, notably south by way of
the N20 and N140 to Figeac (*see pages 172–6*). On the detour,
Les Eyzies-de-Tayac has road links to Montignac (*see pages 123–4*) and
Sarlat-la-Canéda (*see pages 132–4*).

Sharp shopping

Plenty of attractive little shops vie with the historic buildings for the
tourist's attention in Périgueux. If you're self-catering you may want to
stock up with ready-to-eat meats and pies at the *charcuterie* A La
Cathédrale in *r. des Chaînes*. Try choosing from 75 sorts of chocolate at La
Chocolathèque Philippon, *r. Taillefer*.

One of the pleasures of shopping on holiday – even window-shopping – is
finding things you don't see at home. Périgueux has some fine cutlery
shops, or *coutelleries*. There's one in *r. Taillefer* and another in *r. Limogeanne*.
Look for the neat little truffle knives, made in Périgord – a speciality of the
region.

Bookshops – antiquarian and modern – are interesting in any language, and
Périgueux has several. For gifts or something for yourself, browse around
the leather goods at Maroquinerie St-Front, *av. Daumesnil*, near the
cathedral. Maison Léon at *pl. de la Clautre* will also provide ideas for gifts
and souvenirs, including *foie gras*, wines and liqueurs of the region. Cartier,
Gucci and other world-famous names are represented at Bouix jewellers in
pl. de la Clautre. The products of prestigious perfume houses can be found
at Parfumerie Bleue, *pl. Francheville*. For paintings and other works with a
local flavour, take a look into the gallery at *4 r. St-Front* – Créateurs et
Artisans d'Art du Périgord.

Half-day or full-day minibus tours of the countryside around Périgueux can be booked two days ahead. Tours are in air-conditioned vehicles. *Details from the tourist office or contact Allo Taxis, Périgueux; tel: 05 53 09 09 09, or M. Flanchec; tel: 05 53 53 70 47.*

Château de l'Herm €€ *Saint Cernin de Reilhac, Rouffignac; tel: 05 53 05 46 61; e-mail: contact @chateaudelherm.com; www.chateaudelherm.com. Open daily Apr–Nov 1000–1900.*

Route: From **PERIGUEUX** ❶ head south on the N2089 for 5km. At Niversac continue south on the D710 to Les Versannes, where you should pick up the D6 and travel east for a further 9km to La Bouderie.

It's worth stopping here to take a look around **Château de l'Herm**, an atmospheric ruin on top of a wooded hill. Surrounded by a weed-choked ditch that was once a moat, the château was built in the 16th century on the site of a 12th-century structure and has a history of bloody family feuds of Shakespearean magnitude.

Continue on the D6 to **Rouffignac** ❷, a small town that was rebuilt after being burned down in an act of reprisal by the Germans in 1944. The 16th-century church was the only building to survive. The town's main claim to fame, however, is the **Grotte de Rouffignac**, 5km to the south. The cave has some 8km of galleries and chambers decorated with more than 150 engravings of prehistoric animals from about 13,000 years ago. Depressions in the soft floor of the cave were created by hibernating bears, whose claw marks can be seen on the walls.

Grotte de Rouffignac €€ *Tel: 05 53 05 41 71; e-mail: grotterouffignac@ wanadoo.fr; www.grotterouffignac.fr. Open Jul and Aug daily 0900–1130, 1400–1800; Apr–Jun, Sep & Oct daily 1000–1130, 1400–1700 (1-hour guided tours by electric train).*

Just outside Plazac, the leaning Tour de la Vermondie is said to have stooped so that an imprisoned prince and his lover could exchange kisses. Nearer the truth, perhaps, is the belief that the tower was damaged by the Saracens in the 8th century.

Opposite
Cathédrale St-Front

From Rouffignac follow the D32 south for 7km, then turn left on to the D47 and continue for a further 7km to **Les Eyzies-de-Tayac** ❸, an attractive little town lying below an imposing line of cliffs riddled with troglodyte dwellings *(see pages 120–3)*. Leave Les Eyzies on the D706 and travel east for 5.5km to Tursac, where scenes from the daily life of Neanderthal and Cro-Magnon people have been re-created in the **Préhistoparc** *(see page 127)*.

After another 3.5km the road reaches **La Roque St-Christophe** ❹, where more than 100 carved-out dwellings have been found in the 80m-high cliff, which dominates the landscape *(see page 124)*. Cross the River Vézère to Le Moustier and head north on the D6 for 5.5km to **Plazac** ❺, where the Romanesque church with a 12th-century belfry-keep overlooks the village from a cypress-fringed hillock. From Plazac the D6 continues for 6.5km to return to Rouffignac.

From Rouffignac follow the D31 northeast for 13km through the unremarkable town of Thenon, where the N89 will speed you back to Niversac on the outskirts of Périgueux in 24km.

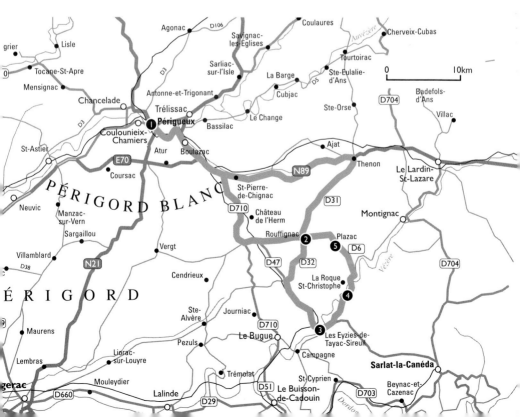

The Isle Valley

Ratings

Food and drink	●●●●●
Historical sights	●●●●○
Restaurants	●●●●○
Villages	●●●●○
Architecture	●●●○○
Scenery	●●●○○
Shopping	●●●○○
Museums	●●○○○

The valleys of the River Isle and its tributary, the Auvézère, are by no means the best-known parts of the Dordogne to tourists, but they are never far from the thoughts of the food-loving French. The two rivers take us through three of Périgord's four regional colours: Périgord Pourpre (purple), Périgord Blanc (white) and Périgord Vert (green). The area may lack the dramatic gorges, cliffs and caves of the Dordogne and Lot valleys to the south, but that's not to say they lack interest. There are stunning châteaux and brooding ruins, history in abundance and fascinating villages hidden in the extensive forests of La Double and Landais. In some woodland areas – local inhabitants will not reveal exactly where – the elusive, delicious and highly prized truffle may be uncovered. Add another regional speciality – *foie gras* – and you have the ingredients for a gourmet's paradise.

HAUTEFORT

ⓗ Château de Hautefort €€
Hautefort; tel: 05 53 50 51 23; www.chateau-hautefort. com. Open for guided tours (45 mins) Apr–Oct 0900–1200, 1400–1900. About half the château is accessible to visitors with disabilities. Grounds and château may be visited separately; combined admission available.

ⓘ Office de Tourisme
Pl. du Marquis Jacques-François de Hautefort; tel: 05 53 50 40 27.

Among the gentle, thinly wooded hills of the Auvézère Valley this small village huddles beneath the grandeur of the **Château de Hautefort**, whose massive bulk is extended by two wings ending in towers resembling the matching pieces of an old-fashioned cruet.

The castle is the latest development of fortifications that have stood on the site since the 9th century. Its most notorious medieval occupant was Bertrand de Born, aka Bertrand the Troubadour, who seems to have been as good with a sword as he was with a song. A family feud kept him on his toes, defending the castle against raids by his brother, Constantine. In 1185 Bertrand secured an endorsement of his claim to the family home by Henry II, but a year later Constantine came back and burned the place down. Bertrand retired to a monastery where he died some time before 1215.

Rebuilt, the castle was strengthened during the 16th century to thwart attacks during the Wars of Religion. A century or so later, Marie

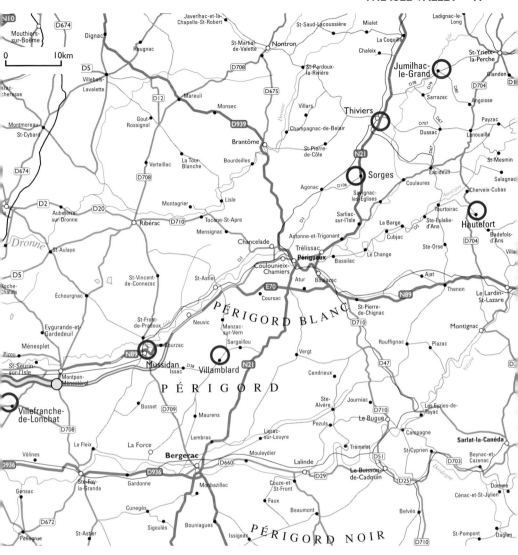

de Hautefort was born there. She became lady-in-waiting to Anne of Austria and earned a place in history by her outrageous and unsuccessful flirting with Louis XIII – even inviting him to retrieve letters 'posted' down the front of her dress, but to no avail.

In 1630 Jacques-François de Hautefort began a reconstruction programme that was to last 40 years. In 1968 the château was badly damaged by fire. Careful restoration work began a year later and the place is now much the same as it was before the disaster, filled with wonderful collections of furniture, tapestries, paintings and porcelain and surrounded by 40 hectares of parkland, which include terraced and formal gardens.

Overleaf
Jumilhac-le-Grand

JUMILHAC-LE-GRAND

Château de Jumilhac €€ *Jumilhac-le-Grand; tel/fax: 05 53 52 42 97, out of summer season 05 53 52 58 62; e-mail: ch.de.jumilhac@wanadoo.fr; www.chateaux-france.com/jumilhac. Open all year, Jun–Sep 1000–1900; rest of year open only at weekends and on public holidays in the afternoon. Guided tour 50 mins.*

Musée de l'Or €€ *Tel: 05 53 52 55 43. Open mid-Apr–mid-Oct Sun and public holidays 1500–1800; Jul and Aug daily 1030–1830.*

The village is an outpost of Périgord Vert, almost at the head of the Isle river and on the edge of the Limousin Plateau. It is dominated totally by the huge **Château de Jumilhac**. The 19th-century illustrator Gustave Doré described the castle as the most romantic in France, but he was inspired more by the fairy-tale conical roofs of the main building than by the rather militaristic style of the whole complex.

The original castle was ruined by Richard the Lionheart's troops but was rebuilt around 1580 by Antoine Chapelle, the first Count of Jumilhac. Flanked by two wings added in the 17th century, the château encompasses a grand staircase, state drawing room, dining room and kitchens and collections of fine furniture and paintings. Terraced gardens enclose the buildings.

Housed in the old cellars of the castle is the **Musée de l'Or**, the only museum in France dedicated to gold and gold-mining. The story of gold is told from the extraction and treatment of the ore to the metal's applications as jewellery, in industry and as currency.

There is a tourist information office in pl. du Château, *tel: 05 53 52 55 43; e-mail: ot.jumilhac@wanadoo.fr; www.pays-jumilhac.fr*

MUSSIDAN

Tourist Office *Pl. de la République, Mussidan; tel: 05 53 81 73 87; e-mail: ot.mussidan@wanadoo.fr; www.tourisme-mussidan.com*

Musée André Voulgre €€ *2 r. Raoul Grassin, Mussidan; tel: 05 53 81 23 55; www.museevoulgre.fr/index.htm. Open Jun–mid-Sep Wed–Mon 0930–1200, 1400–1800; Mar–May, Oct & Nov weekends and hols 1400–1800. Closed last two weeks Sep, and Dec–Feb.*

Château de Montréal €€ *Issac; tel: 05 53 81 11 03. Open Jul–Sep daily 1000–1200, 1430–1830.*

Château du Mellet €€ *Neuvic; tel: 05 53 80 86 65. Open for tours Apr–Sep, 1330–1830; rest of year by appointment.*

Although it stands well downstream of the Isle Valley's most scenic and interesting parts, Mussidan is neatly placed as a gateway to two of the Dordogne region's most extensive forest areas: Forêt de la Double and Forêt du Landais. An old Huguenot city, it was besieged a number of times during the Wars of Religion. The most horrendous siege – that of 1569 – inspired Michel de Montaigne to write *L'heure des parlements dangereuse*, one of his famous *Essays*.

Today, Mussidan's major attraction for visitors is the **Musée André Voulgre**, an eclectic collection of furniture, artefacts and machinery housed in a handsome mansion. Reproduced bedrooms, a kitchen, dining room and drawing room provide a glimpse of 19th-century bourgeois life in the region. There are reconstructions of rural crafts workshops, and a collection of agricultural tools and machinery is housed in a barn. Brass and pewter artefacts, glazed earthenware and examples of the taxidermist's skills are displayed in an exhibition area.

At Issac, 7km southeast of Mussidan, the **Château de Montréal** provided a name for the Canadian city. There are double-fortified curtain walls dating from the 12th century, but the château and chapel, surrounded by formal gardens, are 16th century.

The handsome **Château du Mellet** at Neuvic, 12km northeast of Mussidan, dates from the 15th century and is noted for its ornate machicolations, frescoes and Louis XVI salon. An 18th-century chapel and botanical gardens may also be visited.

SORGES

Ecomusée de la Truffe €€ *Tel: 05 53 05 90 11; e-mail: si.sorges@ perigord.tm.fr. Open Jul and Aug daily 0930–1230, 1430–1830; rest of year Tue–Sun 1000–1200, 1400–1700. 'Truffle Trail' tours Tue and Thu 1530.*

This modest but pleasant little market town is the capital of what many people believe is Périgord's most valued activity: the gathering of that 'black diamond of gastronomy', the truffle. The story of this odd and mysterious fungus is told in the **Ecomusée de la Truffe** with the aid of a diorama, photographs and documents. Twice a week you can join a guided group on a 'truffle trail' along a 3km trail outside the town. A find might recover the cost of your entire trip... A tourist information office is located in the museum (*tel: 05 53 46 71 43; e-mail: si.sorges@wanadoo.fr*).

THIVIERS

Office de Tourisme *Pl. du Maréchal Foch, 24800 Thiviers; tel: 05 53 55 12 50; e-mail: ot.thiviers@ wanadoo.fr. Open daily all year.*

La Maison de l'Oie et du Canard €€ *Pl. du Maréchal Foch, Thiviers; tel: 05 53 55 12 50. Open daily 1000–1200, 1400–1800; Jul and Aug Mon–Sat 1000–1800. Closed Sun.*

A bustling town on the main route between Périgueux and Limoges and Paris, Thiviers is devoted to the production and marketing of *foie gras*, the fattened liver of force-fed ducks and geese: so devoted, in fact, that a special museum – **La Maison de l'Oie et du Canard** – takes pride of place next to the Syndicat d'Initiative, which doubles as tourist office. The museum traces the history of domesticated ducks and geese from prehistoric times, and documents the methods used today in raising and fattening the birds.

Gourmands will doubtless be attracted to the *foie gras* market staged every Saturday morning, Nov–Mar, in the square in front of the museum. Guided tours of the town take place *Jul–Aug Tue–Sat 1000–1130 and 1500–1730.*

VILLAMBLARD

Tourist Office *Château Barrière, 24140 Villamblard; tel: 05 53 82 26 28.*

Just off the N21, about halfway between Bergerac and Périgueux, Villamblard may be a worthwhile stop-off for those who enjoy poring over old ruins – in this case, those of a massive fortress. There's a 15th-century castle at the nearby village of St-Jean-d'Estissac.

VILLEFRANCHE-DE-LONCHAT

Musée d'Histoire Locale €€ *R. de la Liberté, Villefranche; tel: 05 53 80 77 25. Open Sat and Sun 1000–1200 and 1400–1800.*

Left
Thiviers

About 17km northeast of St-Emilion, this large village is the western gateway to the Forêt du Landais, an area with many very attractive villages, some – such as St-Martin-de-Gurçon and Montpeyroux – with Romanesque churches or ruined castles. At **Carsac-de-Gurson**, 3km east of Villefranche, you can see the ruins of a château built by England's King Edward I. In Villefranche itself the **Musée d'Histoire Locale** concentrates on life at the time of the 16th-century essayist Michel de Montaigne. There are collections of paintings and earthenware pottery.

Land of the enlarged liver

Everyone eats well in Périgord, and it isn't only the force-fed ducks and geese who are likely to finish up with enlarged livers. The region is famous throughout France for its highly individualistic cuisine, much of it based on the flesh or innards of those unfortunate domesticated waterfowl.

After three months of free-range living, during which they are fed on a diet of alfalfa and grains, the birds are placed singly in cages and massively overfed for two to three weeks on ground meal and whole corn. A *gaveuse*, a type of funnel, is used to force-feed the birds. The ideal weight for a duck's liver is considered to be 450–500g and 800–900g for a goose liver, three or four times the normal weight in each case.

You can buy *pâté de foie gras* and other duck and goose products directly from farms throughout Périgord and Quercy, and in many places they are only too pleased to show visitors around.

Truffles, the 'black diamonds' of Périgord, are regarded as the peak of gourmet experience – a fact that is reflected in the prices they command. A century or so ago they were plentiful, but today the entire output for the region amounts to a mere 4 tonnes a year.

The truffle is a strange black fungus, weighing some 100g and about the size of a Brussels sprout. Talented sniffer dogs or specially trained pigs are used to find truffles, which grow underground at the base of a tree, usually an oak. Truffle-hunters are notoriously secretive about the sources of their finds.

Despite its mundane appearance, the truffle has a superb aroma and even a few specks or fine slices introduce a unique flavour to many dishes, especially pâtés, *foie gras* and omelettes.

Accommodation and food

B&B Jumilhac € *12 r. des Croix Bancaud, Jumilhac-le-Grand; tel: 05 53 52 53 24; e-mail info@jumilhac.com; www.jumilhac.com/indexGB. htm* (English). Cosy bed and breakfast on the edge of the village overlooking the Isle valley. Six colour-coded rooms. The family room has en-suite facilities. Laundry service. Children welcome and treasure hunts are organised in the woods.

Hôtel Lou Boueiradour €–€€ *pl. du Château, Jumilhac-le-Grand; tel: 05 53 52 50 47. Open all year.* Seven en-suite rooms and a restaurant. Breakfast available.

Auberge de la Belle Isle €€ *route d'Excideuil, Corgnac-sur-l'Isle; tel: 05 53 62 00 80; e-mail: info@la-belle-isle.com; www.la-belle-isle.com. Open all year.* Situated 5km from Thiviers on the D76, the hotel has five rooms and a restaurant specialising in traditional Périgord cuisine.

Camping la Chatonnière €
Jumilhac-le-Grand; tel: 05 53 52 57 36; e-mail: camping@chatonniere.com. Open mid-Jun–mid-Sep. Only 50 pitches but facilities include a waterside setting, tents for hire, places for motor homes, grocery store, takeaway meals, launderette and swimming pool.

Camping de Gurson €
Base de Loisirs, Carsac-de-Gurson; tel: 05 53 80 77 57; e-mail: lac-de-gurson@wanadoo.fr. Open Apr–Oct. The site has 80 pitches and mobile homes and chalets to let. There is a restaurant, disco and bar and takeaway meals are available. Tennis and mini-golf.

Camping Municipal le Pontillou € *Villamblard; tel: 05 53 81 91 87. Open mid-Jun–mid-Sep.* This small, simple site has 40 pitches, including places for motor homes.

Camping Municipal le Port € *RN 89, Mussidan; tel: 05 53 81 20 09. Open mid-Jun–mid-Sep.* This small waterside campground has 25 pitches with facilities for motor homes; swimming pool.

Camping Municipal le Repaire € *Thiviers; tel: 05 53 52 69 75. Open Apr–Oct.* Places with facilities for motor homes are among the 100 pitches on this waterside site, which also has a grocery store, bar and launderette. Swimming and tennis.

Opposite
Hautefort

Auberge du Parc €€ *Hautefort; tel: 05 53 50 88 98. Open all year.* Five en-suite rooms and a restaurant.

Auberge de la Truffe €€ *Av. de Limoges, Sorges; tel: 05 53 05 02 05; e-mail: contact@auberge-de-la-truffe.com; www.auberge-de-la-truffe.com. Open all year.* With a swimming pool, billiard room, sauna, garden terrace and 18 en-suite rooms, the *auberge* is ideal for those seeking a quiet holiday. The restaurant serves modern and traditional cuisine.

Hotel l'Enclos €€ *Pragelier, Hautefort; tel: 05 53 51 11 40; e-mail: rornsteen@yahoo.com; www.hotellenclos.com. Open May–Oct.* B&B accommodation in six cottages on an estate outside Hautefort, each building at least 250 years old and restored and decorated in country style. Guest swimming pool.

Hôtel de France et de Russie €€ *51 r. du Général Lamy, Thiviers; tel: 05 53 55 17 80. Open all year.* The hotel has nine en-suite rooms. No restaurant.

Hôtel du Grand Café €€ *1 av. Gambetta, Mussidan; tel: 05 53 81 00 07; www.chez.com/otmussidan/hotels/hotels.htm. Open all year.* Six of the hotel's ten rooms have en-suite facilities. There is a restaurant and breakfast is available.

Hôtel de la Mairie €€ *Pl. de l'Eglise, Sorges; tel: 05 53 05 02 11.* The hotel has eight en-suite bedrooms and a restaurant. Guests have use of the facilities at Auberge de la Truffe (*see above*).

Hôtel du Midi €€ *Av. de la Gare, Mussidan; tel: 05 53 81 01 77. Closed mid-Oct–mid-Nov.* This small hotel (nine en-suite rooms) has a swimming pool and a restaurant. Breakfast available.

Hotel-Restaurant Le Périgord €€ *37 av. Gambetta, Mussidan; tel: 05 53 81 05 85.* Nine en-suite rooms with TV.

Hôtel des Voyageurs €€ *R. Pierre Semard, Thiviers; tel: 05 53 55 09 66. Open all year.* Centrally located, the hotel has 17 rooms, 15 of which have en-suite facilities. There is a restaurant and breakfast is available.

Suggested tour

Total distance: The main route covers 234km. The detour adds 26.5km.

Time: The route traverses some very pretty countryside, which means winding, hilly roads in places, so allow a good 4½ hours for driving alone – a pretty full day's trip, allowing for stops.

Links: From Mussidan the D709 heads south for 25km to Bergerac (*see pages 66–8*) and north for 24km to Ribérac on the River Dronne (*see pages 111–12*). The Dronne Valley can also be accessed from Thiviers by way of the D707/78 to Brantôme (*see pages 109–11*).

Camping Plein Air Neuvicois *Route de Planeze, Neuvic; tel: 05 53 81 50 77; e-mail: camp.le.plein.air.neuvicois@ libertysuyrf.fr; www. campingneuvicdordogne.com. Open Jun–Sep.* With 121 pitches, the riverside site has a restaurant and bar and offers takeaway meals. There is a launderette, and tennis and swimming are available.

Route: From **MUSSIDAN** ❶ head southeast on the D38, passing through **ISSAC** ❷ after 7.5km. After another 5.5km turn left on to the D4 to reach **VILLAMBLARD** ❸ in a further 3km. Continue on the D4 for 4.5km to Sargaillou then turn right on to the D42, which meets the N21 after 3.5km. Take the N21 north towards Périgueux for 23.5km.

Head east on the bypass for 4km then join the D5, travelling through Bassilac after 5km. The confluence of the rivers Isle and Auvézère comes about 2km east of Bassilac and the road continues to follow the Auvézère, passing through Le Change after 7.5km and Cubjac (6km), where it crosses the river. After another 4km the road crosses the river again, at La Barge, and after a further 4.5km reaches the attractive village of **Ste-Eulalie-d'Ans**, which has an old mill by the river.

Continue on the D5 for a further 8.5km then join the D62 to reach **HAUTEFORT** ❹ in 5.5km. From Hautefort travel north on the D704, which reaches Cherveix-Cubas, where the river passes through an impressive gorge, in 5km. Another 5km along the road, turn left on to the D76, which reaches **Excideuil** in 6km. The village has a château with 12th-century towers.

Detour: From Excideuil head north on the D67, climbing steadily, passing through Dussac after 8.5km and reaching Sarrazac in a further 8.5km. At Sarrazac turn right and follow the very scenic D79 for 9.5km to **JUMILHAC-LE-GRAND** ❺.

On the main route, leave Excideuil on the D705 east and return to the D704 in 5.5km. Head north again for 9.5km and at Angoisse turn left on to the D80 to reach Jumilhac-le-Grand in 12.5km. From there take the winding, undulating D78 west to join the N21 in 14.5km, then head south for 4.5km to **THIVIERS** ❻. Continue on the N21 for 14km to **SORGES** ❼.

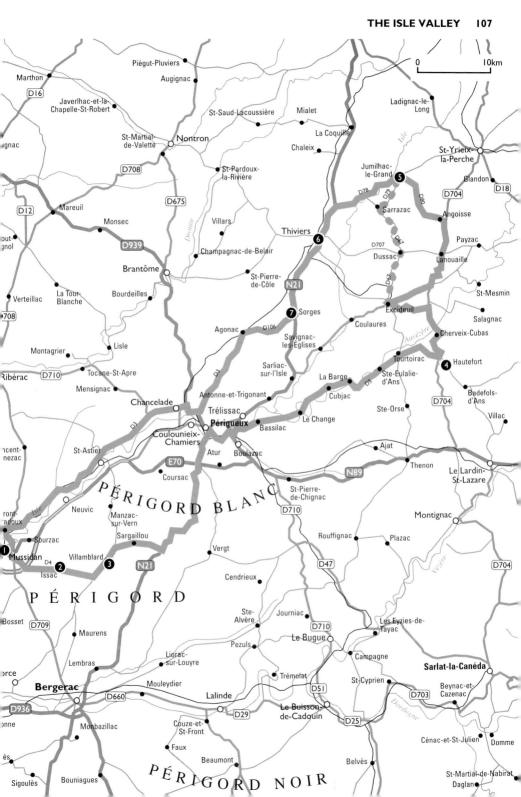

The Dronne Valley

Ratings

Villages	●●●●●
Architecture	●●●●○
Museums	●●●●○
Restaurants	●●●●○
Scenery	●●●●○
Art	●●●○○
Caves	●●●○○
Historical sights	●●○○○

The Dronne is a gentle, slow-moving river, with none of the dramatic scenery found in other parts of the Dordogne region. It passes through quiet meadows and broad-leaved woodlands, whose trees cast cool shadows over the water on tranquil summer days. This is an area for those who like the quiet, contemplative life – a place for relaxed walks and cycle rides; a place where you can find a shady spot beside the river and read a book, or slumber shamelessly. The major tourist attractions are well to the south, but there are still sights to be seen: the ancient abbey at Brantôme, the superb châteaux at Bourdeilles and Villars, where you can also visit one of the largest caves in France, with prehistoric art, stalactites and fantastic rock formations. Ribérac, a lively market town, is at the heart of an area rich in fortified churches.

BOURDEILLES

 Syndicat d'Initiative
Pl. des Tilleuls, Bourdeilles; tel: 05 53 03 42 96; e-mail: si@bourdeilles.com; www.bourdeilles.com. Open Apr–Oct.

Château de Bourdeilles €€
Tel: 05 53 03 73 36. Open for guided tours (45 mins) daily Jul and Aug 1000–1900; rest of the year 1000–1200, 1400–1830. Closed Tue. Access not suitable for wheelchairs.

Set on a gentle curve of the River Dronne, against a backdrop of a cliff bearing two castles in one, compact Bourdeilles (pop. 800) is a gem. Its houses, reaching up to the dominant château, cry out for photography. The **château** is in two quite distinctive parts: an austere feudal fortress dating from the 13th century and a much more relaxed Renaissance palace. The old castle, actually named *château neuf* ('new château') because it was built on the site of an even earlier fortification, has a 14th-century keep with walls 2.4m thick. There are wonderful views to be enjoyed from the top of the keep.

The newer building was created by Jacquette de Montbron, a gifted woman who studied geometry and architecture, in preparation for a visit by Catherine de Medici. As it happened, Catherine failed to appear and Jacquette did not live to see the building completed. Pierre de Brantôme, soldier, adventurer – he accompanied Mary, Queen of Scots, to Scotland in 1561 – abbot and writer of some pretty spicy stories, was born here in 1540.

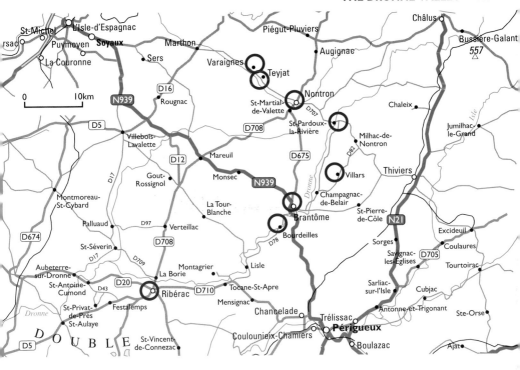

A splendid collection of furniture from the 16th to the 19th centuries is housed in the Renaissance château, which has an extravagantly decorated *salon doré* with a painted ceiling, monumental chimney pieces and a superb tapestry: this is the room in which Catherine de Medici was to stay.

BRANTOME

Tourist Office
Abbaye, Boulevard Charlemagne, Brantôme; tel: 05 53 05 80 52; e-mail: si@ville-brantome.fr; ot.brantome@wanadoo.fr; www.ville-brantome.fr. Open all year. Guided tours and boat trips.

Abbaye de Brantôme including the **Clocher**, the oldest bell tower in France (11th century), and a passage in the rock leading to the Cave of the Last Judgement; *tel: 05 53 05 80 63. Open all year but closed on Tue Apr–Jun.*

Brantôme is charmingly draped along both banks of a picturesque loop in the Dronne: the mellow buildings of the old abbey on one side; the balconied houses, colourful gardens and cafés and bars of the little town on the other. The two sides are connected by a 16th-century arched bridge. Brântome proclaims itself the Venice of the Périgord.

Brantôme Abbey was founded by Charlemagne in 769, sacked by the Normans and rebuilt in the 16th century. Its most famous abbot was the chronicler Pierre de Brantôme (*see opposite*). The present buildings are from the 18th century. The baptistery in the abbey church has a 14th-century stone relief depicting the Baptism of Christ. Another, from the 13th century, shows the Massacre of the Innocents.

The **clocher** (belfry) stands apart from the church on a 12m-high rock over an area riddled with caves, which were used by monks

Caves tour €€
Tel: 05 53 05 80 63.
Open Jul and Aug daily
1000–1900; rest of the year
check with the tourist office
for opening times.

Bateau Maffioletti €€
La Grande Pièce, 24460
Château l'Evêque; tel: 05 53
04 74 71; e-mail:
bateaumaffioletti@free.fr;
http://bateaumaffioletti.free.
fr. Open mid-Apr–mid-Oct
daily 1000–1200,
1400–1800. Boat trips
depart from the Pavilion
Renaissance.

before the abbey was built. Dating from the 11th century, the gabled belfry is one of the oldest in France. Visitors may join a **guided tour of the caves**, including what was once the abbey mill, a dovecote and the Cave of the Last Judgement, a sombre place with a sculpted mural of *The Triumph of Death*.

The old convent buildings of the abbey now house the **Musée Fernand Desmoulin €€** (*tel: 05 53 05 80 63. Open Jul–Aug daily 1000–1200 and 1400–1900; Apr–Jun and Sep Wed–Mon 1000–1200 and 1400–1800*) which has collections of prehistoric art and the works of local painters. The **Musée Rêve et Miniatures €€** (*8 r. Puyjoli; tel: 05 53 35 29 00. Open Jul–Aug daily 1030–1800; Sep–mid-Nov Sat–Thu 1400–1700; early Apr–Jun Sat–Thu 1400–1800*) traces the development of French domestic furnishings from the Middle Ages to the present day in a series of houses built to a scale of 1:12. Meticulously detailed from cellar to attic, the houses even have tiny artefacts fashioned in silver, glass and china. One exhibit, especially for children, depicts an imaginary world of animals.

NONTRON

Nontron 5 r. de
Verdun; tel: 05 53 56
25 50; e-mail:
ot-nontron@wanadoo.fr.
Open all year.

**Musée des Poupées
et Jouets d'Antan**
€€ Château de Nontron;
tel: 05 53 56 20 80. Open
daily in summer season
1000–1900; Mar–May and
Oct, 1000–1200,
1400–1800; rest of the year
1400–1700. Closed Tue
except in high season.

Left
Brantôme

Little remains of old Nontron, the most northerly town in Périgord. There are a few medieval houses, but its château dates only from the 18th century. Here, you will find the **Musée des Poupées et Jouets d'Antan**, an extensive collection of dolls from the past and present, also including such toys as fire engines, sea planes and toy soldiers. There is also a display of games of chance, including board and card games and roulette. Nontron claims to have France's oldest continuously operating cutlery forge. Wood-handled knives have been made by craftsmen in the village for over 500 years, using tools and methods that have changed very little in that time. Each knife is original and the handle is made from wood grown locally and air-dried for at least five years before being carved, shaped and finished with an unusual decorative design.

According to legend, the old castle, which no longer exists, was once terrifyingly attacked by raiders who sent in a herd of goats with flaming torches tied to their horns.

RIBERAC

Tourist Office Pl. du
Général de Gaulle,
Ribérac; tel: 05 53
90 03 10; e-mail:
ot-riberac@wanadoo.fr;
www.riberac.fr. Open all year.

Ribérac is noted as the centre of a region of churches with domed interiors. From outside, the churches look more like fortresses – and this is what they were during times of conflict. The towers served as lookout posts and the construction kept vulnerable windows to a minimum. It also allowed a maximum of interior space – a necessity when the entire village or small town might need to shelter.

Ⓝ Eglise Monolithe d'Aubeterre €
Aubeterre; tel: 05 45 98 65 06. Open daily 0930–1230 and 1400–1800 (1900 Jun–Sep). Closed 25 Dec, 1 Jan. Underground church, the largest in Europe, with vaults higher than 20m.

Collégiale Notre-Dame €€ *Tel: 05 53 90 03 10. Open mid-Jun–mid-Sep daily 1400–1900; by appointment through the tourist office during the rest of the year.* Includes modern art exhibitions.

Most of these churches are very ancient, dating from the 11th and 12th centuries: Ribérac's own Eglise Notre-Dame was built in the year 1000, but suffered badly over the centuries. In 1568, during the Wars of Religion, it was burned down by Huguenot troops, and only the bell tower, the choir and part of the apse survived. Badly restored, it was battered again during the Revolution, when even the vaults were raided and lead coffins used to manufacture ammunition. Today, the church has been completely and more tastefully restored, using some of the original 11th-century stones, and the building is known as the **Collégiale Notre-Dame de Ribérac**, an exhibition centre and concert hall. It contains a collection of 17th-century paintings and has modern stained-glass windows designed by Henri Guerin.

Ribérac tourist office has published a leaflet giving details of a self-guided tour taking in more than 30 domed and fortified churches in the surrounding area. The leaflet, which has a map, is entitled *Le circuit des églises romanes à coupoles du Ribéracois*. A shopping and social centre, especially for many British people who have made their home in the area, the town has a large and lively street market every Wednesday and Friday.

St-Pardoux-la-Riviere

Below
Château de Puyguilhem

Located in a very picturesque part of the Dronne Valley, this small town was once an important stage in the Dordogne–Périgord postal system, a fact that is marked today by the **Musée de la Carte Postale**

Musée de la Carte Postale €€ 46 av. de la Séparation, St Pardoux la Rivière; tel: 05 53 60 76 10; e-mail: bestofperigord@perigord.com. Open Apr–Oct daily 1400–1800. Closed Mon except in Jul and Aug.

Ancienne du Périgord €€. Until 1750 St-Pardoux was the system's fourth most important station, after Périgueux, Bergerac and Sarlat-la-Canéda. Created in 1994, the museum has a collection of postcards and other documents representing the 557 *communes* in Dordogne–Périgord. A philatelic section traces the history of postal services in the region up to 1920. The museum is housed in a former police station and courthouse dating from 1680.

TEYJAT

Espace Muséographique €€ Le Bourg, Teyjat; tel: 05 53 56 23 66; e-mail: varaignes.cedp@perigord.tm.fr. Open all year, but closed Tue, 25 Dec, 1 Jan.

Away from the classic prehistoric sites found elsewhere in the Dordogne, the village of Teyjat proudly displays its own *grotte* – under the town hall. Stuffed with palaeolithic engravings and artefacts from around 10,000 BC, the cavern was discovered towards the end of the 19th century. For conservation reasons, access to the original engravings of bison, bears and other animals is restricted, but the **Espace Muséographique** adjoining the site showcases the highlights and portrays the everyday life of Stone Age people.

VARAIGNES

Office de Tourisme Château de Varaignes, Varaignes; tel: 05 53 56 35 76; e-mail: ot.varaignes@wanadoo.fr

Atelier-Musée des Tisserands €€ Château Communal, Varaignes; tel: 05 53 56 35 76. Open all year daily except Tue 0900–1200, 1400–1800 (Sun pm only). Closed 25 Dec, 1 Jan.

Here's another unexpected discovery in the northwestern edge of rural Périgord. The village is home to **Atelier-Musée des Tisserands et de la 'Charentaise'**, a working museum of the textile industry located in the Renaissance Château de Varaignes. Examples of the weaver's art are on show and there are demonstrations of processes from spinning fibres to the production of 'Charentaise' slippers, a regional speciality. Textile products are on sale in the museum shop. Aspiring weavers can join courses lasting from one to five days.

VILLARS

Office de Tourisme Intercommunal Pl. de l'Eglise, Villars; tel: 05 53 03 50 79; e-mail: siivillars@wanadoo.fr; www.villarstourisme.com. Open all year.

Two attractions just outside the village draw visitors to tiny Villars. The first is the very striking **Château de Puyguilhem**, a 16th-century structure more typical of the Loire Valley than the Dordogne region. Deserted for many years, the château has none of its original furnishings, but there are magnificent chimney pieces, carved panels depicting the Labours of Hercules, coffered beams and massive chestnut beams. The exterior of the building presents a fairy-tale appearance,

Ⓗ Château de Puyguilhem €€
24530 Villars; tel: 05 53 54 82 18. Open daily in summer; daily except Mon in winter.

Ⓒ Camping de la Dronne €€ *Pont du Chalard, 24600 Villetoureix (on the D708 outside Ribérac); tel: 05 53 90 50 08; e-mail: ot.riberac@ wanadoo.fr; www.riberac.com. Open Jun–mid-Sep.*

with towers, conical roofs, sculpted chimneys and balustrades, and there are superb views of it from the surrounding grounds.

The second attraction is much older. **La Grotte de Villars** *(tel: 05 53 54 82 36; e-mail: contact@grotte-villars.com; www.grotte-villars.com)*, an underground network covering some 13km, contains prehistoric paintings said to be around 18,000 years old. Some of these have been covered by a thin translucent film of calcite, which has helped to prove their age. The network also contains impressive calcite streams, fine stalactites and draperies in yellow and ochre.

Accommodation and food

Hôtel Tilleuls € *Bourdeilles; tel: 05 53 03 76 40. Open Apr–mid-Oct.* Handy for the Château de Bourdeilles, this small hotel–restaurant (six rooms) offers simple but comfortable accommodation and traditional cuisine.

Hostellerie le Donjon €–€€ *pl. de la Halle, 24310 Bourdeilles; tel: 05 53 04 82 81; www.hotel-ledonjon.com. Open May–mid-Oct.* Only 25m from the château, the hotel has seven en-suite rooms, a garden and courtyard. Private parking. Swimming, tennis and horse-riding available nearby.

Rev'Hotel €–€€ *route de Périgueux, Ribérac; tel: 05 53 91 62 62; e-mail: contact@rev-hotel.fr; www.rev-hotel.fr. Open all year.* A new hotel in a garden setting, with 17 sound-proofed rooms, each with en-suite facilities. Private parking. There is a restaurant and an outside dining terrace.

Au Fil du Temps €€ *1 chemin du Vert-Galand, Brantôme; tel: 05 53 05 24 12; e-mail: fildutemps@ fildutemps. com; www. fildutemps.com.* Rotisserie specialising in roast Périgord duck, with an outdoor terrace overlooking the river. Twinned with **Au Fil de l'Eau €€** *21 quai Bertin, Brantôme; tel: 05 53 05 73 65; e-mail: fildeleau@fildeleau. com; www.fildeleau.com.* Fish

Left
Rock formation, Villars

ⓘ Grotte des Combarelles €€

On the D47 3km east of Les Eyzies-de-Tayac; tel: 05 53 06 86 00. Open (45-min guided tours, booking at Grotte de Font-de-Gaume essential) 0930–1730. Closed Sat, 1 Jan, 1 May, 11 Nov & 25 Dec.

Grotte de Font-de-Gaume €€ *On the D47 1km east of Les Eyzies-de-Tayac; tel: 05 53 06 86 00. Open (45-min guided tours, booking essential) mid-May–mid-Sep 0930–1730; rest of year 0930–1200, 1400–1730. Closed 1 Jan, 1 May, 1, 11 Nov & 25 Dec.*

Grottes du Roc de Cazelle €€ *Route de Sarlat, Les Eyzies-de-Tayac; tel: 05 53 59 46 09; e-mail: info@rocdecazelle.com; www.rocdecazelle.com. Open daily all year, Jul and Aug 1000–2000; May, Jun & Sep 1000–1900; rest of year 1100–1700.* Reconstructions of daily life scenes where people actually lived in prehistoric times.

Right
Les Eyzies-de-Tayac

Grotte du Grand Roc €€ *On the D47 2.5km northwest of Les Eyzies-de-Tayac; tel: 05 53 06 92 70; e-mail: grandroc@ perigord.com; www. grandroc.com. Open for guided tours (30 mins) in English or French Feb–Nov 0930–1900 in summer season, 1000–1800 out of season. Not accessible for visitors with disabilities.*

Musée National de la Préhistoire €€ *1 r. du Musée, Les Eyzies-de-Tayac; tel: 05 53 06 45 45; e-mail: mnp.eyzies@culture.gouv.fr; www.musee-prehistoire-eyzies.fr. Open all year, for 1-hour visit Jul and Aug 0930–1830, Oct–May 0930–1230, 1400–1730, Jun and Sep 0930–1800.*

Left
Montignac

stunning frieze of bison painted on white calcite. The contours of the rock face have been skilfully utilised to give the animals a three-dimensional form. The threat of environmental damage to the fragile paintings by humidity and carbon dioxide introduced by visitors may mean the cave has to be closed and replaced by a reproduction, as at Lascaux.

For a change of style, try the **Grotte du Grand Roc**, which has an amazing display of stalactites, stalagmites and other formations. There is also an excellent view of the Vézère Valley from the cave's entrance. An exhibition centre at **Habitats Préhistoriques de Laugerie-Basse** (€€ *on the D47 3km northwest of Les Eyzies-de-Tayac; tel: 05 53 06 92 70. Open all year except Jan; Jul–Aug 0930–1900, rest of year 1000–1800. Disabled access. Reduced-price tickets available for visits combined with the caves of Grand Roc*) displays reproductions of prehistoric artefacts and bones discovered on the site beside the Vézère, just upstream of Les Eyzies-de-Tayac. The originals have been scattered among different museums and private collections.

For an overview of the area's prehistory (and, literally, its countryside) climb up to the **Musée National de la Préhistoire**, housed in the recently enlarged and considerably restored 13th-century château poised halfway up the cliff above the village. The museum is a cornucopia of wall paintings, rock carvings and prehistoric artefacts uncovered in the area in the 20th century. For a glimpse into the world of cave exploration, visit **Musée de la Spéléologie** (€€ *Les Eyzies-de-Tayac; tel: 05 53 06 97 15. Open Jul–Aug daily 1100–1800*), where the history of the pursuit, caving equipment, and studies of geological formations and subterranean animal and plant life are exhibited in chambers carved out of the living rock.

MONTIGNAC

Office de Tourisme *Pl. Bertran de Born, Montignac; tel: 05 53 51 82 60; e-mail: ot.montignac@ perigord.tm.fr; www.bienvenue-montignac.com*

Lascaux II €€€ *Off the D704 1km south of Montignac; tel: 05 53 51 95 03. Open (45-min guided tours) Jul and Aug daily 0930–1900; Apr–Jun Tue–Sun 0900–1900; late Jan–Mar and Sep–Dec 1000–1200, 1400–1730. Closed 25 Dec and first three weeks of Jan. Daily limit of 2000 tickets is soon reached in peak season. No disabled access.*

Here is a case of the attraction diminishing the town, for just outside Montignac, a pleasant riverside community on the Vézère, lie the **Grottes de Lascaux**, probably the most important and certainly the most famous prehistoric site in Europe.

The original cave consists of four galleries with more than 1500 coloured paintings and engravings of animals superbly executed up to 17,000 years ago. It was discovered in 1940 by four schoolboys searching for a dog that had fallen into a hole. The cave was officially opened to the public eight years later and in the next 15 years attracted more than a million visitors, but the carbon dioxide and humidity they introduced began to damage the priceless works of prehistoric art. There was only one way to preserve the works – and that was to close the cave.

To avert public disappointment, it was decided to build a replica and **Lascaux II** opened in 1983. The 'copy-cat' cave, about 200m from the original, is the result of painstaking research and exceptionally

Grotte de Régourdou €€
Close to Lascaux site; tel: 05 53 51 81 23; e-mail: micheleconstant@wanadoo.fr; http://regourdou.fr/11.html Open Jul and Aug daily 0900–1800; May and Jun 0900–1200, 1400–1830; Sep–Apr 1000–1200, 1400–1800. Advance booking (14 days) essential.

detailed reconstruction. The cave paintings themselves were carefully photographed and the artist Monique Peytral copied the photographs, utilising the techniques and materials used by the original painters. Lascaux II is a reconstruction of the two major galleries – the Bulls' Hall and the Axial Gallery – which contain the finest examples, and there are displays showing how the original masterpieces were created and telling the history of the cave.

A kilometre east of Lascaux II is **Régourdou**, a prehistoric site where the 70,000-year-old skeleton of a man, together with other bones and artefacts, was unearthed in 1954. 'Régourdou Man' now rests in the Périgord Museum in Périgueux, but a cast of his jawbone and a number of tools and bones found on the site are displayed in a small museum.

LA ROQUE ST-CHRISTOPHE

La Roque St-Christophe €€
Peyzac-le-Moustier, off the D706, 3.5km from Tursac; tel: 05 53 50 70 45; e-mail: contact@roque-st-christophe.com; www.roque-st-christophe.com/indexgb.html. Open all year, Jul and Aug 1000–2000, Apr–Jun and Sep 1000–1830, Oct–mid-Nov and Feb–Mar 1000–1800, mid-Nov–Jan 1400–1700.

Nearly 1km in length and rising 80m above the Vézère Valley between the villages of Tursac and Peyzac-le-Moustier, this imposing cliff is like a prehistoric high-rise apartment block with about 100 caves hollowed out on five levels. Archaeological findings unearthed there suggest that the cliff dwellings were in use from up to 35,000 years ago. Fireplaces, stairways and carved-out passages, as well as post holes, drainage channels and water tanks, provide evidence of continuous human habitation over the millennia.

ST-AMAND-DE-COLY

Abbaye de St-Amand-de-Coly €€ Tel: 05 53 51 04 56; e-mail: info.st.amand@wanadoo.fr. Open Jul and Aug Mon–Fri 1030–1230, 1530–1900; rest of year weekends and public holidays 1500–1800.

Roofed with slabs of limestone, the old houses of this small village (pop. 300) are totally dominated by the fortress-like church that gives the place its name. It is one of Périgord's best-fortified churches – so well protected, indeed, that in the 15th and 16th centuries it was known as the St-Amand Fort. From a chamber above the main door, defenders were able to rain rocks and boiling oil down on to attackers, and in 1575 Protestants occupying the church were able to withstand a six-day siege by 20,000 soldiers backed up with heavy artillery.

In contrast to its militaristic exterior, the church's interior displays the simple, spacious beauty typical of Augustinian architecture – before the Hundred Years War it was part of an Augustinian abbey. An audio-visual presentation on the church and its history is shown in the former presbytery.

Right
St-Amand-de-Coly

St-Leon-sur-Vezere

Le Conquil €€ *Off the D66 across the bridge from St-Léon-sur-Vézère; tel: 05 53 51 29 03. Open May–Sep 1000–1900; rest of year 1000–1800.*

Château de Losse €€ *Off the D706 2km north of Thonac; tel: 05 53 50 80 08; e-mail: chateaudelosse24@yahoo.fr; www.chateaudelosse. com. Open for guided tours (in English) Apr, May & Sep 1100–1800; Jun–Aug 1000–1900. Disabled access over most of the house.*

Espace Cro-Magnon €€ *Le Thot; tel: 05 53 50 70 44. Open Apr–Sep 1000–1900; rest of year 1000–1230, 1400–1730. Closed Mon out of season. Combined ticket with Lascaux II available.*

Charmingly sited on a loop in the river, the village has much to offer, including one of the loveliest Romanesque churches in Périgord. The church's elegantly arcaded bell tower stands over the smoothly rounded apse and chapels like a mother hen guarding her chicks. Inside are sections of Romanesque frescoes. Originally part of a 12th-century Benedictine priory, the church was built on the site of a Gallo-Roman villa, of which some remains may still be seen.

The village has two castles: Château de la Salle, on the square, with a 14th-century keep, and Château de Clérans, dating from the 15th and 16th centuries, overlooking the river. **Le Conquil**, in woodland on the opposite bank of the Vézère, is a limestone cliff into which dwellings were cut in prehistoric times. Visitors can gain an insight into such prehistoric skills as archery, flint knapping and rock painting. They can also enjoy a superb view of the valley.

Visitors may tour the interior of the elegant **Château de Losse**, 4km upstream of St-Léon. Set high above the river and built in the 16th

Right
Tursac's Préhistoparc

century, the château is superbly furnished with 16th-century cupboards and chests from Italy and Louis XIII furniture. For an exciting experience of Prehistoric life, travel another couple of kilometres upstream to Le Thot, where **Espace Cro-Magnon** uses modern technology to re-create the distant past and serves as an introduction to the area's best-known cave sites, especially Lascaux.

Species of animals that have survived from the time of Cro-Magnon man, up to 35,000 years ago – such as bison and Przewalski's horses – roam the surrounding park while animatronics of such extinct animals as the mammoth and woolly rhinoceros give an extra touch of authenticity. The centre's innovative museum includes exhibits on prehistoric art and there are reproductions of paintings and engravings found in remote parts of Lascaux.

SERGEAC

Castel-Merle €€
Near Sergeac; tel: 05 53 50 79 70; www.castelmerle. com. Open for 1-hour guided tours daily Jul and Aug 1000–1900; rest of year closed Sat; Apr–Jun 1000– 1200, 1400–1830; Sep and Oct closes 1730. Nov–Dec groups by appointment only. Disabled access.

Sergeac is a pleasant riverside village with a restored Romanesque church, but its chief attraction, 1km to the west, is **Castel-Merle**, a prehistoric site that until recently was open only to professional archaeologists. A museum near the site displays necklaces and other artefacts from 150,000 years ago to the Gallo-Roman period. Some of the *abris* (shelters) in the area, including one with wall sculptures of animals, can be visited.

TURSAC

Tursac Préhistoparc €€
Le Faure de Reignac, Tursac; tel: 05 53 50 73 19; e-mail: e-mail: prehisto-parc@wanadoo.fr; www.prehistoparc.fr. Open Jul and Aug 1000–1900, Apr–Jun and Sep 1000–1830, rest of year 1000–1730.

The village provides another opportunity for a close-up look at prehistoric life. **Tursac Préhistoparc**, located in a small, steep valley, consists of a discovery trail leading to 20 or so reconstructions of aspects of daily life for Neanderthal and Cro-Magnon people, including cave painting, hunting and food preparation.

Accommodation and food

La Faisandière € *La Baronnie, close to Gouffre de Proumeyssac, Le Bugue; tel: 05 53 07 24 17.* This farm–*auberge* has three double rooms and a 45-seat restaurant (**€€–€€€**) where home-made regional specialities are served.

Les Marroniers € *Pl. de la Gare, Le Bugue; tel: 05 53 07 22 54.* This hotel–bar–restaurant has seven rooms for overnight guests and seating for up to 35 diners. Each room has television. The restaurant serves regional specialities.

Camping La Linotte € *Le Bugue; tel: 05 53 07 17 61; e-mail: infos@campinglalinotte.com; www.campinglalinotte.com. Open Apr–Sep.* The campsite has 88 pitches; mobile homes and chalets are available for hire.

Camping Le Val de la Marquise € *Le Bugue; tel: 05 53 54 74 10; e-mail: valmarquise@wanadoo.fr; www.levaldelamarquise.com. Open Apr–Oct.* Bungalows, caravans, mobile homes and chalets may be rented at this 104-pitch campground.

Les 3 Caupain €€ *Le Port, Le Bugue; tel: 05 53 07 24 60; e-mail: info@camping-bugue.com; www.caupain.net. Open Apr–Oct.* Camping in 4 hectares, including mobile homes. Restaurant and two swimming pools on site.

L'Abreuvoir €–€€ *31 Grand-Rue, Le Bugue; tel: 05 53 03 45 45.* 'Food that looks good, smells good and tastes good' is the boast in this centrally located restaurant. As well as a 50-seat dining room, there is space for 30 more diners on the terrace. Wheelchair access.

Hôtel de Paris €–€€ *14 r. de Paris, Le Bugue; tel: 05 53 07 28 16; e-mail: hoteldeparis24@yahoo.fr; www.hotel-bugue-perigord.com. Open all year.* Each of the hotel's 22 rooms has a direct-dial telephone, and there is a television room for guests.

La Pergola €–€€ *16 av. de la Libération, Le Bugue; tel: 05 53 54 18 05.* Pizzas, Italian cuisine and traditional Périgord dishes are on the menu. The dining room seats 60, the terrace 100. In the evening there is a pub bar and there is space for those who wish to play *pétanque*.

Restaurant Laugerie Basse €–€€ *Near the Grotte du Grand Roc, Les Eyzies-de-Tayac; tel: 05 53 06 97 91; e-mail: contact@laugerie-basse.com; www.laugerie-basse.com.* Traditional cuisine dominates the menu in this restaurant where the dining terrace overlooks the Vézère Valley.

Le Châteaubriand €–€€€ *29 av. de la Préhistoire, Les Eyzies-de-Tayac; tel: 05 53 35 06 11; e-mail: info@leseyzies.com. Closed Jan.* Traditional dishes based on fresh regional produce are served in two large air-conditioned dining rooms and on a pleasant terrace in the tree-shaded garden.

Les Fontenilles €€ *Route de Campagne, Le Bugue; tel: 05 53 07 24 97; e-mail: fontenilles@dordogne-perigord.com; www.hotel-lesfontenilles.*

com. Open all year. The closest a hotel could get to a typically perigourdine home. Six rooms and a restaurant serving local-style, home-cooked fare.

Hôtel de France €€–€€€ *R. du Musée National, Les Eyzies-de-Tayac; tel: 05 53 06 97 23; e-mail: contact@hoteldefrance-perigord.com; www. hoteldefrance-perigord.com. Open all year.* In a quiet location in the centre of the village, the hotel has 25 en-suite rooms with direct-dial telephones and television, a swimming pool, garden and private parking. Its restaurant, Auberge du Musée (€€–€€€), specialises in Périgord cuisine.

Hôtel Royal-Vézère €€–€€€ *Pl. de l'Hôtel-de-Ville, Le Bugue; tel: 05 53 07 20 01; e-mail: royalvezere@wanadoo.fr; http://hotel-royal-vezere.com/ index-gb.htm.* The riverside hotel has 53 en-suite rooms with direct-dial telephones, television and balconies. A terrace where meals may be taken overlooks the river. Private parking. Rooftop swimming pool.

La Roseraie €€–€€€ *Pl. d'Armes, Montignac; tel: 05 53 50 53 92; e-mail: hotelroseraie@wanadoo.fr; www.laroseraie-hotel.com. Open Apr–Oct.* A charming hotel–restaurant at the heart of medieval Montignac. It has 14 well-appointed rooms and offers swimming, mini-golf, horse riding and tennis. Gastronomic meals are served in the garden-restaurant.

Château de Puy-Robert €€€ *Route de Valojoux, Montignac; tel: 05 53 51 92 13. Open May–mid-Oct.* A 15-minute walk from Lascaux, the hotel–restaurant has 38 en-suite rooms, a swimming pool and a well-deserved reputation. Imaginative cuisine is served in elegant surroundings.

Below
The River Vézère

Château de Lacypierre €
Tel: 05 53 29 39 28; e-mail: serge.lebon.arch@wanadoo.fr. Open by appointment (seven days' notice required) Easter–All Saints' Day for guided visits.

Château de Salignac-Eyvignes €€ Tel: 05 53 28 80 06. Open (guided tours) Jun–Sep Wed–Mon 1030–1200, 1400–1800. Last two weeks of Jun and first two weeks of Sep 1400–1800.

Salignac-Eyvignes Office de Tourisme 24590 Salignac-Eyvignes; tel: 05 53 28 81 93; e-mail: ot.salignac@perigord.tm.fr; www.ot-salignac.com/otsalignac/index.asp

Domaine de la Barde €€€ *route de Périgueux, Le Bugue; tel: 05 53 07 16 54; e-mail: hotel@domainedelabarde.com; www.domainedelabarde.com. Open all year.* The 14-room hotel is a restored, elegant 18th-century manor house set in formal gardens. Rooms have television and direct-dial telephones. Amenities include swimming pool, sauna and tennis. In the evening the restaurant is reserved for hotel guests.

Hôtel Cro-Magnon €€€ *54 av. Préhistoire, Les Eyzies-de-Tayac; tel: 05 53 06 97 06. Open May–mid-Oct.* Standing in parkland, this elegant country hotel has 22 en-suite rooms and four apartments. Meals may be taken in the garden or in the rustic dining rooms. Private parking.

Suggested tour

Total distance: The main route covers 127km and the detour 42.5km.

Time: Allow 3 hours' driving time and a full day (or even two, with an overnight stop) for sightseeing.

Links: At Le Bugue you are only 10km north of the D29, part of the route west to Bergerac (*see pages 66–8*). From Les Eyzies-de-Tayac, the D47 heads southeast for 21km to Sarlat-la-Canéda (*see pages 132–4*). From Terrasson-la-Villedieu the N89 goes east for 10km to Brive-la-Gaillarde (*see pages 152–3*) and west towards Périgueux (*see pages 86–97*) 54km away.

Route: From **LE BUGUE ❶** follow the D703 for 4km to Campagne, then take the D706 northeast for 7km to **LES EYZIES-DE-TAYAC ❷**. Next, head east on the D47 and after 4km, in which you will pass the entrances to **Grottes de Font-de-Gaume** and **des Combarelles**, bear left on to the D48, which takes you by **Abri du Cap-Blanc**. After 19km you'll reach **St-Geniès**, just east of the D704. This attractive village of yellow limestone houses has a 15th-century castle, the Gothic Chapelle du Cheylard, with 14th-century frescoes and a church with a 16th-century fortified porch.

Detour: From St-Geniès head southeast on the D61 and after 4km turn right on to the D60, which reaches St-Crépin-et-Carlucet in 2km. Here, the turreted **Château de Lacypierre** may be visited by appointment. Take the D60 west for 4km, then head south on the D704 for 9km to Sarlat-la-Canéda (*see pages 132–4*). Follow the D47 for 8.5km to **Ste-Nathalène**, where you may visit the 16th-century Moulin-de-la-Tour for a free demonstration of the traditional production of walnut and hazelnut oils. Continue on the D47 for 5km and at La Font turn left on to the D61 to reach **Salignac-Eyvignes** in 10km. The village has pleasant streets, a square with a 13th-century convent and an attractive **medieval château** with Renaissance and Louis XIII furnishings.

Right
Sarlat-la-Canéda

century only to be closed during the Revolution. Today, most of its buildings are used as a tobacco warehouse. In 1562 the monastery was pillaged by Huguenots and a decade later its buildings were set on fire; only the church was saved. The **Eglise Ste-Marie**, built in the 12th century, has three domes above the nave and transept and a half dome over the chancel. The best-known feature of the church,

Musée des Attelages de la Belle Epoque €€ R. Paul Chambert, Souillac; tel: 05 65 37 05 75. Open Jul and Aug daily 1000–1200, 1500–1900; Apr–Jun, Sep & Oct 1430–1830.

Musée National de l'Automate €€ Pl. de l'Abbaye, Souillac; tel: 05 65 37 07 07; e-mail: musee.automate@wanadoo.fr; www.souillac.net/musee.automate. Open Jul and Aug daily 1000–1900; Jun and Sept 1000–1200, 1500–1800; Apr, May & Oct Tue–Sun 1000–1200, 1500–1800; Nov–Mar Wed–Sun 1430–1730.

Camping les Acacias € Bourg La Canéda, Sarlat; tel: 05 53 31 08 50; e-mail: camping-acacias@wanadoo.fr; www.acacias.fr. Open May–Sep. Sites for motor homes are among the 89 pitches on this campground, which has a restaurant and bar, takeaway food, launderette and a swimming pool.

Camping le Caminel € Sarlat; tel: 05 53 59 37 16; www.lecaminel.com. Open Mar–mid-Nov. The campground has 100 pitches, with tents, mobile homes and chalets for hire. Full facilities for motor homes; restaurant; grocery store; takeaway meals; bar; launderette. Swimming pool.

Opposite
Souillac

though, is the west doorway, which was rebuilt inside out during restoration in the 17th century. Richly carved reliefs relate the story of the monk Theophilus who was extricated by the Virgin from a pact he had made with the devil.

The **Musée des Attelages de la Belle Epoque** houses 60 19th-century horse-drawn carriages, with harnesses and stable gear displayed in a tack room. If you are travelling with children, you certainly won't want to miss the **Musée National de l'Automate**, a collection of some 3000 mechanical toys, working models and robots. The core of the collection is 1000 automata donated by the family of Jean Roullet, who created spectacular Christmas window displays for the Bon Marché department store in Paris. Appropriately, the museum and the movements of figures in the collection are controlled by computer.

Accommodation and food

Hôtel Altica € 24 av. de la Dordogne, Sarlat; tel: 05 53 28 18 00. Open all year. A 'new generation' hotel offering simple but comfortable accommodation in modern surroundings at a budget price. Each of its 46 en-suite rooms can accommodate up to three people. No restaurant, but breakfast is available.

Auberge du Puits €–€€ 5 pl. du Puits, Souillac; tel: 05 65 37 80 32; e-mail: info@auberge-du-puits.fr; www.auberge-du-puits.fr. Closed Dec–Jan. The hotel has 19 rooms with television and direct-dial telephones. Wine by the glass is available in the restaurant (€€–€€€).

La Couleuvrine €–€€ 1 pl. de la Bouquerie, Sarlat; tel: 05 53 59 27 80; e-mail: lacouleuvrine@wanadoo.fr; www.la-couleuvrine.com. Open all year. The hotel–restaurant is in a listed building with a tower that was once part of the city's ancient ramparts. Its 24 en-suite rooms are individually decorated and furnishings are antiques. There are direct-dial telephones and television. The restaurant (€€) specialises in regional cuisine based on produce obtained locally.

Hôtel des Recollets €–€€ 4 r. J-J Rousseau, Sarlat; tel: 05 53 31 36 00; e-mail: contact@hotel-recollets-sarlat.com; www.hotel-recollets-sarlat.com. Open all year. Built around the cloisters of a 17th-century convent, with an attractive courtyard, the hotel has 18 rooms. There is secure parking for cycles and excursions are organised from the hotel.

Hôtel Le Renoir 2 €–€€ R. de l'Abbé Surgié, Sarlat; tel: 05 53 59 35 98; e-mail: info@hotel-renoir-sarlat.com; www.hotel-renoir-sarlat.com. Two minutes' walk from the historic centre of Sarlat. Twenty-seven en-suite rooms with satellite TV, and a swimming pool on site.

Hôtel Saint Albert €€ Pl. Pasteur, Sarlat; tel: 05 53 31 55 55; e-mail: hotel.stalbert@wanadoo.fr; www.sarlathotel.com. Family-run hotel in a

Camping les Perières € *R. Jean Gabin, Sarlat; tel: 05 53 59 05 84; www.lesperieres.com. Open Apr–Sep.* The ground's 100 pitches include sites for motor homes and there are mobile homes and chalets for hire. Restaurant and bar; takeaway food; grocery store and launderette. Swimming pool.

Camping Le Rivaux € *Sarlat; tel: 05 53 59 04 41; e-mail: aft@francecom.com. Open Apr–Sep.* 100 pitches; simple facilities. Tents and caravans for hire.

former coaching inn, at the gates to the medieval city. Twenty-five rooms and a restaurant serving regional dishes. Car parking in front of the hotel.

Grand Hôtel €€–€€€ *1 allée Verninac, Souillac; tel: 05 65 32 78 30; www.grandhotel-souillac.com. Closed Dec–Mar.* Barely 50m from blvd Louis-Jean Malvy (the N20), the hotel has 42 en-suite rooms with air conditioning, television and direct-dial telephones. There is a terraced dining area and wine is served by the glass in the restaurant (€€–€€€).

Hostellerie-Restaurant la Verperie €€–€€€ *Allée des Acacias, Sarlat; tel: 05 53 59 00 20; e-mail: hotellaverperie@wanadoo.fr; www.laverperie.com. Open mid-Mar–mid-Nov.* Just five minutes from the centre of town, the hotel is in a quiet setting. It has 24 en-suite rooms and offers free, private parking. A large swimming pool is in the grounds. The restaurant (€€–€€€) serves generous portions of home-cooked fare.

Hôtel-Restaurant La Hoirie €€–€€€ *R. Marcel Cerdan, Sarlat; tel: 05 53 59 05 62; e-mail: lahoirie@club-internet.fr; www.lahoirie.com.* The hotel is in a former hunting lodge at the heart of a country park. Nineteen rooms, including two apartments, and a gastronomic restaurant offering regional specialities.

Hôtel de la Madeleine €€–€€€ *1 pl. de la Petite Rigaudie, Sarlat; tel: 05 53 59 10 41; e-mail: hotel.madeleine@wanadoo.fr; www.hoteldelamadeleine-*

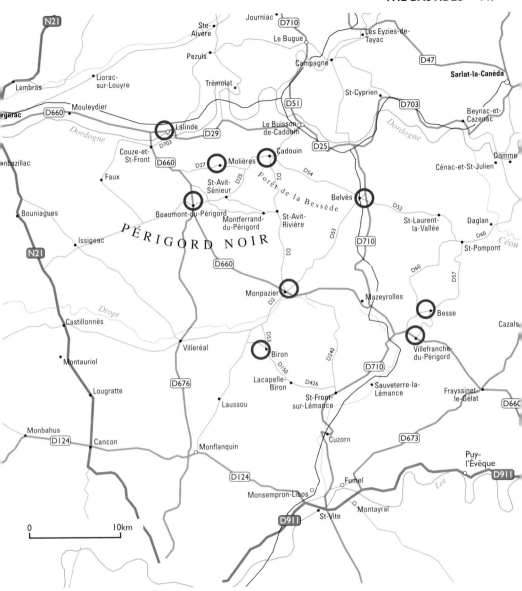

🅗 **Musée de la Préhistoire €€**

Belvès; tel: 05 53 29 10 93. Open all year, admission by appointment.

The Saturday market is a lively affair, with fresh butter and honey among its wares. The covered market, dating from the 15th century, has well-preserved supports of wood and stone. This and the old bell tower are in pl. d'Armes.

Belvès has a **Musée de la Préhistoire**, exhibiting items excavated in the area. The village is in a clearing of the great forest of Bessède, between the Lot and Dordogne rivers. Chestnuts and mushrooms are in abundant supply in autumn.

BESSE

ⓘ Mairie *Le Bourg, Besse; tel: 05 53 29 93 42; e-mail: mairie-besse@wanadoo.fr*

Here is another forest village. It has a château from the 16th and 17th centuries and a **Romanesque church**. Detailed carvings on the west front doorway, believed to be from the 11th century, are of special interest, representing some of the Bible's more lurid scenes, and original sin and damnation.

CADOUIN

ⓘ Le Cloître de Cadouin, Musée de Suaire and Musée du Pélerinage €€ *Tel: 05 53 63 36 28; e-mail: contact@semitour.com; www.semitour.com/pages. php?p=Cadouin. 45-min guided tours Jul and Aug daily 1000–1900; shorter hours rest of year. Closed Jan.*

Musée du Vélocipède €€ *Ancient Couvent de l'Abbaye, Cadouin; tel: 05 53 63 46 60. Open all year 1000–1900.*

Grottes de Maxange *Mestreguiral, Le Buisson-de-Cadouin; tel: 05 53 23 42 80; e-mail: contact @lesgrottesdemaxange.com; www.lesgrottesdemaxange. com. Open daily Jul and Aug 0900–1900, Apr–Jun and Sep 1000–1200, 1400–1800 (closes 1700 in Oct).*

The town's market and old houses grew up around the famous Cistercian abbey, the **Cloître de Cadouin** in the Bessède Forest, though the village itself remained small. The abbey dates from the 12th century. Mention Cadouin and people think of the Cadouin Holy Shroud, which brought pilgrims to the abbey for centuries, and is still something people go to see. The embroidered linen cloth was believed to have been used to wrap Christ's head and to have been brought to Cadouin, probably by 1214, by a priest from Périgord. During times of danger, as in the Hundred Years War, it was sent to places of safety to be looked after by monks. It was not until the late 15th century that it was returned to Cadouin.

A scientific study of the shroud in the 1930s suggested a connection with a caliph who had ruled in Egypt in the 11th century, and a 1982 study virtually confirmed the date, proving that it could not have enshrouded Christ's head. The shroud is exhibited in the abbey today in the **Musée du Suaire**. The abbey, in golden stone, is very beautiful, with many points of interest, notably the carved capitals in the cloisters, with four galleries, built in Flamboyant Gothic style in the 15th and 16th centuries.

Cadouin has a **Musée de Pélerinage** (Pilgrimage) and a **Musée du Vélocipède** (Bicycle). The bicycle museum claims to be the biggest in France, with more than 100 cycles on show, from penny-farthings to a bicycle that took part in the first Tour de France in 1901 and another that competed in a race from Paris to Brest and back in 1893.

The **Grottes de Maxange** at nearby Mestreguiral are known as the 'caves of stars' because of the presence of short, spiky deposits of calcite crystals rather than the more usual limestone. The Maxange caves are easy to visit as there is little difference in height between the caves.

CHATEAU DE BIRON

ⓘ Château de Biron €€ *On the D53 road; tel: 05 53 63 13 39. Guided tours. Open Jul and Aug daily 1000–1900; rest of year closed Mon, times vary.*

This massive structure – one of the biggest châteaux in the Périgord region – commands a great view from its lofty seat. It is about 7km southwest of Monpazier. They say pride comes before a fall, and Charles de Gontaut, a member of the Biron family in the time of

Henri IV, provides a good illustration of this: it was his head that fell. As a so-called friend of the king, he received one exalted office after another and, in the late 16th century, the Barony of Biron was created. Charles was made a duke, and before long Governor of Burgundy. Showing no gratitude at all, he plotted to overthrow the kingdom of France. He was found out, and inconceivably forgiven by Henri. But he soon resumed his plotting. This time Henri was still prepared to forgive him on condition that he confessed. Charles was too proud to confess, so his head was cut off.

The castle was built over a period of several centuries by successive generations of the Gontaut-Biron family, starting with a 12th-century fortress. The result is a whole complex of buildings in different styles. It was rebuilt after Simon de Montfort knocked it down in the 13th century, and for years it bounced back and forth between the English and French. When maintenance costs became prohibitive for private owners more than 20 years ago, the Dordogne *département* bought it and carried out extensive restoration work.

LALINDE

Château de Lanquais €€ *Tel: 05 53 61 24 24; e-mail: chateaudelanquais@wanadoo.fr; www.pays-de-bergerac.com/assos/pays-bergerac/lanquais.asp. Open daily Jul and Aug 1000–1900; rest of year to 1830.*

Hôtel du Château €€–€€€ *1 r. de la Tour; tel: 05 53 61 01 82; www.jpmoser.com/lechateau.html.* A small, well-equipped 3-star hotel with restaurant (**€€–€€€**) and swimming pool. The seven guest rooms are en suite. *Closed Jan.*

Lalinde, by the Dordogne to the east of Bergerac, was one of the first of the royal English *bastides*, having been founded by King Henry Plantagenet III in 1267. Even though the town has been quite heavily industrialised it still shows its *bastide* beginnings.

Near Lalinde, south of the river, is the **Château de Lanquais**, most of which was built in the 14th and 15th centuries, an addition to the fortification being built during the Wars of Religion. Two of the fireplaces are decorated with fine carvings. Visitors can tour the kitchens, laid out and equipped as in medieval times, and frequently filmed for TV programmes and the movies. If you are in Lalinde on a Thursday morning you may like to buy some wine, cheese, fruit and vegetables from the market. In the season (November to March) you can buy fresh truffles there.

MOLIERES

Maison de la Noix *Tel: 05 53 73 90 33. Open Jul and Aug 1000–1300, 1430–1900; rest of year by appointment.*

Molières is a *bastide* whose population has shrunk over the centuries from about 1200 to 300. But it still has its central square and the nucleus of its grid-system streets. It also has its **Maison de la Noix** or House of Nuts, which is a place where you can learn about how nut oil is made and about the cultivation, harvesting and use of the nuts. The fortress built to protect Molières still stands. Part of it is a dungeon.

MONPAZIER

ℹ **Office de Tourisme**
Pl. de Cornières,
Monpazier; tel: 05 53
22 68 59; e-mail:
ot.monpazier@perigord.tm.fr;
www.pays-des-bastides.com

Opposite
Monpazier

Here is a showpiece *bastide* that people want to revisit and persuade their friends to visit. Founded in 1284, it was declared a listed national monument in 1991. It is the archetypal village that time left untouched, yet is gratifyingly lacking in self-consciousness. Perhaps it is because it is also a workaday place in which the locals go about their business, accepting tourism without rancour.

Its streets are of the classic grid pattern and the square has its medieval covered market with little arcaded shops around it. The *cèpes* (Boletus mushrooms) are piled up on the market stalls in autumn.

VILLEFRANCHE-DU-PERIGORD

Below
Villefranche-du-Périgord

This *bastide* ranks close to Monpazier for its well-preserved state. Also like Monpazier, it is a great centre for wild mushrooms – there is a

**ⓘ Syndicat
d'Initiative** *Rue
Notre Dame, Villefranche-du-
Périgord; tel: 05 53 29 98
37; e-mail: ot.villefrancepgd@
perigord.tm.fr; www.
tourisme.perigord-fr.com*

mushroom nature trail – and for chestnuts harvested in the woodlands in the area. The **Maison du Chataignier, Marrons et Champignons** (*tel: 05 53 29 98 37*) presents exhibits on chestnuts, chestnut trees and mushrooms. Villefranche-du-Périgord was founded in 1261. It has a large covered market and some of its arcades remain.

Fortress villages

From a light aircraft flying over Aquitaine it's easy to pick out the *bastide* towns and villages by their 'noughts and crosses' streets and central squares. There are about 250 *bastides* in Aquitaine, a number of which are clustered in the southern part of the Dordogne.

During the 13th and 14th centuries, when the *bastides* were being built, the central focus of each became the village square instead of the church. The churches were built as strategically placed fortifications, and were used as a place of shelter for the people in times of invasion. From time to time some of the churches served as prisons.

Markets and trade fairs were held on the central square, and many medieval covered markets, with strong stone or stone and wood pillars, exist in fine condition today. Many still have the old grain measures in place. Around the square, buildings had arcaded fronts where tradesmen carried out their work.

The demographic growth of the time led to the regrouping of dispersed populations and according them franchises. For many decades the French and the English battled for supremacy, and founding the *bastides* was very effective from a military point of view – even more so from an economic angle. The citizens benefited from having the protection of their local seigneurs.

Among the founders of *bastides* during the two centuries were the counts of Toulouse, the royal dukes of Aquitaine, regional lords and the kings of France and the kings of England. As well as being centres of commerce, the squares had the civic and municipal buildings on their borders. The house of the seneschal or governor was always on the central square.

Accommodation and food

Camping La Bastide € *Route de Cahors, Villefranche-du-Périgord; tel: 05 53 28 94 57; www.camping-la-bastide.com. Open Jun–mid-Sep.* Forty pitches (tents, caravans, mobile homes and chalets); motor homes accommodated. The site has restaurant, takeaway food, bar, launderette and pool.

Camping Moulin de la Guillou € *Route D703, Lalinde; tel: 05 53 61 02 91; e-mail: mairie@ville-lalinde.fr. Open May–Oct.* Waterside campground with 100 pitches with bar, swimming and tennis.

Camping Le Moulinal € *Biron; tel: 05 53 40 84 60; e-mail: lemoulinal@perigord.com; www.lemoulinal.com/GB_welcome.htm. Open mid-Apr–mid-Sep.* Quality campground by the water with 250 pitches and just about every amenity – locations for tents, caravans, mobile homes, chalet, places for motor homes. On site are a restaurant, food store, takeaway, bar, disco, childcare, launderette, internet café, swimming and tennis.

Camping Municipal Panoramique € *Le Buisson-de-Cadouin; tel: 05 53 63 46 43. Open Jun–Sep.* This is a basic site with 33 pitches.

Camping Les Nauves € *Bos Rouge, Belvès; tel: 05 53 29 12 64; www.lesnauves.com. Open June–mid-Sep.* There are 100 pitches (tents, mobile homes, caravans, chalets). Amenities include restaurant, takeaway, bar, launderette, tennis and swimming.

Camping Le Parc € *Sauveboeuf, Lalinde; tel: 05 53 61 02 30; e-mail: sylvie@camping-le-parc.com; www.camping-le-parc.com. Open Jun–mid-Sep.* Small site (27 pitches), with tents, caravans, mobile homes and chalets and places for motor homes. Bar and swimming pool.

Camping Le Pont de Vicq € *Le Buisson de Cadouin; tel: 05 53 22 01 73; www.campinglepontdevicq.com. Open mid-Apr–Sep.* Waterside site with 130 pitches (tents, caravans, mobile homes, chalets), space for motor homes. Bar, restaurant, food store and takeaway on site.

Domaine de Fromengal € *Le Buisson-de-Cadouin; tel: 05 53 63 11 55; e-mail: fromengal@domaine-fromengal.com; www.domaine-fromengal.com/ gb/bienvenue.htm (English). Open Apr–Oct.* This quality site has 98 pitches (tents, caravans, chalets, mobile homes); motor homes accommodated. It has a grocery store, takeaway food, bar, tennis and swimming pool.

La Grande Veyière € *Molières; tel: 05 53 63 25 84; e-mail: la-grande-veyiere@wanadoo.fr; www.lagrandeveyiere.com. Open Apr–mid-Nov.* There are 64 pitches (tents, caravans, mobile homes, chalets); motor homes accommodated. Grocery store, takeaway, bar and laundry facilities on site.

Le Moulin de la Pique *Route D710, Belvès; tel: 05 53 29 01 15; e-mail: info@rcn-lemoulindelapique.fr; www.rcn-campings.fr/ lemoulindelapique/gb/index.htm (English). Open May–mid-Sep.* Well-equipped waterside ground (tents, caravans, mobile homes, chalets), places for motor homes. Restaurant, grocery store, takeaway food, bar, swimming, tennis, launderette.

Hôtel Les Bruyères €–€€ *Route de Cahors, Villefranche-du-Périgord; tel: 05 53 29 97 97. Closed two weeks in Feb.* The hotel has a swimming pool, 10 en-suite rooms and a restaurant (€–€€).

Hôtel La Forge €€ *Pl. Victor Hugo, Lalinde; tel: 05 53 24 92 24. Closed two weeks in Dec.* Fourteen en-suite rooms and a restaurant (€–€€).

Hôtel du Périgord €€ *Pl. du 14 Juillet, Lalinde; tel: 05 53 61 19 86; e-mail: philippe.amagat@wanadoo.fr; www.hotelduperigord.com. Open all year.* All 16 rooms have private facilities and there's a restaurant (€€).

Hôtel La Petite Auberge €€ *Les Peyrouillines, St-Capraise-de-Lalinde; tel: 05 53 29 91 01. Closed two weeks in Nov and Feb.* The hotel has a restaurant (€–€€) and 10 en-suite rooms.

Hôtel Relais St-Jacques €€ *Pl. de l'Eglise, St-Capraise-de-Lalinde; tel: 05 53 63 47 54. Open year round.* Only five rooms, but all have private facilities. There is a restaurant (**€–€€**).

La Salvetat €€ *Route de Belvès, 24480 Cadouin; tel: 05 53 63 42 79; e-mail: contact@lasalvetat; www.lasalvetat.com. Open Feb–mid-Dec.* Twelve en-suite rooms, a restaurant (**€€**) and swimming pool.

Hôtel Manoir de Bellerive €€€ *Route de Siorac, Le Buisson-de-Cadouin; tel: 05 53 22 16 16; e-mail: manoir.bellerive@wanadoo.fr; www.bellerivehotel.com. Open Mar–mid-Dec.* The 21 rooms are en suite. The 3-star hotel offers tennis, swimming and a restaurant (**€€–€€€**).

Suggested tour

Total distance: The route covers 117km.

Time: Driving time will be about 2½ hours, but give yourself a day for this fascinating trip through forests and ancient villages.

Links: At Lalinde, Bergerac (*see pages 66–8*) is only 19km to the west on the D660. From Belvès, travelling south, Villefranche-du-Périgord can be reached in 24km by way of the D710 and the D660.

Route: From **LALINDE** ❶, cross the Dordogne river, head west on the D703 for 3km to Couze-et-St-Front, then turn south on to the D660 for 6km, joining the D27 east, which reaches **MOLIERES** ❷ in 9km and **CADOUIN** ❸ 2km after that. Take the D54 southeast out of Cadouin, crossing the northern edge of the Forêt de la Bessède and arriving at **BELVES** ❹ after 12km.

Next, follow the D52 southeast for 9km, passing through the village of St-Laurent-la-Vallée and continuing for a further 4.5km to **St-Pompont**, a village of typical Périgord houses. The English built a castle here in the 15th century, but now only a doorway remains. A cairn built on a hilltop on the western edge of the village is said to be a prehistoric burial mound. Take the D57 southwest for 9km to **BESSE** ❺, passing first through areas of scattered cultivation, then into an extensive forest of pines and chestnut trees. From Besse the road descends, twists and turns, then climbs again to reach **VILLEFRANCHE-DU-PERIGORD** ❻ in 6km.

Leave Villefranche on the D660 west and in 3.5km take the D710 south for 9km and at St-Front-sur-Lémance turn right on to the D240, reaching Lacapelle-Biron in 6.5km. From here, the D150 takes you to **BIRON** ❼ and its imposing château. Continue north for 3km on the D53, turning right on to the D2 just beyond the small village of St-Cernin. The D2 leads to **MONPAZIER** ❽ in 5km.

Continue north for 8.5km to St-Avit-Rivière. The river on which the village stands is the Couze, which joins the Dordogne after a very pretty run of some 18km. Turn left on to the D26 and in 2km arrive at **Montferrand-du-Périgord**, where there are stunning views to the south, looking over the river. The village itself is delightfully terraced and has a ruined château with a 12th-century keep. From the north bank of the Couze, follow the signs to **St-Avit-Sénieur** 4km north of Montferrand. The village name honours Avitus Senior, who served as a soldier in the army of the Visigoth king Alaric II, then became a hermit. A huge church and monastery buildings are the remains of an 11th-century Benedictine abbey.

Heading west, the D25 crosses a rustic landscape with some handsome manor houses and reaches **BEAUMONT-DU-PERIGORD** ❾ in 5km. From Beaumont the D660 travels north, staying close to the Couze and taking you back to Lalinde in 13.5km.

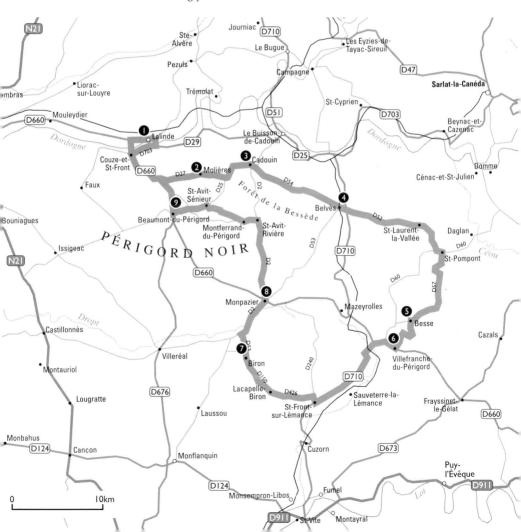

Around Brive-la-Gaillarde and Rocamadour

Ratings

Caverns	●●●●●
Churches	●●●●○
History	●●●●○
Scenery	●●●●○
Walks	●●●●○
Architecture	●●●○○
Art	●●●○○
Children	●●○○○

For those spending their holiday touring the Dordogne and the Lot it's worth considering getting there by Motorail with the car on board. Brive is a main railway junction just over the Dordogne border in the Corrèze *département*. You could pause to see the museum in Brive's finest Renaissance town house, then leave the industrial conurbation for the pastoral expanses, green hills, lush valleys and walnut plantations of the region. Small medieval towns, the amazing pilgrimage destination of Rocamadour (teeming uncomfortably with visitors in summer), shops selling local foods and crafts, villages of rose-red stone – there's plenty to see. A 36-hectare lake for swimming and windsurfing, perhaps. A wildlife park. A monkey forest. Birds of prey demonstrating their soaring and nose-diving techniques at the Rock of Eagles. And aeons of nature's sculptures far beneath the ground in strange grottoes and gorges.

BRIVE-LA-GAILLARDE

ⓘ **Brive** *Pl. du 14 Juillet, Brive-la- Gaillarde; tel: 05 55 24 08 80; e-mail: service-accueil@ brive-tourisme.com; www.brive-tourisme.com. Open all year Mon–Sat 0900–1800.*

Brive, or to use its full name, Brive-la-Gaillarde (the Bold), is not your typical tourist town, though if you dropped by parachute into its centre you could be forgiven for thinking so. Many of the 50,000 population work in the town's canning industry, but Brive's old heart beats with the gentle throb of past ages. Narrow twisting streets of well-restored tall buildings and new ones in gold sandstone live cheerfully together. You'll find good little cafés and interesting shops.

The **Eglise St-Martin**, right in the city's heart, has a 14th-century nave and is believed to have developed from a monastery community 200 years earlier. The chancel was rebuilt in the 18th century, and the font has been dated as belonging to the 12th century. Archaeological excavations have suggested that previous places of worship on the site go back to the 5th century. Why Brive-the-Bold (or Brive-the-Brave)? Apparently the local people stood up gallantly to the many sieges they had to face.

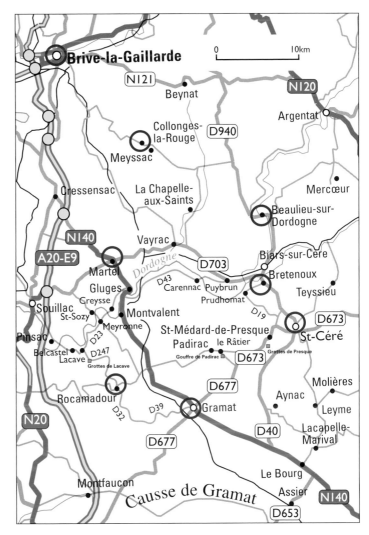

Musée d'Art et d'Histoire €€ *Hôtel de Labenche, 26bis blvd Jules Ferry, Brive; tel: 05 55 18 17 70; e-mail: claire.moser@ brive.fr; www.musee-labenche. com/defaulta.htm (English). Open Apr–Oct 1000–1830; Nov–Mar 1000–1800. Closed Tue (90-minute guided tours available).*

Centre d'Etudes Edmond Michelet €
4 r. Champanatier, Brive; tel: 05 55 74 06 08. Open all year Mon–Sat 1000– 1200, 1400–1800 except public holidays.

The **Musée d'Art et d'Histoire** is in the Hôtel de Labenche, a fine example of a Renaissance town house, and not only exhibits ancient items unearthed in the area but also reproduces some of the excavations that yielded them. The 17th-century Mortlake tapestries form a prized collection, showing rural scenes in rich colours.

In the **Centre d'Etudes Edmond Michelet**, documents, photographs, maps and pictures relate to the work of the Resistance Movement locally and the camps to which local people were deported. Dachau gets special coverage as the prison camp where De Gaulle's minister, Michelet, was held.

BEAULIEU-SUR-DORDOGNE

ℹ️ **Beaulieu** *6 pl. Marbot; tel: 05 55 91 09 94; e-mail: mairie.beaulieu@wanadoo.fr; www.beaulieu-sur-dordogne.fr. Open Apr–Sep daily; rest of year closed Sun.*

🏛️ **Chapelle des Pénitents €€**
Beaulieu; tel: 05 55 91 11 31; e-mail: chapelle.penitents. beaulieu@wanadoo.fr; http:// perso.wanadoo.fr/chapelle. penitents.beaulieu. Open Jul and Aug daily 1000–1200, 1500–1800; Sep 1030–1200, 1500–1730; rest of year by appointment (five days' notice required).

Below
Château de Castelnau

Apart from its natural beauty and narrow streets of thick-walled old buildings, Beaulieu has been put firmly on the tourist map by its 12th-century riverside church, with its marvellous Last Judgement sculpture and other points of interest: at the **Eglise St-Pierre**, a conglomeration of rooftops of chapels, towers, the octagonal belfry and accoutrements gives the church distinction. Even as you approach the porch you discover why this Romanesque church, once part of a Benedictine abbey, gets special attention.

The sculpture depicting a vision of the Last Judgement at the south doorway provides much to absorb: Christ with trumpet-blowing angels and others bearing the Cross, Crown of Thorns and nails. Apostles, then the dead rising from their graves and a veritable chamber of medieval horrors. The well-preserved sculpture dates from the 1120s and was part of the work of some of the sculptors who carved the south doorway at Moissac (*see pages 212–21*). The interior has much to interest the connoisseur, and there is also a Trésor, a locked room containing such treasures as a 12th-century Virgin and ancient items of value from the 10th to 14th centuries. To view the Trésor you will need to make a special application to the tourist office. Downstream of the Eglise St-Pierre is another much-photographed **Chapelle des Pénitents**, now a small museum of local history.

BRETENOUX

ℹ️ **Bretenoux** *Av. de la Libération; tel: 05 65 38 59 53; e-mail: ot.bretenoux@wanadoo.fr; www.ot-bretenoux.com. Open all year 0900–1200, 1400–1800, Sun high season 1000–1300; rest of year closed Sun and holidays.*

🏛️ **Château de Castelnau-Bretenoux €€**
Prudhomat; tel: 05 65 10 98 00; http://castelnau-bretenoux.monuments-nationaux.fr/en. Guided tours Jul and Aug daily 0930–1900; Apr–Jun and Sep 0930–1215, 1400–1815; Oct–Mar Wed–Mon 1000–1215, 1400–1715. Ticket office closes 45 min before closing times.

The *bastide* village founded in the 13th century still has its square, covered arcades and parts of the ramparts. The big landmark near here – and big's the word – is the **Château de Castelnau**. Its red stone bulk fills the sky above the little community of Prudhomat, and is the second largest fortification in southern France. The keep dates from the 13th century, additions being made during the Hundred Years War. Visitors on the guided tour learn about the Castelnau family who occupied the castle in medieval times.

COLLONGES-LA-ROUGE

Mairie *Tel: 05 55 25 41 09; e-mail: mairie@collonges-la-rouge.fr. Open daily 0900–1200.*

All the stonework in this much-visited village blushes deep red. Collonges gets so busy in summer that cars are banned from its streets. A large parking area for cars and coaches is provided. People go to see the large, ornate houses, spiky with turrets and architectural whims, built mainly in the 16th century. The village has 426 residents and 700,000 visitors per year.

GRAMAT

Gramat *Pl. de la République, Gramat; tel: 05 65 38 73 60; e-mail: gramat@wanadoo.fr; www.tourisme-gramat.com. Open all year, Apr–Sept 0930–1230, 1400–1900, Oct–Mar closes 1800.*

Centre de Cynophilie (Police Dog Training Centre) *Le Ségala Gramat; tel: 05 65 38 71 59. Open house every Thu mid-Jun–mid-Sep 1500–1730. Free entry.*

Parc Animalier de Gramat €€ *Tel: 05 65 38 81 22; e-mail: gramat.parc. animalier@wanadoo.fr; www. gramat-parc-animalier.com. Open Easter–Sep daily 0900–1900; rest of year 1400–1800.*

This is a commercial centre of some 4000 people and the main town of the Gramat Causse, the limestone plateau that extends from the Dordogne Valley in the north to the Lot and Célé valleys in the south. The town has a sports centre, swimming pool and tennis courts. Horse races are held at a festival in early August. Local specialities in the shops include pewter and wrought-iron items, goose liver and truffles.

If you are in Gramat on a Thursday afternoon in summer you may like to watch a demonstration of **police dog handling**. Creatures of European origin, some species known from prehistoric times, can be seen in their natural habitat at the **Parc Animalier de Gramat**: ibex, bison, wild oxen, an ancient breed of horse and domestic poultry, pigs and other farmyard animals are among the species roaming the 36-hectare park. Trees, shrubs and plant specimens of the Gramat Causse are also on show.

GROTTOES AND GORGES

Gouffre de Padirac €€€ *Gramat; tel: 05 65 33 64 56; e-mail: info@gouffre-de-padirac.com; www.gouffre-de-padirac.com. Open (guided tours) Apr–Nov 0900–1800 (1700 in Oct, Nov) daily.*

For experiences of sheer wonder, visit some of the grottoes and gorges of the region. Three of the most spectacular are worth deviating for. At **Gouffre (gorge) de Padirac** in the limestone Causse de Gramat, you take a boat ride along a river 103m underground to see the Lac de la Pluie (Lake of the Rain) and the vast stalactites hanging eerily above it. You go on to see another lake at a higher level and a vaulted chamber 94m high. You follow a path around the chamber's nooks and crannies, and get a good view of the lake and river, then return by boat through a series of galleries before disembarking. The bad news is that it's a climb of 455 steps to the surface; the good news is that you can take the lift if you prefer.

ⓘ **Les Grottes de Lacave €€** *Near Souillac; tel: 05 65 37 87 03; e-mail: grottes-de-lacave@wanadoo.fr; www.grottes-de-lacave.com. Open Mar–Oct daily (guided tour by electric train); Mar 1000–1200, 1400–1700; Apr–Jun 0930–1200, 1400–1800; Jul 0930–1230, 1330–1800; Aug 0930–1800; Sep and Oct 0930–1200, 1400–1700.*

Grottes de Presque €€ *St-Médard-de-Presque; tel: 05 65 38 07 44; e-mail: grottesdepresque@yahoo.fr; www.grottesdepresque.com. Open (guided tours 40 mins) Jul and Aug daily 0930–1830; mid-Feb–Jun and Sep–mid-Oct 0900–1200, 1400–1800; Oct and Nov 1000–1200, 1400–1700.*

Prehistologia €€ *On the D247 near the Grottes de Lacave; tel: 05 65 32 28 28; www.prehistologia.com.* An imaginative display of prehistoric reconstructions including a Neolithic village showing scenes of everyday life, set in a forest park.

Visiting the beautiful **Grottes de Lacave** near Souillac involves a ride in a little open-top electric train and a lift to 12 caves with lakes, mirages and weird formations. Technology makes a bid to outdo nature in a 2000sq m cave. Visual effects provide 'black light' and present a curious phosphorescent quality. A little imagination brings strange figures and scenes to visitors' minds in the sometimes grotesque, sometimes beautiful formations.

Stalagmite columns up to 10m high in various colours can be seen in several chambers at the **Grottes de Presque**, 5km from St-Céré. The walls are thick with fascinating shapes and folds – a veritable wonderland.

Right
Rocamadour

MARTEL

Martel *Palais de la Raymondie; tel: 05 65 37 43 44; e-mail: martel2@wanadoo.fr; www.martel.fr/public*

Palais de la Raymondie €€
Martel; tel: 05 65 37 30 03. Open Jul and Aug daily 1000–1200, 1500–1800.

Reptiland €€ *N140, Puy Lombry, 46600 Martel; tel: 05 65 37 41 00; e-mail: info@reptiland.fr; www.reptiland.fr. Open Jul and Aug daily 1000–1800; rest of year 1000–1200, 1400–1800. Closed Mon Nov–Mar.*

This place is close to paradise for the student of medieval architecture. It is a lovely little town, capital of the 11th-century Viscounty of Turenne and known as the Town of Seven Towers. Parts of the 12th-century ramparts may be seen. Architectural treasures include the 13th-century **Palais de la Raymondie**, built as a fortress and converted to a residential mansion in the 14th century. It now houses the town hall and a small museum displaying Roman items excavated at a site near the town.

Most of the streets have ancient buildings – a 12th-century tower here, a Renaissance doorway there. The 13th-century turreted Hôtel de la Monnai was where coins were minted. The Eglise St-Maur, built to double as a fortification, dating from the 13th and 14th centuries, has some fine 16th-century stained glass. A covered market at the pl. des Consuls belongs to the 18th century.

Reptiland, on the N140 at Martel, presents nearly 90 reptile species, including snakes, crocodiles and lizards, with some scorpions and spiders.

ROCAMADOUR

L'Hospîtalet, *Rocamadour; tel: 05 65 33 22 00; e-mail: rocamadour@wanadoo.fr; www.rocamadour.com. Open daily all year except 25 Dec and 1 Jan.*

It is an incredible sight as you approach from L'Hospîtalet or the Colzou road and see Rocamadour hanging on the cliffside, all red roofs and pale amber walls, with a castle on top. This is one of the great centres of pilgrimage of the Middle Ages and the most famous site in the Lot, poised on its perch in a narrow valley of the River Alzou. There is a great deal to see in Rocamadour, and in summer a continuous congestion of people trying to see it. Try to visit out of peak season when it should be less jam-packed.

Another downside: the souvenir shops. Most have shelf upon shelf of crudely fashioned pottery figures and so-called crafts, which detract from the reason that put the town on the map more than 700 years ago. This was the discovery of the mummified body of St-Amadour in a niche in the limestone in 1166.

Rocamadour's narrow streets are lined with buildings from the 12th to 15th centuries. The long sweep of the Pilgrims' Staircase is dramatic, with its slow procession of people, the most devout on their hands and knees, making their way towards the Chapelle de la Vièrge Noire. It contains the small statuette believed to be from the 12th century, and the Basilique St-Sauveur, where the body of the hermit saint was found, since which momentous discovery, miracles are said to have occurred. There are seven chapels in all, and they can be visited only with a guide. Unless you are a true pilgrim ask yourself how eager you are to take the tour, because in summer it can mean a lot of waiting about.

Forêt des Singes
€€ *L'Hospitalet,
Rocamadour; tel: 05 65 33
62 72; e-mail: info@la-foret-
des-singes.com; www.la-foret-
des-singes.com. Open
Apr–Oct daily and some days
in Nov; Jul and Aug
0930–1830; rest of year
times vary.*

Rocher des Aigles €€
*Rocamadour; tel: 05 65 33
65 45; e-mail:
rocherdesaigles@wanadoo.fr;
www.rocherdesaigles.com.
Open Apr–Aug daily
afternoons only.*

Féérie du Rail €€
*L'Hospitalet, Rocamadour;
tel: 05 65 33 71 06;
e-mail: contact@la-feerie.com;
www.la-feerie.com/
voyage_an.html. Open daily
Apr–mid-Nov. Demonstration
shows at various times from
1100–1800 (1630
Sep–Nov).*

**Musée du Jouet Ancien
Automobile** *Pl. Ventadour,
Rocamadour; tel: 05 65 33
60 75. Open daily mid-
Mar–mid-Nov 1000–1200,
1400–1800.*

Aquarium €€
*L'Hospitalet, Place de
l'Europe; tel: 05 65 33 73
61. Open Jun and Sep
1000–1200, 1400–1800;
Jul and Aug 1000–1900.*

The most amazing sight in Rocamadour for many is the view of it hanging on to its cliff. With such great crowds drawn by Rocamadour, it is obvious that other diversions and entertainments will have been introduced. If you have children with you (and if you don't), this is where the fun starts. About 150 Barbary macaques live freely in 10 hectares of trees and open spaces of the **Forêt des Singes**. People can mingle with the monkeys, study them, take their photographs and feed them with popcorn sold at the entrance. The **Rocher des Aigles**, near the Château de Rocamadour, presents the big stars of the sky – eagles, vultures, owls and other birds of prey – flying freely to great heights and returning to their handlers' wrists. The **Féérie du Rail** is more than a model railway system. It has scenery, sound effects and all sorts of things moving in its midst, from the rise and fall of hot-air balloons to football matches. The **Musée du Jouet Ancien Automobile** is a nostalgia trip among gleaming pedal cars made between 1910 and 1960 and a great collection of Dinky cars. The **Aquarium** showcases flora and fauna of cold continental waters, with fish and curious crustaceans.

Right
Rocamadour's rue de la
Couronnerie

Right
Rocamadour's St-Sauveur

St-Cere

ℹ️ **St-Céré** Pl. de la
République; tel: 05 65
38 11 85; www.tourisme-saint-
cere.com. Open daily in high
season 0900–1230,
1400–1900, Sun and public
hols 1000–1230; rest of year
1000–1200, 1400–1800
(closed Sun).

The centre of St-Céré has some venerable buildings in its little
streets, having been lucky in surviving the Hundred Years War with
comparatively little plunder. Streets such as pl. du Mercadial and r.
St-Cyr have houses from the Middle Ages to the 15th century. It
was the hilltop fortification 2km north of St-Céré that defended the
town from onslaught. Most of the castle has gone now, but two
medieval towers – the Tours de St Laurent – can be seen long before
you reach them.

Atelier Musée Jean Lurçat €€ *Tours de St-Laurent, St-Céré; tel: 05 65 38 28 21; e-mail: affaires-culturelles@cg46.fr. Open mid-Jul–Sep daily 0930–1200, 1430–1830.*

Galerie du Casino € *av. Jean Mouliérat, St-Céré; tel: 05 65 38 19 60; e-mail: contact@le-casino.fr; www.le-casino.fr. Open daily 0900–1200, 1400–1900. Closed Tue from Oct–Jun.*

This is where cubist artist Jean Lurçat made his home after World War II, having been introduced to the Lot region by his work in the Resistance Movement. He worked in several media, including ceramics and mosaics, and was responsible for restoring an interest in tapestries through his impact-making, sometimes strange, designs. Lurçat died in 1966, aged 74. His studio, examples of his work and some downstairs rooms of his home form a fascinating **museum**. In St-Céré, just off blvd Jean Lurçat, is the **Galerie du Casino**, exhibiting a large collection of Lurçat's imaginative tapestries. Temporary exhibitions are also held at the Casino.

Accommodation and food

Hôtel-Restaurant Ste-Marie €€ *Rocamadour; tel: 05 65 33 63 07; e-mail: hotelsaintemarie@wanadoo.fr; www.hotel-sainte-marie.fr.* One of a dozen 2-star hotels in Rocamadour, most with restaurants, the Ste-Marie has 23 rooms (17 en suite).

Les Charmilles €€–€€€ *20 blvd St-Rodolphe de Turenne, Beaulieu-sur Dordogne; tel: 05 55 91 29 29; e-mail: contact@auberge-charmilles.com; www.auberge-charmilles.com/anglais/hotel.html.* Hotel with eight en-suite guest rooms.

La Segalières holiday village €
Route de Cajarc, Gramat; tel: 05 65 38 76 92. Open Jun–Sep. Quality campsite with boulodrome, mini-golf, volleyball, tennis, swimming and a children's playground. 75 pitches.

Château de la Treyne €€–€€€ *Lacave; tel: 05 65 27 60 60; e-mail: contact@chateaudelatreyne.com; www.chateaudelatreyne.com. Closed mid-Nov–mid-Dec.* The 4-star hotel–restaurant is air conditioned and has 14 well-equipped rooms, swimming pool and tennis courts.

Hôtel Domaine de la Rhue €€–€€€ *Near Rocamadour; tel: 05 56 65 33 71 50; e-mail: domainedelarhue@wanadoo.fr; www.domainedelarhue.com.* The hotel is in a quiet location 6km on the road towards Brive. It has 14 rooms with direct-dial telephones.

Hôtel-Restaurant Les Charmilles €€–€€€ *20 bd St-Rodolphe de Turenne, 19120 Beaulieu-sur-Dordogne; tel: 05 55 91 29 29; e-mail: contact@auberge-charmilles.com; www.auberge-charmilles.com.* Country house with eight guest rooms, each named after a variety of strawberry grown in the region.

Château du Doux €€€ *Altillac, Corrèze; tel: 05 55 91 94 00; e-mail: info@chateaududoux.com; www.chateau-du-doux.com.* A castle renovated in 1995 providing 4-star accommodation in 19 rooms, and 11 apartments for up to six guests. Located directly north of Beaulieu and 50km from Brive. Courtesy car available.

Suggested tour

Total distance: The main route covers 112km. The detour totals 25km.

Time: Much of the main route and the detour is over winding, very hilly roads, through picturesque and at times spectacular scenery, so allow 4 hours for driving time alone. Allow an hour for the detour.

Links: At Martel the N140 goes north for 33km to Brive-la-Gaillarde and southeast for 58km to Figeac (*see pages 172–6*). The D703 heads west for 15km to Souillac (*see pages 134–6*).

Route: From **MARTEL ❶** take the N140 south, crossing the Dordogne at Gluges, and after 5km head east on the D43 which reaches Carennac in a further 12.5km. **Carennac**, one of the most attractive villages along the river, was where François de Fénelon (*see Château de Fénelon, page 80*) spent 15 years as senior prior before becoming archbishop of Cambrai. The **Maison de la Quercynoise** is a museum featuring the Dordogne and the people who live along its course. The restored cloisters of the old priory and the 12th-century Eglise St-Pierre are also worth a visit.

At the eastern end of the village cross the river, then follow the D3 to Puybrun, a distance of 5km. Next take the D703 east for 5km to **BRETENOUX ❷**. From here head west again, this time on the D14, bearing south on to the D19 at Prudhomat, beneath the bulk of the **Château Castelnau-Bretenoux**, to reach **ST-CERE ❸**, then on to the D673 west, passing through Montal and near the **GROTTES DE PRESQUE ❹**.

At the hamlet of Le Râtier, 12.5km from St-Céré, the D90 takes you for 2.5km to the **GOUFFRE DE PADIRAC** ❺. Return to Le Râtier and follow the D60 south for 3km then turn right on to the D677 to reach **GRAMAT** ❻, a busy agricultural centre, in 8km. From Gramat the most spectacular way to **ROCAMADOUR** ❼ is by way of the D39 west and the D32 north, a distance of 17km. Leave Rocamadour on the D247 and travel north for 10km to reach **GROTTES DE LACAVE** ❽.

Detour: From Lacave take the D43 west to Belcastel, where a restored medieval castle is perched dramatically at the top of a sheer cliff overlooking the confluence of the Dordogne and Ouysse rivers. Pass the Château de la Treyne, another clifftop castle dating from the 14th century and now a hotel, to reach **Souillac** ❾ (*see pages 134–6*) in a total of 10.5km. From Souillac head east on the D703 and after 7km turn right on to the D15, crossing the Dordogne from St-Sozy to reach Meyronne after a further 5.5km.

From Lacave the main route continues along the D23 through a striking terrain of rocks, cliffs and small fields to the lovely riverside village of Meyronne, one-time domain of the Bishops of Tulle, 7km away. Cross the river to Creysse, another very charming village of narrow streets and red-roofed houses. Next, after another 4.5km, comes Gluges, stunningly set at the foot of steep cliffs overlooking the river. From Gluges, Martel is 7km north along another scenic section of the D23.

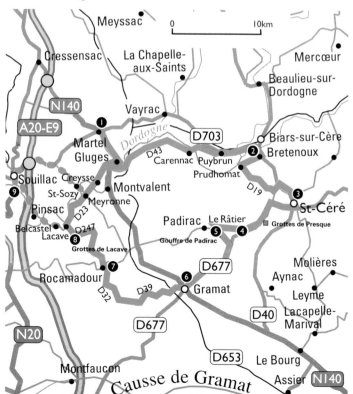

Opposite
St-Céré

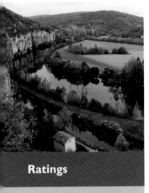

The Célé and Lot valleys

Ratings

Scenery	●●●●●
Caves	●●●●○
Villages	●●●●○
Architecture	●●●○○
Boating and canoeing	●●●○○
Castles	●●●○○
Walking	●●●○○
Children	●●○○○

The countryside embraced by the rivers Lot and Célé is among the most striking in the whole of Southwest France. It is very much a region of contrasts, though there is a common theme of rural tranquillity. There are mountainous areas, traversed by white-knuckle, corniche-style roads. There are sheer cliffs hanging over villages whose peaceful ambience draws a veil over centuries of bloodshed. There are delightful meadows and shady woodlands. And there are the two rivers, each quite different from the other. The Lot is the mightier – broad, fast-flowing and navigable – its power awesomely obvious as it plunges savagely over a weir. Here and there it is squeezed between cliffs and near its confluence with the Célé it provides an artistic touch to the towering village of St-Cirq-Lapopie. The Célé is the quiet one, gently tumbling over rocks and flowing serenely through ancient woods.

CABRERETS

ⓘ **Office de Tourisme**
*Tel: 05 65 31 27 12;
Open Apr–Sep; rest of year
refer to office de tourisme,
Saint-Cirq Lapopie; tel: 05 65
31 37 02.*

🏠 **Grotte de Pech
Merle** €€€ *Cabrerets;
tel: 05 65 31 27 05; e-mail:
gpechm@free.fr;
www.pechmerle.com. Open
Apr–Nov daily 0930–1200,
1330–1700. Visitor numbers
limited to 700 per day.
Booking advised Jun–Sep.*

Cabrerets is in a stunning position, set against a background of rocky cliffs where the rivers Sagne and Célé meet. Nearby are the ruins of the Château du Diable, which is also known as the Castle of the English for it was from here during the Hundred Years War that an English occupying force used to set out on raids. Also on the edge of the village is the massive Château Gontaut-Biron, built in the 14th and 15th centuries.

The real attraction here, however, is the **Grotte de Pech Merle**, discovered by two 14-year-old boys in 1922 and a close rival to Lascaux in the quality of its prehistoric paintings and engravings. More than 1km of chambers and galleries are open to the public. Among the works of art created more than 10,000 years ago is a frieze 7m long and 3m high with drawings of mammoths and bison. Elsewhere there are silhouettes of horses, with a pattern of dots, the engraving of a bear's head and handprints made by placing hands flat against the rock and tracing their shapes in various pigments. You can

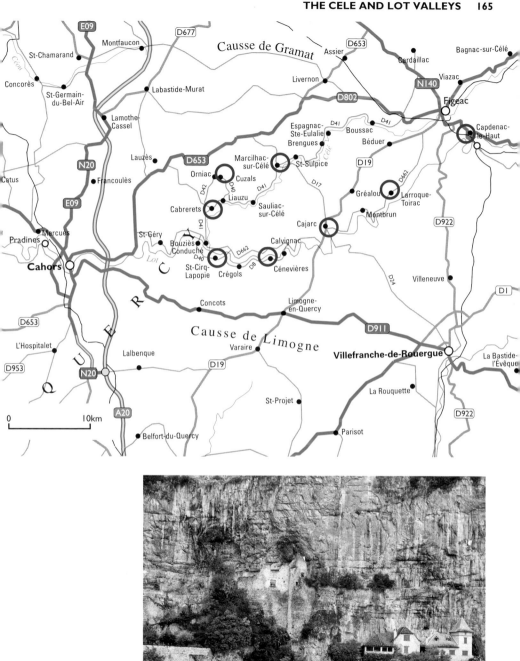

Right
Cabrerets

Musée Amédée Lémozi €€
Cabrerets; tel: 05 65 31 27 05; www.pechmerle.com. Open Palm Sunday to All Saints' Day daily 0930–1200, 1330–1700. Combined entry ticket for cave and museum available.

also see the footprints of a prehistoric visitor to the cave, set forever as he or she trudged through what was then mud. One of the chambers contains the bones of bears that once sheltered there.

Adjoining the entrance to the cave is the **Musée Amédée Lémozi**, named after the Abbé Lémozi, a local priest with a special interest in prehistory and speleology. It was his work that inspired the two youths who found the cave in 1922 and it was he who recognised its importance. The museum houses a display of works of art, tools, weapons and other artefacts from 160 prehistoric sites in France.

CAJARC

Bureau de Cajarc *La Chapelle, Cajarc; tel: 05 65 40 72 89. Open daily Jul and Aug 1000–1230, 1430–1900, Apr–Jun and Sep Mon–Sat 1530–1830, Sun 1000–1230.*

Maison des Arts Georges Pompidou
€€ Route de Figeac, 46160 Cajarc; tel: 05 65 40 78 19; e-mail: magp.cajarc@ wanadoo.fr; www.magp.fr. Open daily 1400–1800. Closed Tue.

This small town, which has more of the ambience of places closer to the Mediterranean, has two special distinctions: it was the birthplace of the writer Françoise Sagan and is the former home of President Pompidou, and it is thanks to M. Pompidou that Cajarc has become an important centre of contemporary art. The works of leading European artists displayed in exhibitions are staged in the **Maison des Arts Georges Pompidou**. Temporary exhibitions of contemporary art are also held in the gallery, **L'Acadie** (*€€ pl. de l'Eglise, Cajarc; tel: 05 65 40 76 37. Open mid-Mar–Nov Tue–Sun 1000–1900*).

CAPDENAC-LE-HAUT

Office de Tourisme et Musée Capdenac-le-Haut *Pl. Lucter; tel: 05 65 50 01 45. Open Jul and Aug Mon–Sat 0930–1230, 1430–1830, Sun 1430–1830; Sep–Jun Tue–Sat 1400–1800. Closed Sun, Mon.*

With ramparts dating from the 13th and 14th centuries, including ancient gateways and the bulk of a turreted square keep, the village has changed little over the centuries. Set on a promontory in a meander of the Lot, it gazes down on Capdenac-Gare, a busy rail junction on the opposite bank. The community's history, with the emphasis on Gallo-Roman and medieval times, is related in the **Musée**, housed in the old keep, where you will also find the tourism office.

CENEVIERES

Overlooking the village and the River Lot is the imposing **Château de Cénevières**. The site, some 70m high, has held fortifications since the 7th century, but the present structure, considerably altered during the Renaissance period, dates from the 13th century. The oldest part is the

Château €€
Cénevières; tel: 05 65 31 27 33; www.chateau-cenevieres.com. Open (guided tours) Easter–Sep daily 1000–1200, 1400–1800; Oct daily 1400–1700.

Right
Cuzals open-air museum

keep and there are 15th-century wings connected by a Renaissance gallery with Tuscan columns. A beautiful painted ceiling dominates the drawing room, which also contains Flemish tapestries. Visitors touring the castle are also taken into the kitchens, the keep and an alchemy room which has an alchemist's oven and 16th-century frescoes showing scenes from Greek mythology. The terrace affords superb views along the Lot Valley.

CUZALS

Musée de Plein Air du Quercy €€€
Cuzals; tel: 05 65 31 36 43. Open Jul and Aug Sun–Fri 1100–1900; Sep 1400–1800, closed Mon.

The big attraction in this village in the rocky hills above the valley is the entertaining and informative **Musée de Plein Air du Quercy**, which traces life in the region between the French Revolution and World War II. The open-air museum covers some 50 hectares and there are reconstructions of a milliner's shop, a bakery and a dentist's surgery of 1900. Examples of Quercy architecture are also on show and there is a collection of old agricultural equipment. In July and August some of the machinery, the mill and the baker's oven are operated by local people in period costume. There are ox-cart rides for children.

LARROQUE-TOIRAC

Château de Larroque-Toirac
€€ Larroque-Toirac; tel: 06 12 37 48 39; e-mail: contact@chateautoirac.com; www.chateautoirac.com. Open (guided tours) Jul–Oct daily 1000–1200, 1400–1800.

Grottes de Foissac €€€
Larroque-Toirac; tel: 05 65 64 77 04; e-mail: Grotte. de.Foissac@wanadoo.fr; www.grotte-de-foissac.com. Open for guided tours Jun–Sep 1000–1800; Apr, May & Oct 1400–1900. Other times by appointment.

One of a number of charming villages on the river's north bank, Larroque-Toirac has a major attraction in the form of the **Château de Larroque-Toirac**, which was rebuilt by Louis XI after being razed at the end of the 14th century. The castle was built by the powerful Cardaillac family in the 12th century and during the Hundred Years War frequently changed hands between the English and the French forces. Inside, there are fine 15th-century fireplaces, 16th-century frescoes and furnishings from the early 17th century.

A child's footprint, left in clay some 4000 years ago, can be seen along with human skeletons in the **Grottes de Foissac**, near the village. Items found in the caves suggest that they were inhabited about 2700 years ago and were used as quarries and catacombs. They were rediscovered in 1959. There are 8km of galleries with beautiful rock formations and white stalactites. The roof of one gallery is covered with bulbous stalactites known as 'the onions'. The caves are drained by an underground stream that joins the Lot.

Marcilhac-sur-Cele

① Office de Tourisme
Maison du Roy, Le
Bourg, Marcilhac-sur-Célé;
tel: 05 65 40 61 43;
e-mail: marcilhac@quercy.net;
www.quercy-tourisme.com/
marcilhac/index.htm. Open
Jul and Aug daily 1100–1730.

Grotte de Bellevue
46160 Marcilhac-sur-Célé;
tel: 05 65 31 28 77; e-mail:
contact@grotte-bellevue.com.
Open Jul and Aug.

Set against a backdrop of cliffs, Marcilhac is an enchanting village collected around a ruined **Benedictine abbey** founded in the 11th century. The abbey flourished until it was very badly damaged in raids by English and French troops during the Hundred Years War. Although parts of the abbey today are roofless, there are some well-preserved medieval features, including some fine carvings in stone and wood and 15th-century frescoes.

Above the village, 1.5km to the northwest, is the **Grotte de Bellevue**, discovered in 1964. The cave contains an amazing range of stalactites, stalagmites, columns and 'streaky bacon' formations of ochre and white calcite. Slim, candle-like stalagmites stand in contrast to Hercules' Column, a pillar 4m high and 3.5m in circumference.

St-Cirq-Lapopie

① St-Cirq-Lapopie Pl.
du Sombral; tel: 05 65
31 29 06; e-mail: saint-cirq-
lapopie@wanadoo.fr;
www.saint-cirqlapopie.com.
Open all year.

**① Château de St-
Cirq-Lapopie €€**
Le Bourg St-Cirq-Lapopie; tel:
05 65 31 27 48;
e-mail: info@
chateaudesaintcirqlapopie.
com; www.
chateaudesaintcirqlapopie.
com. The château has
exhibitions of modern art
and is fitted out with five
guest rooms.

**Maison de la
Fourdonne €€** R. de la
Fourdonne, St-Cirq-Lapopie;
tel: 05 65 31 21 51. Open
Tue–Sun 1400–1800.
Guided tour 1500 daily.
Closed Jan.

One of the most beautiful villages in the region – some say in the whole of France – St-Cirq (pronounced 'San-sear') stands dizzyingly on a rocky escarpment that plunges vertically for 80m to the left bank of the Lot. It looks like an illustration in a book of fairy tales, but has had more than its fair share of violence over the centuries. Occupied since Gallo-Roman times, the village is named after St Cyr who was martyred along with his mother in Asia Minor during the reign of Diocletian. St Amadour is said to have brought the martyr's relics to the area. The Lapopie part of the name comes from a family of local lords who occupied the castle at the top of the rock in the Middle Ages.

The castle attracted the attention of many invaders and was repeatedly besieged. Among those who tried and failed to seize it was Richard the Lionheart in 1198. It was demolished on the orders of Louis XI in 1471, but the ruins were still fought over during the Wars of Religion. Henri de Navarre put an end to the site's importance in 1580 when he had the remaining walls flattened. Today, the village is a delightful jumble of steep, narrow streets of cheerful red-roofed houses.

Until the 19th century the main industry was wood-turning and many craftsmen worked in small shops. An exhibition of the objects they produced and the tools they used is in the **Maison de la Fourdonne**. A collection of antique furniture and *objets d'art* from Europe, Africa and China is housed in the **Musée Rignault**.

Accommodation and food

Hôtel des Grottes €–€€ *Cabrerets; tel: 05 65 31 27 02; e-mail: hotel.grottes@wanadoo.fr; www.hoteldesgrottes.com. Open Apr–mid-Oct.*

Musée Rignault €€
*Château de la
Gardette, St-Cirq-Lapopie;
tel: 05 65 31 23 22. Open
Jun–Oct daily 1000–1230,
1430–1800 (Jul and Aug
1900). Closed Tue.*

**Camping de la
Plage €** *St-Cirq-
Lapopie; tel: 05 65 30 29
51; e-mail: camping-
laplage@wanadoo.fr;
www.campingplage.com.
Open all year.* The
campground has 120
pitches; caravans and
mobile homes are available
for hire. Activities include
boating, canoeing, caving
and horse riding.

Camping La Truffière
€ *Route de Concots, St-Cirq-
Lapopie; tel: 05 65 30 20
22; e-mail: contact@
camping-truffiere.com;
www.camping-truffiere.com.
Open May–Sep.* The site
has 96 pitches, with
caravans and chalets for
hire. Special events for
children.

Below
St-Cirq-Lapopie

The main feature here is a riverside terrace. The hotel's 18 en-suite rooms have direct-dial telephones and there is a swimming pool and private parking. The restaurant (€€) serves wine by the glass.

Auberge de la Sagne €€ *Route Grotte de Pech Merle, Cabrerets; tel: 05 65 31 26 62; e-mail: contact@hotel-auberge-cabrerets.com; www.hotel-auberge-cabrerets.com. Open mid-May–Sep.* The hotel has 10 en-suite rooms with direct-dial telephones. There is private parking, a pool and outdoor dining area. The small restaurant (€€) serves dinner only.

Les Gabarres €€ *Tour-de-Faure, near St-Cirq-Lapopie; tel: 05 65 30 24 57; e-mail: infos@hotel-les-gabarres.com; www.hotel-les-gabarres.com. Open all year.* No restaurant, but 28 en-suite rooms with direct-dial telephones. The hotel has private parking, a garden and swimming pool.

Hôtel Ségalière €€ *380 av. F. Mitterrand, Cajarc; tel: 05 65 40 65 35; e-mail: hotel@lasegaliere.com; www.lasegaliere.com. Open mid-Mar–Oct.* The hotel has 24 en-suite rooms with direct-dial telephones and television and has a garden, swimming pool and private parking. The restaurant (€–€€€) serves wine by the glass, and a budget lunch is available. There is an outside dining terrace.

Auberge du Sombral €€–€€€ *St-Cirq-Lapopie; tel: 05 65 31 26 08. Open Apr–mid-Nov.* Primarily a restaurant, where you can get a budget lunch and dine outside, the establishment also has eight guest rooms (€€–€€€) with en-suite facilities and direct-dial telephones.

Hôtel de la Pélissaria €€-€€€ *St-Cirq-Lapopie; tel: 05 65 31 25 14; e-mail: hoteldelapelissaria@wanadoo.fr; http://perso.orange.fr/ hoteldelapelissaria. Open May–Nov.* Ten very different rooms in a 16th-century house, with views over the medieval village and the Lot valley. Terraced garden and a swimming pool.

Suggested tour

Total distance: The route covers 100km.

Time: Driving time is around 2 hours, but allow a whole day for this absorbing trip.

Links: From Figeac the D922 south reaches Villefranche-de-Rouergue (*see page 177*) in 35km. From Conduché the D662 heads west for Vers in 14km, then the D653 continues for 15km to Cahors (*see pages 182–91*).

Route: From **Figeac** (*see pages 172–81*) follow the D13 (signposted Cahors) for 4km to the big railway viaduct, then take the D41 towards Boussac, which is reached in a further 5km. This first stretch is over a wide valley with wooded hills and the river clinging to the roadside. At Boussac the valley begins to close in and the road and river start to wind, running between cliffs from time to time.

Espagnac-Ste-Eulalie, 8km beyond Boussac, is a charming village of turreted houses set against cliffs and surrounding the Ancien Prieuré Notre-Dame, a convent founded in the 12th century, badly damaged during the Hundred Years War and rebuilt in the 1400s. It now serves as a rural centre. Another attractive village, reached after 4km of pleasant countryside dotted with typical pigeon houses, is Brengues, where the D38 crosses the Célé.

Continue west on the D41 for 5.5km to St-Sulpice, lying at the foot of a cliff and guarded by a private castle, which has stood here since the 12th century. Another 3.5km and you reach **MARCILHAC-SUR-CELE ❶**, where the Grotte de Bellevue can be found 1.5km northwest of the village. After a further 6.5km the D41 passes through Sauliac-sur-Célé, huddled beneath a dramatic cliff riddled with caves in which the villagers took refuge in times of strife. At the hamlet of Liauzu, 3km beyond Sauliac, you turn away from the river at last, heading north on the D40 for 3km to **CUZALS ❷**.

Just north of Cuzals, turn left and travel 2km to Orniac, then head south on the D42, reaching **CABRERETS ❸** in 5.5km. At Conduché, 4km south of Cabrerets, the Célé joins the River Lot. Take the D662 west for 1km then cross the Lot to **Bouziès**, where you can follow the GR36 footpath for 500m to visit a section of towpath carved out of solid rock when the river was a commercial waterway and now decorated with a relief of fish and crustaceans, the work of the contemporary sculptor, D. Monnier.

From Bouziès head east on the D40 and after 5km, climbing steadily all the way, stop at the viewpoint on the left – there is a car park – for a superb view of the confluence of the two rivers and, even more spectacular, **ST-CIRQ-LAPOPIE ❹**, towering over the Lot. The village is reached in a further 1.5km. At Crégols, 2km upstream, continue to follow the river on the D8, reaching **CENEVIERES ❺** in 5km.

Cross the river at Calvignac, 4.5km upstream, then head east on the north bank, following the D662 for 6.5km to **CAJARC** ❻. The next village, Montbrun, 7km along the D662, overlooks the Lot from a rocky promontory and is itself dominated by a ruined castle that was once the home of a brother of Pope John XXII. Beyond Montbrun, the countryside softens into a patchwork of fields and the river and valley both widen. Within 6km you reach **LARROQUE-TOIRAC** ❼ and beyond there the D662 moves away from the river and reaches Figeac in 13km.

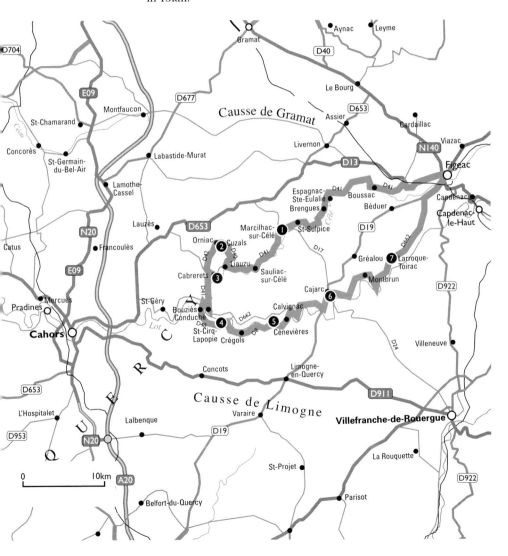

Figeac

Ratings

Scenery	●●●●●
Architecture	●●●●○
Museums	●●●●○
Walks	●●●●○
Children	●●●○○
History	●●●○○
Outdoor activities	●●●○○
Villages	●●●○○

What connection has a medieval French town with Ancient Egyptian art works and a replica of the Rosetta Stone? The answer is Jean-François Champollion, born in Figeac in 1790, who devoted much of his life to deciphering Egyptian hieroglyphics. Situated on the River Célé, a tributary of the Lot, Figeac is a friendly little town set in a region of green heights, rugged limestone plateaux and tree-lined streams. The town's old quarter has narrow alleys twisting between tall, well-preserved sandstone houses from the 13th to 15th centuries. Figeac developed around a monastery in the 9th century; the abbot and seven consuls governed the town. Early in the 14th century the king intervened and Figeac was given a licence to print money – literally. The Mint Museum and the tourism office are in the same fine 13th-century building, the Hôtel de la Monnaie.

FIGEAC

ℹ️ **Figeac** *Hôtel de la Monnaie, pl. Vival, Figeac; tel: 05 65 34 06 25; e-mail: info@tourisme-figeac.com; www.tourisme-figeac.com. Open daily Jul and Aug 1000–1930, Sep–Jun 1000–1200, 1430–1800, closed Sun.* The office is in one of the town's finest 13th-century *soleilho* buildings, which also houses the Mint Museum.

Right
Figeac

History

Students of architecture will find much to catch their attention in this attractive little town (pop. about 10,000), which has known periods of considerable prosperity through the ages. There are carved façades, sculpted décors, a few octagonal stone chimneys, Renaissance doorways, and numerous half-timbered houses with decorative brickwork.

For the interested amateur and the specialist alike, the big appeal is the *soleilho*, fine examples of which can be seen in the old

Tourist train €€
Tel: 05 65 34 49 86.
For a fun way to tour the old town and the waterside area – and get a commentary into the bargain – climb aboard *Lou Fijagal*, the tourist train, for a 40-minute ride. *Runs Jul–mid-Sep. Departures from tourist office between 1000 and 1200 and 1500 and 1900. In peak season there's a nocturnal tour at 2130.*

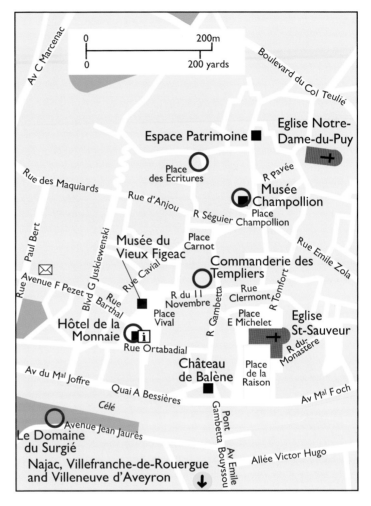

quarter. These are the tall houses of pale amber sandstone with open attics, typical of the 13th to 15th centuries. Goods would be stored at ground-floor level in workshops with open archways. The middle floor was the living quarters and the open attic – the *soleilho* – was where such items as vegetables and woollen cloth were stored. The roof was supported by pillars.

A stroll through the old quarter reveals much of Figeac's past, century by century, though the Hundred Years War and the Wars of Religion took their toll. World War II was disastrous, too, with more than 500 Figeac people being deported by the Nazis. The River Célé, more intimate than the wide Lot or Dordogne, runs along the southern part of the town.

Commanderie des Templiers €€
41 r. Gambetta, Figeac; tel: 05 65 50 27 08; e-mail: francois@templiers-figeac. com; www.templiers-figeac. com. Daily 1-hour guided tours are held Jul–Sep between 1000 and 1300 and 1400–1930. There are also Tue and Thu evening tours; rest of year by appointment.

The former abbey church of St-Sauveur was founded near the river in 838. Parts of the present building date from the 11th century. The font is supported by four Romanesque capitals from another part of the church. Because of the richness of its architectural heritage and its fine state of preservation, Figeac was declared a *Secteur sauvegardé* (protected sector). In 1990 it became one of France's network of Cities of Art and History.

Sights

Le Centre Nautique € Tel: 05 65 34 18 76. Open Jun–Sep. For canoe or kayak hire contact Figeac Eau Vive (base at Domaine du Surgié, Jul and Aug); tel: 05 65 50 05 48.

Domaine du Surgié €
Route de Roussilhe, Figeac; tel: 05 65 34 59 00; e-mail: surgie.camp.lois@ wanadoo. fr; www. domainedesurgie.com/gb/ index2.htm (English). Open Apr–Sep.

Commanderie des Templiers
The Order of the Knights Templars was established in Figeac in the 1180s, when the Commanderie was built. The wooden staircase to the guardroom was put up in the 15th century.

Domaine du Surgié
This is Figeac's riverside leisure park and nautical centre. The leisure park has trampolines, inflatable animal models, an adventure course, *pétanque*, mini-golf, swimming pool, pedaloes and kayaks. The nautical centre provides a wave pool, large swimming pool, water skiing and other water activities. The park has a bar-restaurant with brasserie, snackbar and a spacious terrace. Tourist accommodation and a campsite with 103 pitches are in the northern part of the park.

Guided tours
The tourist office runs general guided tours (€€) from Sunday to Friday in July and August at 1700. Themed tours are offered on designated dates in July and August. *Figeac Yesterday and Today, Merchants of Figeac in the Middle Ages* and *Medieval Art and Architecture* are among the themes. Trips to four historic villages near Figeac (one village

Above
Figeac's Rosetta Stone

**ⓘ Musée
Champollion €€**
*4 r. des Frères Champollion,
Figeac; tel: 05 65 50 31 08;
e-mail: musee@ville-
figeac.com; www.ville-
figeac.fr/musee. Open daily
Jul and Aug 1030–1830,
Mar–Jun and Sep–Oct same
hours but closed Mon,
Nov–Feb Tue–Sun
1400–1800. Closed 1 Jan,
1 May, 25 Dec. Guided visits
are held on Tue in school
summer holidays at 1030.
Visits year round in English
can be arranged for groups.*

Musée du Vieux Figeac
*€€ Pl. Vival, Figeac; tel: 05
65 34 06 25. Open daily Jul
and Aug 1000–1300,
1430–1900, May, Jun & Sep
1000–1200, 1430–1800,
same hours in Apr except
closed Sun, Oct–Mar
1100–1200, 1430–1730.*

visited on each tour) are held on occasional Wednesdays, departing at 1030. There are also twice-monthly themed torchlight visits in Figeac.

Information about a children's programme of activities organised in July and August is available from the tourist office. From April to June and in September a *Discover Figeac* visit is arranged on occasional Saturdays at 1630, and there's a choice of three occasional themed tours. Throughout the year the tourist office organises visits and themed tours of the town for groups, by arrangement.

Musée Champollion

The bookshop run by Jean-François Champollion's father is now the Musée Champollion – three floors of Egyptian vases, jewellery, statuettes, documents, papyrus fragments, funeral objects including mummy wrappings, sarcophagi and other items, many bearing hieroglyphics.

Champollion, born in 1790, spoke six languages by the age of 14. He went on to develop some interpretative work on hieroglyphics by Thomas Young, an Englishman, and worked on deciphering the Rosetta Stone (*see Place des Ecritures, below*). During his expedition to Egypt he spent much time deciphering texts. He died, aged 42, a year after becoming curator at the Egyptology Museum, which he had founded at the Louvre in Paris.

Musée du Vieux Figeac

Housed in the same late 13th-century building as the tourist office, the museum displays old coins, Figeac town seals from more than 700 years ago, grain measures and sculpture work from local ancient buildings.

Museum village

A 12th-century fortification perched on rocks above the village of Cardaillac, 11km north of Figeac, may be visited: two towers remain, only one of which is open to the public. You climb a spiral staircase to the two-room tower, which has vaulted ceilings, and you are rewarded by a glorious view of the countryside and the River Drauzou running through it.

Much of Cardaillac itself is a museum, the Musée Eclat, which is spread over several sites. The two-hour guided tour is packed with interest. You find out about the craft of making winegrowers' baskets – once an important rural industry in the village – and see other local crafts. Other exhibits illustrate the part the school plays in local affairs and the general way of life in the village, and how day-to-day modern living fits in with Cardaillac's history.

Guided tours take place *daily in July and August, 1500–1800. In September there is just one departure at 1500.* Group visits the rest of the year are by arrangement (*place de la Tour, Cardaillac; tel: 05 65 40 10 63*). There is no set charge: you are asked to make a donation at the end of the tour.

Place des Ecritures

(**€** *off pl. Carnot*) This is a tranquil and shady haven moments from Figeac's busy streets – a greatly enlarged replica of the black granite

Espace Patrimoine
5 r. de Colomb, Figeac;
tel: 05 65 50 05 40;
e-mail: service.patrimoine@
ville-figeac; www.ville-figeac.fr.
Open daily Jul–Sep
1000–1230, 1500–1900;
Apr–Jun and mid-Sep–Oct
1000–1800. Closed Mon.
Nov–Mar open on request.
Free entry.

Egyptian Rosetta Stone set into the floor of a courtyard enclosed by typical medieval architecture of the town. The setting, close to the Champollion Museum, was created by the American artist Joseph Kosuth, and unveiled in 1991. An adjacent small courtyard has a French translation of the hieroglyphics on the Rosetta Stone, engraved on the glass front of a vaulted cellar. Steps lead up to a terraced garden in which are growing papyri, the plant from which the Egyptians made 'paper'.

Portrait d'une Ville: Figeac

A permanent exhibition in the Espace Patrimoine, offering lectures on Figeac and a summer programme of discovery visits and year-round events for local people, students and those interested in learning about the town, one of a network of 120 Cities of Art and History in France.

NAJAC

Office de Tourisme
Pl. du Faubourg, Najac;
tel: 05 65 29 72 05;
e-mail: otsi.najac@wanadoo.fr

Forteresse Royale €
Najac; tel: 05 65 29 71
65; e-mail: camillede.
montalivet@wanadoo.fr. Open
daily. Guided visits daily Jul and
Aug 1000–1300, 1500–1900,
closes 1800 in Jun and 1700 in
Apr, May & Sep. Rest of year
open by appointment; contact
tourist office Villefranche-de-
Rouergue, tel: 05 65 45 13 18.

This medieval village sits loftily on the narrow ridge of a rocky promontory overlooking a bend in the River Aveyron. Its one street leads about 1km along the ridge to a wider part on which sits solidly

Right
Najac

the ruins of a 12th-century castle, the **Forteresse Royale**, of which the great circular keep is 33.5m high. Najac and its castle are an impressive sight from the river. Equally, to look down on the curved sweep of the Aveyron from the village is a scenic treat.

VILLEFRANCHE-DE-ROUERGUE

Office de Tourisme
Promenade du Guiraudet, Villefranche-de-Rouergue; tel: 05 65 45 13 18; e-mail: infos@villefranche.com

Chartreuse St-Sauveur € *Tel: 05 65 45 13 18. Open Jul–Sep daily 1000–1200, 1400–1800.*

This is a fine example of a *bastide* village, with its narrow streets in a grid pattern and its arcaded central square and marketplace. The square is dominated by the great hulk of the Eglise Notre-Dame with its 55m belfry. The town, on the River Aveyron, was founded in 1252 by Alphonse de Poitiers, brother of King Louis IX. On the river just south of the town is the former **Chartreuse (charterhouse) St-Sauveur** and cloisters. The 15th-century Carthusian foundation, now a hospital, is claimed to be the only complete charterhouse open to the public in France.

VILLENEUVE D'AVEYRON

Syndicat d'Initiative *Pl. des Conques, Villeneuve; tel: 05 65 81 79 61.*

Anyone interested in medieval ecclesiastical art should make a point of looking at the frescoes in this *bastide* village 18km south of Figeac. They depict 14th-century pilgrims on their way to Compostela beneath the figure of Christ. The picturesque village has neat and tidy streets of well-preserved old stone houses.

Accommodation and food

Hôtel-Restaurant Chez Marcel € *R. du 11 mai 1944, Cardaillac; tel: 05 65 40 11 16. Open all year.* The five-room property 11km north of Figeac has a terrace for outdoor dining.

Hôtel-Restaurant le Toulouse € *4 av. de Toulouse, Figeac; tel: 05 65 34 22 95. Open all year.* The eight-room hotel has a bar and parking for guests' cars.

Pizzeria del Portel € *9 r. Ortabadial, 46100 Figeac; tel: 05 65 34 53 60. Closed Mon.* As well as a satisfying pizza you may find some entertainment laid on here.

Brasserie-Restaurant Le Sphinx €–€€ *7 pl. Carnot, 46100 Figeac; tel: 05 65 14 05 81.* Good range of savoury dishes in pleasant atmosphere. There's a bar and a large terrace.

● **Camping à la Ferme** € *Chez Mme Therondel, 16 r. de Puits-Ste-Marie, Bagnac-sur-Célé (15km northeast of Figeac); tel: 05 65 34 95 81. Open Jun–Sep.* This is a 'Welcome to the Farm' site with eight pitches for tents, caravans or motor homes.

Camping Les Rives du Célé € *Domaine du Surgié, Figeac; tel: 05 65 34 59 00; e-mail: contact@marc-montmija.com; www.lesrivesducele.com. Open Apr–Sep.* Tents, caravans, mobile homes and chalets to rent. There are 103 pitches on the partly shaded campground. Amenities include restaurant and takeaway food, grocery store, swimming pool, mini-golf and entertainment.

La Dinée du Viguier €–€€ *4 r. Boutaric, 46100 Figeac; tel: 05 65 50 08 08.* Popular restaurant with seating for 100 inside or on the terrace. Accessible by wheelchair.

L'Oustal del Barry €–€€ *Pl. du Bourg, Najac; tel: 05 65 29 74 32; e-mail: oustaldelbarry@wanadoo.com; www.oustaldelbarry.com. Open late Mar–late Oct. Closed Mon except Jul–Sep.* In a beautiful setting overlooking the River Aveyron, the hotel has 21 mainly small rooms, most with bath or shower, and a renowned restaurant.

La Puce à l'Oreille €–€€ *5–7 r. St-Thomas, 46100 Figeac; tel: 05 65 34 33 08. Closed Sun evening and Mon except in high season.* Comfortable restaurant with terrace.

Le Sarrasin €–€€ *6 r. Balène, 46100 Figeac; tel: 05 65 34 76 44; e-mail: monique@restaurant-sarrasin-figeac.com; www.restaurant-sarrasin-figeac.com. Closed Sun and Mon (Mon only in peak season).* Relaxing crêperie, in the pedestrian zone of the old city.

Hôtel des Bains €–€€€ *1 r. du Griffoul, Figeac; tel: 05 65 34 10 89; e-mail: figeac@hoteldesbains.fr; www.hoteldesbains.fr. Closed for two weeks Dec–Jan.* The 19-room hotel has a range of amenities, including garage parking, bar and terrace.

L'Hostellerie de l'Europe €€ *51 allée Victor Hugo, 46100 Figeac; tel: 05 65 34 10 16; e-mail: de4605@inter-hotel.com; www.hotel-europe-figeac.com.* Recently renovated, the hotel is air-conditioned and has 80 rooms. Its restaurant partner is **La Table de Marinette** €–€€ *at the same address, tel: 05 65 50 06 07; e-mail: restaurant.marinette@wanadoo.fr; www.latabledemarinette.com.* Popular restaurant and bar with up to 50 covers indoors and terrace seating for another 100. The restaurant is run by a matriarchal chef, Marinette Baldy.

Hôtel Champollion €€ *3 pl. Champollion, Figeac; tel: 05 65 34 04 37; hotelchampillon@orange.fr. Open all year.* A terrace, bar and cable TV are among the facilities at this centrally situated 10-room hotel.

Hôtel-Bar La Courtepaille €€ *12 pl. Carnot, Figeac; tel: 05 65 34 21 83. Open all year.* Only six rooms, but guests have the benefit of a brasserie and bar.

Hôtel du Faubourg €€ *56 r. du Faubourg du Pin, 46100 Figeac; tel: 05 65 34 21 82; e-mail: contact@hoteldufaubourg.fr; www.hoteldufaubourg.fr.* A 22-room hotel located in the east of Figeac close to the exit towards Aurillac, and 600m from the centre of the medieval city.

Hôtel-Restaurant le Terminus St-Jacques €€ *27 av. Georges Clémenceau, 46100 Figeac; tel: 05 65 34 00 43; e-mail: contact@hotel-terminus.fr; www.hotel-terminus.fr. Open all year.* South of the river, the hotel has 11 rooms with garden, cable TV and bar.

Château du Viguier du Roy €€€ *R. Emile Zola (r. Droite), Figeac; tel: 05 65 50 05 05; e-mail: hotel@chateau-viguier-figeac.com; www.chateau-*

viguier-figeac.com. Closed Oct–Apr. This is Figeac's 4-star 20-room hotel, with restaurant (**€€–€€€**), bar, garden, swimming pool, Jacuzzi®, tennis and cable TV.

Hôtel Le Pont d'Or €€€ *2 av. Jean Jaurès, 46100 Figeac; tel: 05 65 50 95 00; e-mail: contact@hoteldepontdor.com.* Located in the centre of Figeac overlooking the river. An elegant hotel in a 13th-century building combining modernity and tradition. Thirty-five rooms, some overlooking the river.

Suggested walk

Total distance: The walk covers a little over 1km. There is a fairly steep climb up to pl. du Puy.

Below
Villefranche-de-Rouergue

Time: Allow 1½ hours.

Route: The walk takes you through the narrow medieval streets of Figeac's old town. From the tourist office in pl. Vival head across the car park and follow r. du 11 Novembre to the right. Turn left into r. Gambetta, the main street of the old town, where the 12th-century **COMMANDERIE DES TEMPLIERS** ❶ will be found on the left. Continue into pl. Carnot, which has a covered marketplace. Follow the square round to the left and turn right into r. Séguier then cross the street, turning into r. de la Monnaie, an alley leading into **PLACE DES ECRITURES** ❷, with the huge replica of the Rosetta Stone tucked away among a surrounding of medieval buildings. The archway on one side of the square leads into r. des Frères Champollion and the entrance to the **MUSEE DU CHAMPOLLION** ❸.

Follow the very narrow lane to the end, then turn left into r. de Colomb. Ruelle St-Jacques, a narrow street on the right, climbs to pl. du Puy, where there are views of the town. Here, too, is the **Eglise Notre-Dame-du-Puy**, which was used as a Protestant fortress during the Wars of Religion. The church has a massive walnut altarpiece, carved in the 17th century. At the right-hand end of pl. du Puy take the steps down to r. Bantaric, which leads into pl. Champollion, dominated by an infirmary founded in the 14th century by the Knights Templars. The street running to the left out of the square is r. Emile Zola, the town's oldest thoroughfare with arcades and houses with fine Renaissance doorways.

Below
Figeac old town

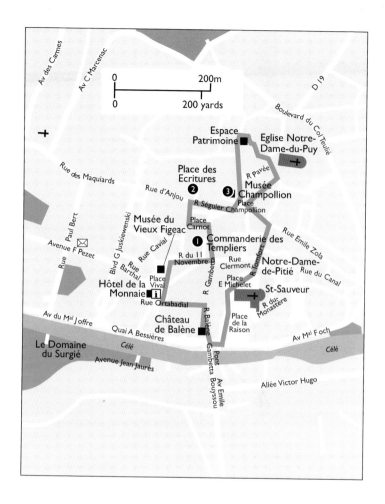

Less than 50m along r. Emile Zola turn right into r. Tomfort. This leads to pl. Edmond Michelet and the **Eglise St-Sauveur**, founded as an abbey church in the 11th century. The neighbouring church is **Notre-Dame-de-Pitié**, formerly a chapterhouse, which became a place of worship in 1623 when Protestants left the town. It contains fine examples of painted wooden panels, including one of the Infant Jesus foreseeing the Crucifixion. From pl. Edmond Michelet follow r. Capote into pl. aux Herbes and turn left into the lower section of r. Gambetta.

Almost at the river end of the street turn right into r. Balène, where the 14th-century **Château de Balène** is now a public hall and exhibition centre. Follow the street round to r. Ortabadial and cross the road to return to the tourist office.

Cahors

Ratings

Architecture	●●●●●
Food and wine	●●●●●
History	●●●●○
Scenery	●●●●○
Shopping	●●●●○
Art	●●●○○
Nightlife	●●●○○
Tours	●●●○○

Cahors is the chief town in the *département* of the Lot in the Midi-Pyrénées. Most of the city is within a great loop of the River Lot, which is crossed by the Pont de Valentré complete with its three towers and regarded as the best-preserved medieval bridge in France. Many buildings of the same period still stand. The earliest site, though not intact, is the Arc de Diane – remains of Gallo-Roman baths. St Etienne's Cathedral reflects periods between the 11th and 17th centuries. Modern history is recorded in the Resistance Museum. The celebrated 'black' Cahors wines spread the city's name around the world. A wine museum opens from July to September, and a number of local vineyards are open to the public. With its wide squares, its Old Quarter and its riverside gardens, Cahors is a place of charm and character.

History

Office de Tourisme Cahors Pl. François Mitterrand, Cahors; tel: 05 65 53 20 65; e-mail: officetourisme@ mairiecahors.fr; www.mairie-cahors.fr. Open all year Mon–Sat (open Sun in Jul and Aug).

Comité Départmental de Tourisme de Lot 107 quai Cavaignac, Cahors; tel: 05 65 35 07 09; e-mail: info@tourisme-lot.com; www.tourisme-lot.com. Open all year.

The city (pop. 20,000) owes its existence to a spring by the River Lot. The spring, fed by an underground well 20km away, is said to have been discovered by Carthusian monks and was used by the Gauls and later the Romans. The discovery in 1991 of hundreds of coins from the dawn of Christianity supports the theory that the spring was considered sacred. It is the source of Cahors's drinking water supply to this day.

The Pont Valentré, a magnificent and well-preserved bridge, is the city's top attraction for most visitors. Cahors honours its famous sons, notably Pope John XXII, whose papacy was from 1316 to 1334. He founded the University of Cahors and was the power behind the taming of the River Lot, having sluices and dams installed and the Pont Valentré built, giving new impetus to local commerce. A 34m tower serves as a monument to the Pope.

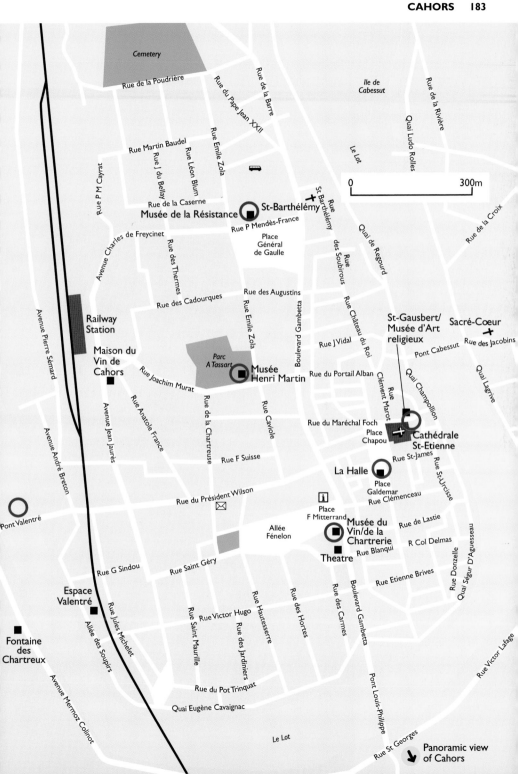

Cemetery

Rue de la Poudrière

Rue de la Barre

Rue du Pape Jean XXII

Rue Emile Zola

Ile de Cabessut

Rue de la Rivière

Quai Ludo Rolles

Rue Martin Baudel

Rue P M Cayat

Rue J du Bellay

Rue Léon Blum

Le Lot

0   300m

Rue de la Caserne

Musée de la Résistance   St-Barthélémy

Rue St-Barthélémy

Rue de la Croix

Rue P Mendès-France

Rue des Soubirous

Quai de Regourd

Avenue Charles de Freycinet

Rue des Thermes

Place Général de Gaulle

Rue des Cadourques

Rue des Augustins

Rue J Vidal

St-Gausbert/ Musée d'Art religieux

Sacré-Cœur

Railway Station

Boulevard Gambetta

Rue Château du Roi

Pont Cabessut

Rue des Jacobins

Avenue Pierre Sémard

Maison du Vin de Cahors

Parc A Tassart

Rue Emile Zola

Musée Henri Martin

Rue du Portail Alban

Rue Clément Marot

Quai Champollion

Quai Lagrive

Rue Joachim Murat

Rue du Maréchal Foch

Cathédrale St-Etienne

Avenue Jean Jaurès

Avenue André Breton

Rue Anatole France

Rue de la Chartreuse

Rue Caviole

Place Chapou

Rue St-James

Rue St-Urcisse

La Halle

Place Galdemar

Rue F Suisse

Rue Clémenceau

Pont Valentré

Rue du Président Wilson

Place F Mitterrand

Musée du Vin/de la Chartrerie

Rue de Lastie

R Col Delmas

Allée Fénelon

Rue Blanqui

Quai Ségur D'Aguesseau

Théâtre

Espace Valentré

Rue G Sindou

Rue Saint Géry

Rue Etienne Brives

Rue Donzelle

Fontaine des Chartreux

Allée des Soupirs

Rue Jules Michelet

Rue Saint Maurille

Rue Victor Hugo

Rue Hautesserre

Rue des Jardiniers

Rue des Hortes

Rue des Carmes

Boulevard Gambetta

Rue Victor Lafage

Avenue Mermoz Collinot

Rue du Pot Trinquat

Quai Eugène Cavaignac

Pont Louis-Philippe

Le Lot

Rue St Georges

Panoramic view of Cahors

A guide giving the addresses of more than 500 restaurants offering authentic local cooking in the Lot region, from village inns to prestigious establishments, is available from the Departmental Committee of Tourism (*see address page 182*). For a free publication giving information about the Association des Bonnes Tables du Lot – it lists 22 places of high reputation run by talented head chefs – contact the **Chambre de Commerce et Industrie du Lot-et-Garonne** *52 cours Gambetta, tel: 05 53 77 10 00.* Their list of hotels and restaurants is also on a website, *www.hotel-restaurant47.com/anglais/ welcome.htm*

Cathédrale St-Etienne € *Pl. Chapou, Cahors. Open daily.* **Chapelle St-Gausbert** €€ *Tel: 05 65 23 07 50; http://architecture.relig. free.fr/cahors.htm. Open daily in summer 1000–1200, 1400–1800.*

Maison du Vin de Cahors *430 av. Jean Jaurès, Cahors; tel: 05 65 23 22 24; e-mail: uivc.cahors@free.fr; www.vindecahors.fr.* Very informative about the wine-producing area around Cahors. Located opposite the rail station.

The main thoroughfare in Cahors is the Boulevard Gambetta, home of the 19th-century Hôtel de Ville (City Hall) and the Palais de Justice (Palace of Justice). The street is named after Léon Gambetta, born in Cahors in 1838, who became a lawyer in Paris and a flamboyant republican prime minister. He died in 1882 at the age of 44.

In the Old Quarter of Cahors are narrow lanes, mansions, gates and the Henry IV house where the king once stayed. Today, visitors find much to enjoy, from medieval architecture to local food products and vineyard tours.

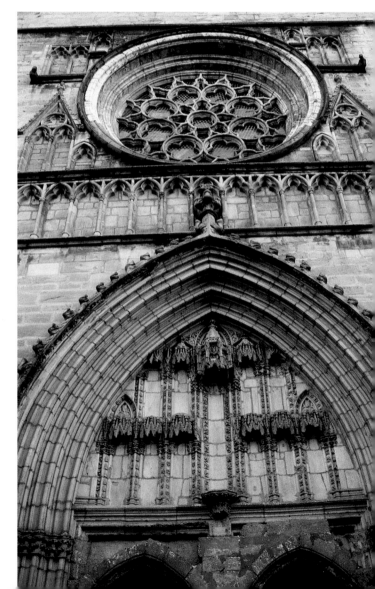

Right
Cahors Cathédrale St-Etienne

Guided tours €€
These are arranged all year for groups by the tourist office. For individuals, two themed guided tours of the medieval city are held at 1600 on Mon Jul–Sept, also in Jul and Aug at 1700 on Mon, Tue, Thur and 1030 Fri. They take in the Cathedral and parts of the old town dating back centuries. Tours last 2½hrs including a visit to the Mont St-Cyr military school which gives a panoramic view of the town; a shorter tour lasts 1½hrs and includes the medieval streets, the Cathedral, Maison Henri IV, the Ramparts, the Arc of Diane and the Pont Valentré. Tours begin at the Tourist Office, Place François Mitterrand. Booking and information from the tourist office.

Tourist Train, Le Petit Train de Cahors €€
Tel: 05 65 30 16 55; e-mail: le-petit-train-de-cahors@ wanadoo.fr. 40-min tours of the old town and its monuments daily 1000–1900, starting from allée des Soupirs (200m from Pont Valentré).

QuercyRail €€ Pl. de la Gare; tel: 05 63 40 11 93; www.trains-fr.org/unecto/ quercyrail. Offers day or half-day trips in the Lot Valley using old rolling stock restored by a conservation group.

Les Bateaux Safaraid
€€ Tel: 05 65 35 98 88; e-mail: bateaux.safaraid@ club-internet.fr. 90-min boat trips depart from quai Pont de Valentré, Apr–Nov. Commentary in English on request

Historic foundations

Arc de Diane: The most ancient parts of Cahors are the remains of the Gallo-Roman thermal baths and the foundations of a theatre beneath the present Chambre d'Agriculture. The **Cathédrale St-Etienne** was built as a fortress in which people could find refuge from attackers. Work began in 1110, and by the 14th century ramparts had been built, turning the city into a virtual island. Parts of these are still visible: one of the surviving fortifications is a great tower at the western end of the city.

In the 1300s Cahors began to prosper greatly and expand: Lombard bankers, merchants and men of international business affairs moved in and the city became the finance centre of Europe. Houses and mansions were built of brick; stone was used for great arcades. It was in this period that Cahors-born Jacques Duèse became Pope John XXII. He endowed the University of Cahors and enhanced commerce by installing dams, sluices and mills along the River Lot. Building of the great **Pont Valentré** began as early as 1308. Much of the present-day city belongs to this era and the Renaissance period that followed, from the 1500s.

Sights

Cathédrale St-Etienne

With a history of barbarian invasions of Cahors, safety and defence were uppermost in the minds of those building the cathedral, on the site of a 6th-century church, and they made a fortress of it. A number of periods covering some six centuries are represented, accentuated by 19th-century restoration work.

Within the cathedral precincts the **Chapelle St-Gausbert** contains portraits of nearly 100 bishops from the 3rd to the 16th centuries, a fresco of the Last Judgement, and 16th-century ceiling paintings. A carving around the north doorway, dating from about 1135, depicts the Ascension. The cathedral's two great domes are 16m in diameter, rising above the 20m-wide nave. The fine cloisters were added in the early 16th century. Sculptures of a pilgrim – Cahors is near the route to Compostela – and a garland of sea shells may be seen here.

City tours

You can take a guided tour of the Old Quarter or get a general introduction to Cahors by taking a half-hour narrated trip on the **Tourist Train**. Because the River Lot flows around three sides of the city, you can see many of the sights from the deck of a trip boat. For an excursion into the picturesque Lot Valley, take a break from the car and let **QuercyRail** escort you.

Galleries of Art

Paintings of the French landscape and other works of art from the 19th and 20th centuries are displayed in the **Musée Henri Martin**.

Musée du Vin *R. de la Chartrerie; tel: 05 65 23 99 70. Open Jul and Aug daily 1000–1200, 1500–1900. Closed Tue. Free entry.*

Le Bowling (10 lanes) *Belle Croix; tel: 05 65 35 71 46. Open Sun 1600–0200, Tue–Sat 1900–0200.*

Discos are held at **La Palmeraie**, Fontanès, Lalbenque, near Cahors; *tel: 05 65 21 86 64. Open Fri and Sat 2230–0500* and **Le Look**, *route de Paris, Cahors; tel: 05 65 22 57 19. Check opening hours.*

Nightlife Cahors music bars and discos stay open until the early hours: **Biscot 'O' Rock** (*r. St-James; tel: 05 65 53 18 26. Open Mon–Fri 1900–0200, Sat 1700–0200*); **Le Duplex** (*r. Gustave Larroumet; tel: 05 65 22 14 56; http://leduplex.free.fr. Open daily to 0100 and to 0200 in summer*); and **The Irish Pub** (*pl. des Consuls; tel: 05 65 53 15 15. Open Mon–Sat 1800–0200*). **Club Oxygène** (*La Beyne, Cahors; tel. 06 77 13 15 36. Open Wed–Sat 2300–0500*); **Le Diam's** (*route de Paris, Cahors; tel: 05 65 23 00 79; http://diams46.free.fr. Open Thur–Sun from 2300*); **Le Latino** (*quai Lagrive, Cahors; tel: 05 65 35 54 68; www.el-latino.net. Open Thur–Sat from 2300*).

Temporary exhibitions are staged at the **Tourist Office Gallery** and at **La Chartrerie** (*35 r. de la Chartrerie; tel: 05 65 37 11 03*) in the **Musée du Vin**, which is also a cultural centre. Exhibitions of paintings and sculptures by contemporary artists are held at the **Compagnie des Arts** (*44 r. St André; tel: 05 65 22 57 41. Open Tue–Sat 1500–1900*).

Museums and markets

Musée Henri Martin €€ *R. Emile Zola, Cahors. Tel: 05 65 20 88 66. e-mail: musee@mairie-cahors.fr; www.mairie-cahors.fr/musee. Open Jun–Oct daily except Tue 1100–1800 (Sun 1400–1800);* Landscapes and modern art.

Tourist Office Gallery € *Pl. F. Mitterrand; tel: 05 65 53 20 65. Open daily except Sun and public holidays, Dec–Mar 0930–1230, 1330–1800, Apr–mid-Jun and mid-Sep–Nov, 0900–1230, 1330–1830, mid-Jun–mid-Sep 0900–1900. Free entry to temporary exhibitions.*

Maison Henri IV €€ *R. St-Urcisse, Cahors; tel: 05 65 35 04 35. Open Easter–Sep 1000–1200, 1400–1730; to 1800 in Aug.*

Henry de Navarre, later to become Henry IV, stayed in this 16th-century private house, which is a listed monument. It has furniture from the 15th to 18th centuries, and stone fireplaces.

La Halle *Pl. Galdemer. Open Tue–Sat 0800–1230, 1500–1900, Sun 0900–1200.*

Every day except Monday is market day in Cahors. Traders offer regional wines and food products, fruit, vegetables, fish, shellfish, bread, conserves, nuts, pizzas, *foie gras* and meat and dairy products.

Musée de la Résistance € *Pl. Bessières; tel: 05 65 22 14 25; e-mail: cahors.musee-de-la-resistance@libertysurf.fr. Open daily all year, except 25 Dec, 1 Jan, 1 May.*

An illuminating insight into the perilous work of the Resistance Movement in the wild, often remote, terrain of the Lot *département* in World War II. Each of five rooms is devoted to a different aspect of the movement's work.

Musée du Vin/de la Chartrerie

Housed in the cultural centre, one of Cahors's principal monuments, the museum presents information on the history, culture, tradition and production of the region's celebrated wines, with displays of the final product.

Musée d'Art religieux

Access from the Cathedral cloister. A collection of religious artefacts in the St Gausbert chapel, with beautifully preserved 15th-century murals. One curiosity is a piece of cloth displayed in a reliquary and claimed to be the linen cap that covered Christ's head in the tomb. It was brought from the Holy Land by a 12th-century bishop and was instrumental in Cahors being granted the status of a cathedral city.

Pont Valentré €€
Tel: 05 65 53 20 65.
Pedestrian bridge.
Exhibitions open daily Jul and Aug 1000–1230, 1430–1830.

Below
Cahors Pont Valentré

A devil of a job

The long time that it took to build the Pont Valentré is blamed on the devil. According to legend, the bridge's architect, exasperated by the demands on his time, decided to sell his soul to the devil in return for speeding up progress. Presumably the devil did his bit, as matters improved. But as the work neared completion, the architect got cold feet, fearing for his eternal future. So he asked the devil to fetch water in a sieve. The devil made some gallant attempts but couldn't oblige, and took his revenge by breaking off the topmost stone of the central tower. Every time it was replaced he knocked it off again. The tower is still known as the Devil's Tower. During bridge restoration work in 1879, the top stone was firmly fixed once and for all, and a carved figure of the devil trying to dislodge it was added.

Panoramic view of Cahors

Take a 7km drive from Cahors leaving by the Pont Louis-Philippe to Mont St-Cyr: from a viewing platform here you get a bird's-eye view of the city, with blvd Gambetta forming a clear dividing line between medieval and modern Cahors.

Pont Valentré

It took nearly 70 years for the bridge to be completed (1308–1370s). It was an impressive and beautiful structure, and still is today, although it has undergone considerable alteration through the centuries. The bridge has six arches and three towers, and is a prime example of medieval defence architecture in Europe. Exhibitions and displays depicting the bridge's history are presented in summer in the central tower. The bridge is a UNESCO World Heritage monument.

Buying local products

A map showing 600 growers throughout the region producing the *grand vins de Cahors* is available free from tourist offices, hotels and other outlets. The tourist office can supply a list of nearly 50 vineyards and châteaux with their appellations that welcome visitors. Food products of the area can be bought direct from specialists in the villages and countryside of the region, and in Cahors itself. Some concentrate mainly on one item, such as truffles, offered fresh in season (Nov–Mar), and conserves, sold in Cahors at **Pébeyre**, *66 r. Frédéric Suisse; tel: 05 65 22 24 80*. Others offer a veritable Aladdin's Cave of delights: *foie gras* of goose and duck, goose and duck *confit*, pâté, juniper berry liqueur, nut oil, cassoulet, mushrooms, smoked duck breast, conserves and an assortment of apéritifs, liqueurs and the wines of Cahors and the Southwest.

Among those in Cahors with varied gastronomic fare are **Le Cèdre Valentré**, *32 av. A. Breton; tel: 05 65 22 66 16*, and **Franche Lippée**, *22 r. de la Préfecture; tel: 05 65 35 56 79*.

Accommodation and food

Auberge de Jeunesse de Cahors (Youth Hostel) € *Espace Frédéric Suisse, 20 r. Frédéric Suisse; tel: 05 65 35 64 71; e-mail: fjt46@wanadoo.fr; www.hihostels.com/dba/hostel20075.en.htm. Open 24 hours.* In an old convent building, the hostel, 500m from the station, has rooms ranging from two beds up to 11 beds. There is a restaurant service as well as a kitchen for guests' use. The hostel has a bicycle garage.

Le Bistrot de Cahors € *46 r. Daurade; tel: 05 65 53 10 55.* Popular small bistro serving good regional food.

La Bourse € *7 pl. Rousseau, Cahors; tel: 05 65 35 17 78. Closed Sun.* A small hotel with eight guest rooms, a restaurant and a terrace.

Crêperie au Coeur de Lot € *71 r. du Château du Roi, Cahors; tel: 05 65 22 30 67. Crêpes* and salads, à la carte.

Le Melchior € *Pl. de la Gare, Cahors; tel: 05 65 35 03 38; e-mail: lemelchior@wanadoo.fr; www.lemelchior.com.* Twenty rooms with TV and telephone, and a restaurant in this 2-star property.

Le Soleil Ho € *36 r. Mordaigne, Cahors; tel: 05 65 22 02 52. Closed Mon.* Chinese food, modestly priced.

Auberge du Vieux Cahors €–€€ *144 r. St-Urcisse, Cahors; tel: 05 65 35 06 05; e-mail: aubcahors@free.fr; www.aubcahors.free.fr. Closed Tue evening and Wed except in high season.* Regional cuisine, fish and *fruits de mer* are the specialities of this restaurant in the south of the city.

Le Grill de l'Archipel €–€€ *Ile de Cabessut, quai Ludo-Rolles; tel: 05 65 35 95 64. Closed Sun evening and Mon except in peak season.* On an island

Camping: Rivière de Cabessut € *R. de la Rivière, Cahors; tel: 05 65 30 06 30; e-mail: contact@cabessut.com; www.cabessut.com. Open Apr–Sept.* Amenities at this site north of the city include a bar, food, mini-golf, swimming pool and events. 103 pitches.

in the Lot on the eastern side of the city, the restaurant offers an interesting Mediterranean cuisine.

La Taverne €–€€€ *Pl. Escorbiac, Cahors; tel: 05 65 35 28 66. Closed weekends except in season.* Proprietor-chef Jean-Luc Ratier serves regional food and gastronomic specialities in his restaurant near the tourist office.

Hôtel de France €€ *252 av. Jean Jaurès, Cahors; tel: 05 65 35 16 76; e-mail: hdf46@wanadoo.fr; www.hoteldefrance-cahors.fr.* Located in the centre; 79 rooms and furnished apartments for short letting.

Hôtel Gril-Campanile €€ *Rond Point de Regourd Sud, RN20 Cahors; tel: 05 65 22 20 21.* The 49-room, 2-star hotel has lifts, access for travellers with disabilities and a restaurant.

Hôtel de la Paix €€ *30 pl. Saint Maurice, Cahors; tel: 05 65 35 03 40; e-mail: hoteldelapaix-cahors@wanadoo.fr; www.hoteldelapaixcahors.com.* Located in the heart of old Cahors. Seventeen en-suite rooms. The stylish *salon de thé*, The Blue Angel, opens on to the marketplace from where to watch the world go by.

Grand Hôtel Terminus €€–€€€ *5 av. Charles de Freycinet, Cahors; tel: 05 65 53 32 00.* This 3-star hotel has lifts, wheelchair access, garage parking and a restaurant. The 22 rooms have TV and phone. **Restaurant La Balandre** €€–€€€ (*www.balandre.com*).

La Bergerie €€€ *Route de Brive, RN20, Cahors; tel: 05 65 36 82 82; e-mail: hotel.bergierie@wanadoo.fr; www.labergierie-lot.com.* Ten rooms and a restaurant. Located a few minutes' drive north of Cahors, a château in the hills of the Causse countryside.

Château de Mercuès €€€ *Mercuès; tel: 05 65 20 00 01; e-mail: mercues@relaischateaux.com; www.chateaudemercues.com. Open Easter–end Oct, closed Wed except in Jul and Aug.* The 4-star château in its own extensive grounds is about 5km from Cahors in the direction of Villeneuve-sur-Lot. There are 30 rooms, a restaurant, tennis courts and a pool, and access for disabled guests.

Restaurant Le Marché €€€ *27 pl. Chapou, Cahors; tel: 05 65 35 27 27; email: restaurant.le.marche@cegetel.net; www.restaurantlemarche.com.* Regional cuisine using produce fresh from the local markets.

Suggested tour

Total distance: The route covers just over 102km.

Time: Allow 2½ hours for driving – say a good half day for sightseeing and drinking in the scenery.

Links: The D911 at the start of the route continues from Rostassac for 50km to Villeneuve-sur-Lot (*see page 197*). The N20 connects Cahors

Musée Zadkine €€
Les Arques, Cahors; tel:
05 65 22 83 37. Open daily
1000–1300, 1400–1900.
Closed 25 Dec, 1 Jan, 1 May
& 1 Nov. The key to
Chapelle-St-André is
held at the museum.

Eglise St-Laurent €
Les Arques; No tel.
Open Jun–Sep daily
1000–1900; rest of year
1400–1700.

Below
Cahors vineyards

and Souillac (*see pages 134–6*). From Vers you can travel to Figeac (*see pages 172–6*) by way of the D653 or the Lot and Célé valleys (*see pages 164–71*).

Route: Leave **CAHORS** ❶ on the D911 and head for **Mercuès** ❷, 5km northwest, where the Hôtel Château de Mercuès is exactly that – the town's old castle, built in 1212, enlarged 200 years later and the scene of numerous conflicts during the Hundred Years War and the Wars of Religion. Continue on the D911 for a further 10.5km to Rostassac, then take the D660 for 4.5km to **Les Junies** ❸, which has a 15th-century castle with round towers and a massive 14th-century church.

Turn right on to the D37 and in 3km reach **Lherm** ❹, an attractive village of limestone buildings. Its church, in woodland just outside the village, has a Romanesque apse and a carved altarpiece decorated with gold. Another 4km along the D37 you reach **Les Arques** ❺, a tiny village (pop. 160) with a **museum** celebrating the work of the internationally acclaimed sculptor Ossip Zadkine (1890–1967). The Russian-born Cubist lived in Les Arques from 1934. Two of his most important pieces – *Christ* and *Pietà* – can be found inside the 11th-century **Eglise St-Laurent** in the centre of the village. The nearby **Chapelle St-André-des-Arques** contains a series of 15th-century frescoes discovered by Zadkine in 1954.

From Les Arques take the D46 west for 4km, then turn right on to the D673 to reach Montcléra in another 2km. **Château de Montcléra** ❻ has a 15th-century gate, a square keep and round towers with machicolations. The *bastide* village of **Cazals** ❼, built by the English, comes after a further 3km. **Salviac** ❽, another 7km along the D673, has a Gothic church with attractive stained-glass windows. Leave Salviac on the D2 east and after 2km turn right on to the D6 at Dégagnac; after another 2km, head east on the D2 again for 9.5km to St-Chamarand, where the D2 crosses the N20. 3km beyond the N20 turn right on the D17 to reach **Labastide-Murat** ❾ in 7km.

Standing at more than 400m, Labastide-Murat is on one of the

Musée Murat €€
Labastide-Murat;
tel: 05 65 31 11 86. Open
Jul–Sep daily 1000–1200,
1400–1800.

highest points on the Gramat-Causse. The town's name honours Joachim Murat, who was born here in 1767.

The son of an innkeeper, he became a soldier whose heroism brought him to the attention of Napoleon. Later he became the Emperor's brother-in-law and the king of Naples. He was shot in 1815 when the Bourbons returned to Naples. His story is told in the house where he was born, now the **Musée Murat**.

From Labastide-Murat head south on the D32, which merges with the D653 after 13.5km. For the next 7.5km the roads descends, scenically following the River Vers to its confluence with the Lot at the village of Vers. From here the D653 continues west, affording some very pleasant views of the Lot, which it follows for 15km, returning you to Cahors.

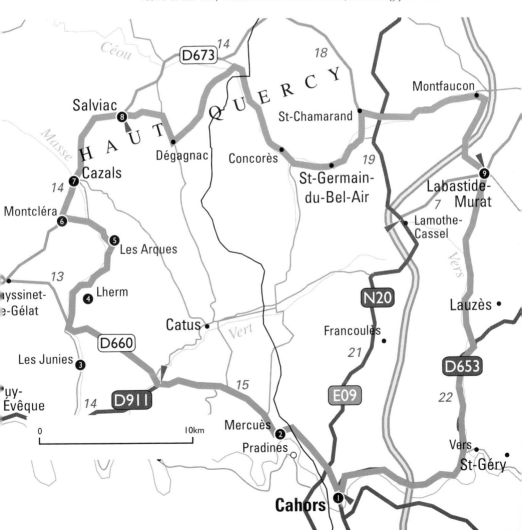

Cahors–Villeneuve-sur-Lot

Ratings

Botanic gardens	●●●●●
Dolmens	●●●●○
History	●●●●○
Scenery	●●●●○
Walks	●●●●○
Wine	●●●●○
Art	●●○○○
Children	●●○○○

There are serene places to be found in this part of the winding River Lot, even in high summer. You can stroll around old villages unsullied by crowds and climb hills high above the river for wonderful views. From a hilltop at Luzech you can survey just about the entire town and the meander of the Lot that almost encloses it. Take a walk from the wine centre of Prayssac, a cheerful town, to prehistoric dolmens. Your camera will probably be put to good use in most of the small towns and villages interspersed with vineyards and orchards on the banks of the Lot. Picturesque Puy-l'Evêque has houses built into the steep river bank. When you've had your fill of long-past history visit Villeneuve-sur-Lot. It retains a few ancient features but it's mostly modern, and it's the biggest metropolis between Cahors and Agen.

Catus

D660

D911

E09

Mercues
Pradir

D673   Puy-
l'Évêque

Cahors

Monflanquin

D710

D124

Cuzorn

Monsempron-
Libos

Fumel

Prayssac   Castelfranc

Lot

Douelle

Albas   Luzech

D911

St-Vite

Montayral

Mauroux

Sauzet

D653

N20

Trentels

D102

asseneuil
Bias

Villeneuve-
sur-Lot

Tournon-
d'Agenais

D656

St-Pantaléon   D653   L'Hospitalet

Pujols

Penne-
d'Agenais

D661

Lot

Montcuq

Q
U
E
R
C

Grottes de
Lestournelle

St-Antoine-
de-Ficalba

D656

Montaigu-
de-Quercy

St-Cyprien

Grottes de Fontirou

Hautefage-la-Tour

Frespech

Roquecor

D953

gnac

N21

Laroque-
Timbaut

Beauville

Touffailles

D2

Castelnau-
Montratier

ulayronnes

D656

Bourg-de-
Visa

Lauzerte

Montpeza
de-Quer

Pont-du-Casse

Cazes-
Mondenard

Boé

N113

Barguelonne

D957

Mirab

Layrac   Caudecoste

D953

D927

Lafrançaise

L'Honor-
de-Cos

ALBAS

Previous page
Albas

This beautiful old village in a neat hillside setting above the Lot's south bank sits amid dense woodland. The narrow streets, old houses and the remains of the bishops' castle are all well worth exploring, for the views and the timeless atmosphere.

CASTELFRANC

This is a *bastide* village. It had a lucky escape in the early 1500s when the plague had been rampant but stopped short of the town walls. A small chapel commemorates the fact.

DOUELLE

This village is about 15km from Cahors. If you want to stretch your legs in pleasant surroundings, take a look at the giant mural by Didier Chamizot on the river bank.

LUZECH

Luzech *Office de Tourisme Maison des Consuls, r. de la Ville, tel: 05 65 20 17 27; e-mail: office.de.tourisme.de.luzech @wanadoo.fr; www.ville-luzech.fr*

Boat trips including a wine-tasting are organised by *Cie Navilot, Caïx Boating Centre; tel: 05 65 20 18 19. Cruises 1630–1830 daily mid-Apr–Oct. Alternatively, canoes and kayaks can be hired by the hour or day or longer from Safaraid, Albas. Tel: 05 65 30 74 47; e-mail: safaraid@aol.com*

This is the first town of any size on the Lot west of Cahors. Like Cahors it was built within a horseshoe formed by a large river meander, making it almost an island. Luzech originally had two castles; the 12th-century square keep of one still exists.

Go to the top of Côte de l'Impernal if you want an excellent view of Luzech. The hill formed a naturally defended site, which was first exploited by the area's Neolithic inhabitants. Later the Gauls built strong defences there. Wander around the old quarter of Luzech among little alleys and the quays and buildings that survive from the Middle Ages. The Penitents' Chapel is from the 12th century.

Luzech's **Musée Archéologique Armand Viré** is housed in a vaulted cellar at the Maison des Consuls, rue de la Ville, an atmospheric home for articles excavated in the area. They include tools and artefacts from the palaeolithic era through to Gallo-Roman times. If you have time, enjoy a two-hour **boat trip** on the Lot.

PRAYSSAC

Office de Tourisme *1 blvd de la Paix,*

This is another place where you can walk to some dolmens. The little town always seems busy – it is a noted centre for the wine trade.

Prayssac; tel: 05 65 22 40 57; e-mail: contact@ tourisme-prayssac.com

Several châteaux offer guided tours. Prayssac has a farmers' market on *Sundays* at pl. de la Liberté, *from 0800 to 1300.*

PUJOLS

ⓘ **Office de Tourisme** *Le Bourg, Pujols; tel: 05 53 36 78 69; e-mail: contact@otpujols47.info; www.otpujols47.info*

Below
Puy l'Evêque

Barely 1km from the southwest gate of Villeneuve is this medieval walled town. From its elevated position you can get a good view of Villeneuve's *bastide* qualities. Pujols's church of St-Foy-le-Jeune, which has some 15th-century frescoes, is used for art exhibitions. After all the medieval churches seen in this part of France, it is a change to come across one that has no ancient origins at all. The Eglise Ste-Catherine was consecrated in 1937, having been erected on the site of a previous church from which some notable stained glass was conserved for use in its successor. The 17th-century Chapelle des Pénitents contains a large collection of processional staffs and some fine glassware.

PUY-L'EVEQUE

ⓘ **Puy-l'Evêque** *Office de Tourisme, pl. de la Truffière, Puy-l'Eveque; tel: 05 65 21 37 63; www.puy-leveque.fr/ uk_index.htm. Open all year.*

A pretty little town in a pretty cliff-side location, capped by the church and the remains of the castle. The 14th-century fortified church is known for its great belfry porch and the ancient tombs in the churchyard. The castle keep still shelters the houses below it. Near Puy-l'Evêque is St-Martin-le-Redon, known for its spring water, which is said to be beneficial for those with skin problems.

Into the action

The Cahors area, with the Lot Valley, is a useful centre if you enjoy sporting activities. Whether you fancy a half-day bicycle ride or a parachute jump, it's easy to organise in this region. If you have the time for a long-distance ride on horseback or mountain bike, or a canoe exploration along the River Lot, you can try a new category of accommodation introduced in the Lot *département* – the Rando-Etape.

Rando-Etapes are stopping points specially for the non-motorised. Rando is short for *randonnée* – a long-distance walk or ride – and *étape* means stage. Rando-Etapes may be a *gîte d'étape*, *chambre d'hôte* (bed and breakfast) or other type of lodging. It has to be open from Easter to the end of October and to accommodate at least 10 people. A bike shelter and enclosure for horses are required. 'Tourisme Equestre' approved places have to provide stalls or horseboxes. Meals may be provided or there may be a kitchen for self-catering.

Long-distance accompanied horse rides from two to seven days are provided by a Cahors establishment that also offers rides by the hour. Lessons for novices are available. Contact the **Association Départementale de Tourisme Equestre du Lot** *Cahors; tel: 05 65 35 80 82; e-mail: otlot@cheval-lot.com*

Footpath walks up to 175km and shorter circular walks of a few hours are suggested throughout the Lot region by the **Comité Départemental du Lot** (*107 quai Cavaignac, Cahors; tel: 05 65 35 07 09; e-mail: rando@tourisme-lot.com; www.tourisme-lot.com*). More than 150 shorter walks are outlined in a collection entitled *Promenades and Randonnées*, on sale at tourist offices.

Mountain bike rides by the day, or for between four and 12 days, are organised by **Cap Liberté** *Conduché, 46330 St-Cirq-Lapopie; tel: 05 65 24 21 02; e-mail: vtt@cap-liberté.fr; www.cap-liberte.fr (in French only)*. The company also has mountain bikes for hire. For details of all road cycling and mountain biking, contact the **Comité Départemental de Cyclotourisme du Lot** *Résidence Souihol, St-Céré; tel: 05 65 10 98 90; e-mail: codepffct46@free.fr; http://randocyclovtt46.free.fr*

Canoes may be hired by the day, half day or hour from **Lot Navigation Nicols** *Le Bourg, Bouziès; tel: 05 65 24 32 20; e-mail: info@lotnavigation.com; www.lotnavigation.com*. Two-person canoes and one-person kayaks are available from **Club Canoë-Kayak MJC**, who run day-long accompanied descents and longer trips (*Base Canoë-Kayak, 1 pl. Chico Mendes, Cahors; tel: 05 65 22 62 62*). The season covers about seven weeks in July and August. For a list of canoeing clubs and/or a list of activities, contact the **Comité Départemental de Canoë-Kayak** at *pl. Chico Mendes, Cahors; tel: 05 65 35 91 59, e-mail: cdck46@9online.fr*

Water-skiing is another option. Contact **Cahors Sport Nautique** *Base Nautique de Regourd, Cahors; tel: 05 65 30 08 02, open every afternoon in July and August, Monday, Wednesday and Saturday afternoons in June and September, weekends and public holidays in May and October.*

VILLENEUVE-SUR-LOT

ⓘ Villeneuve-sur-Lot
*3 pl. de la Libération,
47304 Villeneuve-sur-Lot;
tel: 05 53 36 17 30; e-mail:
tourisme.villeneuve-sur-
lot@wanadoo.fr;
www.tourisme-villeneuve-sur-
lot.com. Open 0900–1200,
1400–1800; Jul and Aug
0900–1900. Closed Sun.*

ⓜ Aquatic Garden
*(Latour-Marliac) €€
Etablissement Botanique, Le
Temple-sur-Lot; tel: 05 53
01 08 05; e-mail: contact@
latour-marliac.com;
www.latour-marliac.com.
Open May–Sept Fri–Sun
1000–1800. Shop opens
Mar–Sep 1000–1800.*

Musée de Gajac €
*2 r. des Jardins; tel: 05 53
40 48 00. Open daily except
Tue 1000–1200, 1400–
1800, Sat, Sun afternoon
only. Closed public holidays.*

The River Lot sees no
point in taking the
shortest route from A
to B. It likes to wriggle
along creating delightful
views and making big
loops, which were ideal
for the establishment of
communities.

**ⓒ Club de Vacances
Duravel €–€€**
*Route de Vire; tel: 05 65 24
65 06; e-mail: clubduravel@
wanadoo.fr;www.clubdevacan
ces.eu. Open late Apr–end
Sep.* This site takes
caravans and mobile homes
and provides swimming,
tennis and entertainment.
237 pitches.

A popular overnight stop for visitors and a lively, mainly modern, town, though it was founded in 1264 and was considered one of the most important *bastide* towns in the Southwest. The town has managed to retain many of the little streets of half-timbered and brick houses of past centuries. Pl. de la Fayette is a good example of this preservation. Stone houses from the 18th and 19th centuries mingle comfortably with modern developments. In the shelter of hills around the town are orchards and vineyards. Villeneuve is known for its regional market and the sweet, plump plums used to make Agen's famous plum brandy.

The Villeneuve area claims to be the birthplace of the water lily. Whether or not this is so, the **Latour-Marliac Aquatic Garden** is a marvellous place to visit. The ornamental lake dates back to 1870. A lake fed by a natural spring contains France's national collection of water lilies, and there is a waterfall. A greenhouse contains tropical plants and some amazing giant water lilies from the Amazon.

Villeneuve's original fortifications have disappeared except for two brick and stone gates in the ramparts, the Porte de Pujols (southwest) and the Porte de Paris (northeast).

The **Château de la Sylvestrie** is one of France's rare medieval courts, dating from the 12th to 15th centuries. In the romantic setting of an old riverside windmill, a municipal museum, the **Musée de Gajac**, has recently opened, exhibiting archaeological items, displays relating to the Lot's history, the *bastide* of Villeneuve and a collection of art works mainly of the 18th to 20th centuries.

Accommodation and food

Ferme Auberge La Roseraie € *Chemin Ginestre, Duravel; tel: 05 65 24 63 82. Closed Mon and Thur lunchtimes. Open late Jun–early Sept.* Traditional regional cuisine is served here in the restaurant or on the terrace.

Hôtel-Restaurant Henry € *23 r. Docteur Rouma, Puy-l'Evêque; tel: 05 65 21 32 24; e-mail: contact@hotel-henry.com; www.hotel-henry.com.* The restaurant (€–€€) seats 120 and there are 75 places on the terrace. The hotel has 19 rooms.

Hôtel des Ramparts € *1 r. Etienne Marcel, Villeneuve-sur-Lot; tel: 05 53 70 71 63.* Nine-room hotel, five en suite.

Aquitaine Hôtel €–€€ *29 av. Lazare Carnot, Villeneuve-sur-Lot; tel: 05 53 49 00 50; e-mail: aquitainehotel@wanadoo.fr; http://aquitainehotel.com/index-gb.htm (English).* The hotel has 22 en-suite rooms and a restaurant (€–€€).

L'Auberge Imhotep €–€€ *Rivière Haute, Albas; tel: 05 65 30 70 91.* This country restaurant specialises in the traditional fare of the region.

◑ Camping de l'Ecluse € *Le Payras, 46140 Douelle; tel: 05 65 30 95 79. Open Apr–mid-Sept.* On the river, with canoes and kayaks, the site has a restaurant, tennis and entertainment. 17 pitches.

Camping Municipal le Rooy € *N21, Villeneuve-sur-Lot; tel: 05 53 70 24 18. Open mid-Apr–Sept.* The basic campground has 63 pitches.

Below
Villeneuve-sur-Lot

Auberge Malique €–€€ *L'Ormeau, Douelle; tel: 05 65 20 02 03. Closed two weeks in Dec–Jan.* The restaurant (€–€€) seats 30, with seating for 60 more on the terrace. There are 17 guest rooms with TV and phone. There's a swimming pool and children's playground.

Les Gardes €–€€ *46220 Prayssac; tel: 05 65 22 41 98; e-mail: prayssac@valvvf.fr. Open Apr–Oct. Gîte* offering various sports and games and swimming. There is a garden and parking. Wheelchair accessible.

Hôtel Le Glacier €–€€ *11–13 blvd G. Leygues 47300 Villeneuve-sur-Lot; tel: 05 53 70 70 14.* Bath or shower in 19 of the 28 rooms.

Hôtel des Platanes €–€€ *40 bd. de la Marine, Villeneuve-sur-Lot; tel: 05 53 40 11 40. Closed the last week in Aug.* Small family hotel in a quiet residential area close to the town centre. 20 rooms, bed and breakfast or full board.

Hôtel la Résidence €–€€ *17 av. Carnot, Villeneuve-sur-Lot; tel: 05 53 40 17 03.* Of the 18 rooms, five are en suite. In summer, breakfast can be taken in the pretty garden.

Hôtel Terminus €–€€ *2 av. M^{al} Foch, Villeneuve-sur-Lot; tel: 05 53 70 94 36.* The hotel has a restaurant (**€–€€**) and 12 guest rooms, each with bath or shower.

La Carrière €€ *Albas; tel: 05 65 36 74 98; e-mail: bookings@lotfrance.com; www.lotfrance.com. Open all year.* Bed & breakfast and gîtes in the village of Albas, run by an English couple. Sleeps up to 10 guests.

La Maison de Velours €€ *21 r. de Velours, 47300 Villeneuve-sur-Lot; tel: 06 73 54 57 47; e-mail: ifls-france@wanadoo.fr; www.maison-de-velours.com/index_ang.php (English).* Cosy guesthouse in the centre of Villeneuve. Five studio rooms equipped with self-catering facilities. The owner also operates a language school down the street.

La Truffière €€ *3 r. des Scafegnous, Puy-l'Eveque; tel: 05 65 21 34 54. Closed two weeks each in Mar and Oct. Open all year.* The 10-room hotel has a restaurant (**€–€€**) and terrace.

Pilgrims' bridge

In the 16th century the crews of three boats were planning to sail down the River Lot at Villeneuve, but for some inexplicable reason they could make no headway. Some mysterious force seemed to prevent them from moving forward. Utterly perplexed, one of the sailors dived over the side to try and locate the problem. Eventually he emerged with a statuette of the Virgin Our Lady of All Joy. Presumably the boats were then able to make progress, because the men vowed to build a chapel at the spot where the incident occurred. That is why one of the places of worship in Villeneuve-sur-Lot is the Chapelle du Bout du Pont (the chapel at the end of the bridge). It became a place of pilgrimage for the boatmen on the Lot, and is still there. The bridge is the Pont Vieux, or Pont de Cieutats, built by the English in the 13th century. Its three defence towers were destroyed in the 17th century.

ℹ Along the Lot are a number of vineyards and wine cellars open to visitors: a list of these is available from the tourist office in Cahors: *pl. François Mitterrand; tel: 05 65 53 20 65.*

Suggested tour

Total distance: The route covers 57km.

Time: Some of the roads are steep and narrow. Allow 2½ hours for driving and at least half a day to include sightseeing.

Route: From **VILLENEUVE-SUR-LOT** ❶ follow the D661 east for 10km to **Penne-d'Agenais** ❷, a popular riverside destination for tourists and pilgrims paying homage to the Virgin. Originally an English possession, it was involved in many conflicts and suffered badly during the Wars of Religion. It was so badly battered over the years that it was largely in ruins by the 20th century. Restored in recent years, it is now a great place for strolling around. Notre-Dame-de-Peyragude is a modern Romanesque-Byzantine sanctuary where pilgrimages are held. It is built on a hilltop where there is a wonderful panoramic view of the Lot Valley from Villeneuve to Fumel in the east. A number of splendidly restored half-timbered houses are to be seen in r. de Ferracap and adjoining streets. Porte de Ricard is named after Richard the Lionheart who ordered the building of the town's first defences.

Leave Penne by the D103, climbing steadily into the region known as the Serres du Bas-Quercy, where peaceful, fertile valleys lie between chains of steep limestone hills. After 9km the road reaches **Hautefage-la-Tour** ❸. The tower that gives the village its name is an elegant hexagonal belfry, part of Notre-Dame-de-Hautefage, a Gothic-style church. The village square, shaded by plane trees, contains an ancient wash house and a pilgrims' fountain.

At the southern end of the village turn left and follow the unclassified road that winds down steeply for 5km to reach the delightful small village of **Frespech** ❹, where some of the houses date from the 11th century, as do the surrounding defensive walls and the Romanesque church. Head south out of Frespech, descending to join the D656 after 3km. Turn right and travel on the D656 for 5km, where another right turn, this time on to the D110, leads in 2km to **Laroque-Timbaut** ❺, a picturesque village with a covered market and ancient houses huddled against the remains of castle walls.

Continue north on the D110, climbing again for 5km to join the N21, just beyond Bayle. Turn right on to the N21 and after 2km, at

CAHORS–VILLENEUVE-SUR-LOT 201

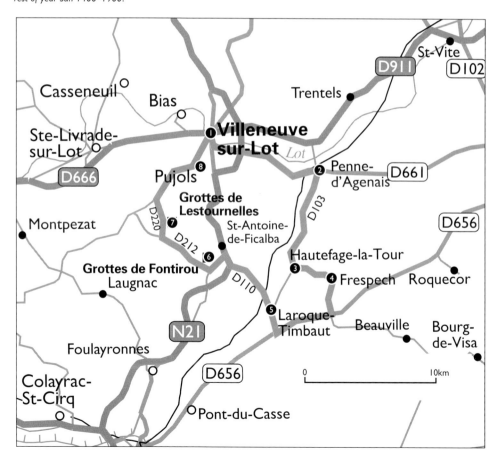

Grottes de Fontirou and Parc Préhistorique €€ *Off the N21, Castella; tel: 05 53 40 15 29; www.grottes-fontirou.com. Open for guided tours Apr–Jun and first half Sep 1400–1730; Jul and Aug 1000–1230, 1400–1800.*

Grottes de Lestournelles €€ *Ste-Colombe-de-Villeneuve; tel: 05 53 40 08 09. Open mid-Jun–mid-Sep daily 1000–1200, 1400–1900; rest of year Sun 1400–1900.*

St-Antoine-de-Ficalba, follow the signs to **Grottes de Fontirou** and **Parc Préhistorique de Fontirou** ❻. The caves have white stalagmites strikingly set against the ochre and grey walls of the galleries. The park leads visitors on a woodland tour through some 4.5 billion years and there are scenes showing dinosaurs and other extinct animals, birds and reptiles. A Neolithic village gives an insight into life at the dawn of human history. Turn right on leaving the park, then take the D212 then D220 north for 6km to the **Grottes de Lestournelles** ❼, where seven chambers with stalactites and huge pillars are open to visitors.

Head north on the D220 and after 2km turn right on to the D118, then in 6km arrive at **PUJOLS** ❽, a village with Renaissance and timber-framed houses surrounded by the remains of 13th-century ramparts. Continue on the D118, returning to Villeneuve in 2km.

Montauban

Ratings

Art	●●●●●
Markets	●●●●●
Food specialities	●●●●○
Museums	●●●●○
Architecture	●●●○○
Historical sites	●●●○○
Scenery	●●●○○
Children	●●○○○

Montauban's pinkish-red brick buildings and beautiful old arcades represent much history. The *bastide* town was founded in 1144. The Pont Vieux, grandly spanning the wide River Tarn, was built nearly 700 years ago. The Musée Ingres displays the works of Jean-Auguste-Dominique Ingres (1780–1867), born in Montauban, and other artists. The town was handed to the English in the Hundred Years War, later to be reconquered by the French. During England's regime the Black Prince built on the ruins of a château (now the Ingres Museum). The cellar contains the Black Prince's room, where instruments of torture and other items are now displayed. The Musée de la Résistance poignantly displays Montauban's World War II history. Two acacia trees in the town were used by the Reich to hang martyrs of the Resistance. The big and boisterous Saturday market draws people from the surrounding fruit-growing country.

History

ⓘ Montauban Office de Tourisme *4 r. du Collège, Montauban; tel: 05 63 63 60 60; e-mail: officetourisme@ montauban.com; www.montauban-tourisme.com/ eng/index.htm (English). Open Mon–Sat 0930–1230, 1400–1830; Jul and Aug Mon–Sat 0900–1900, Sun 1000–1200, 1500–1800. Guided tours of the town daily 1000 and 1600 (not public holidays).*

Fortified towns and villages known as *bastides*, developed in Southwest France in the Middle Ages, are regarded as the earliest examples of urban planning. Each had a covered market and the streets were laid out symmetrically. Montauban, founded in 1144, is considered to be the prototype for later *bastides*. The Old Town, with the pl. Nationale at its core, has 17th-century covered walkways or arcades of timber, providing welcome shade in the heat of summer.

Once a centre of the weaving industry, Montauban has been the principal town of the Tarn-et-Garonne region since 1808. The local economy is based on agriculture and fruit production, supported by a diversity of other industries. Prior to its 1144 charter – by which Alphonse Jourdain, Count of Toulouse, created Montauban – a small farming community existed near the River Tarn. Major building work took place in periods of prosperity. These included the **Eglise St-**

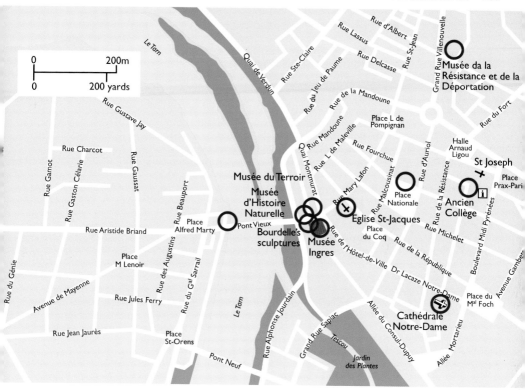

ℹ Comité Départemental de Tourisme de Tarn-et-Garonne (for information on the region) *2 blvd de Midi-Pyrénées, Montauban; tel: 05 63 21 79 65; e-mail: info@tourisme82.com*

Reservations *Service départemental de réservations, Loisirs Accueil Tarn-et-Garonne, 2 blvd de Midi-Pyrénées, Montauban; tel: 05 63 21 79 61; e-mail: sla82@wanadoo.fr; www.resinfrance.com/tarn-et-garonne*

Jacques, begun in 1230, and the great bridge over the River Tarn, begun in 1311, both still existing.

The Hundred Years War, the plague and a great famine took their toll, and it was not until the 15th and early 16th centuries that Montauban got back on its feet. Building, commerce, agriculture and artistic culture revived and flourished. In the 16th century Montauban emerged as a Protestant stronghold from a series of religious wars between 1562 and 1598. The 18th-century **Cathédrale Notre-Dame** contains an Ingres masterpiece, *Louis XIII's Pledge*.

Sights

Bourdelle's sculptures

Six years before the death of the acclaimed local artist Dominique Ingres, the gifted sculptor Emile-Antoine Bourdelle (1861–1929) was born in Montauban. His works can be seen around the town, notably the *Dying Centaur* in bronze, adjacent to the Musée d'Histoire Naturelle, and a dramatic battlefield scene – a memorial to the 1870 war – near the Ingres museum and pl. Bourdelle.

Ancien Collège *In Montauban tourist office complex. For opening times contact tourist office.*

Cathédrale Notre-Dame € *R. Notre-Dame. Open daily (donations welcome).*

Eglise St-Jacques € *R. de la République, Montauban (donations welcome).*

Farm visits €€ *La Tome Le Ramier, near Montauban; tel: 05 63 03 14 49; e-mail: helene. depierre@wanadoo.fr. Open all year. Advance booking advised.*

Musée Ingres €€ *Palais Episcopal, 13 r. de l'hôtel-de-Ville, Montauban; tel: 05 63 22 12 91; e-mail: contact@amis-museeingres. com; www.amis-museeingres. com. Open Jul and Aug daily 0930–1200, 1330–1800; rest of year 1000–1200, 1400–1800, but closed Tue and Sun am.*

Ancien Collège

You will see the former Jesuits' College if you call at Montauban tourist office – it is housed there. Originally a private house, the brick-built structure was bought by the Jesuits who founded their college there at the end of the 17th century. It has been put to several uses since, including a cannon foundry and, more recently, a primary school. There was talk of demolishing the building when a fire caused considerable damage in 1961, but eventually it was restored and re-opened as a cultural centre. The tourist office occupies a spacious hall.

Cathédrale Notre-Dame

Built to celebrate the triumph of the Catholic religion in a Protestant city, following the Revocation of the Edict of Nantes, the classical-style cathedral was designed by noted architects of the day, François d'Orbay and Robert de Cotte. It was constructed in pale stone and inaugurated in 1739. In the left side of the transept is the Ingres painting *Louis XIII's Pledge*.

Eglise St-Jacques

Dating from 1230, the church, with its distinctive octagonal bell tower, was partially destroyed and rebuilt in the first half of the 18th century. Marks of cannonballs, relics of the 1621 siege, may be seen at the bottom of the bell tower. One of the three chapels off the nave contains an altar and a sculpture by Joseph Ingres, father of Dominique. The cost of the original building was raised partly by donations and also by fines imposed on well-to-do individuals who were considered to be too finely dressed.

Farm visits

A 'Welcome to the Farm' agricultural tourism booklet is available from the tourist office. Fruit farms, wine estates, honey farms, goat herds and specialists producing flowers, *escargots*, *foie gras* and traditionally made breads and cheeses may be visited in the Tarn-et-Garonne region. At La Tome du Ramier, 3km from Montauban, you can see how milk from 160 cows is transformed into hundreds of maturing cheeses. The farm routine and the rearing and care of the cows and heifers are outlined.

Musée Ingres

Built on the site of a 12th-century castle owned by the counts of Toulouse, the impressive red-brick edifice that houses the Ingres Museum was developed as the Bishop's Palace (begun in 1664), following three centuries of neglect. Before this long period of decay the Black Prince, son of the king of England, began to build on the old castle ruins in 1342. Part of the cellar was the Black Prince's guardroom. Today instruments of torture and various artefacts and relics from the distant past are displayed in the room. Artworks by Jean-Auguste-Dominique Ingres (1780–1867) and other artists are exhibited on five floors.

Musée d'Histoire
Naturelle €€ 2 pl.
Bourdelle; tel: 05 63 22 13
85. Open Tue–Sat 1000–
1200, 1400–1800, Sun pm.

Musée du Terroir €€
2 pl. Bourdelle; tel: 05 63 66
46 34. Open daily except Mon
1000–1200, 1400–1800,
Sun pm only. Closed on public
holidays.

The devotee will want to spend a good two to three hours here, although improvements to lighting and labelling would be appreciated. Ingres and other Montauban-born artists, and some who painted local landscapes, are represented on the ground floor. Bronzes by Montauban resident Antoine Bourdelle (1861–1929) are exhibited. On the top floor are drawings and paintings by Ingres and some of his pupils. There's a reconstruction of the room where Ingres relaxed with his violin, with the instrument in pride of place.

Among the artist's best-known paintings on display are *Jesus Among the Doctors*, *Ossian's Dream*, *Portrait of Madame Gonse* and the nude *Angelique*. Ingres bequeathed many paintings and 4000 drawings and made generous donations to the museum, which opened in 1843. Separate areas in the museum are devoted to the French, Spanish and Flemish schools of the 17th and 18th centuries. In the museum's courtyard are terracotta figures by Joseph Ingres, father of Dominique.

Musée d'Histoire Naturelle

Four thousand birds, mammals (including primates), reptiles and fish reflect the taxidermist's art. Palaeontology and mineral collections are housed in the museum, established in the mid-19th century.

Musée du Terroir

Below the Natural History Museum, this 'museum of the soil' presents one man's collection over a period of 40 years of artefacts, implements and household items relating to the lives of peasants in the region in days gone by.

Above
Musée Ingres

Musée de la Résistance et de la Déportation €€ 33 Grand Rue Villenouvelle, Montauban; tel: 05 63 66 03 11. Open Tue–Sat 0900–1200, 1400–1800. Closed Aug.

Pont Vieux €€ For a change of perspective on the town, hire an electric boat on the River Tarn. Boats are moored near the Pont Vieux, and are available daily from mid-Jun to mid-Sep.

Below
Montauban and the banks of the Tarn

Musée de la Résistance et de la Déportation

This new museum provides a moving insight into the dedication of the Resistance Movement in this region of France in World War II during the German occupation and the supreme sacrifice made by many local people. Photographs, documents, letters, reports and other exhibits ensure that the memory of the Resistance workers' courage lives on.

Place Nationale

A centre of urban life since the 12th century, this is the heart of Old Montauban, a forerunner of *bastide* towns and villages, with an early 'grid system' of streets at right angles to one another, leaving a large open square in the middle – pl. Nationale. Fire destroyed two of the adjoining timber arcades in 1614 and the other two in 1649, but all were rebuilt to the original design and survive today. Wednesday and Saturday markets are held there in winter and theatrical performances take place there in summer.

Pont Vieux

A bridge – the enduring Pont Vieux crossed by countless vehicles daily – was built between 1311 and 1335 over the River Tarn. Originally it had three towers: one at either end and a triangular central one that contained an altar dedicated to Ste Catherine. Opposite the central tower was a balance that operated a metal cage. Blasphemers were put into this cage and dipped three times in the river as a punishment.

Pigeon houses

Pigeonniers are a feature of the landscape in Southwest France generally and Tarn-et-Garonne in particular. They come in many styles of architecture and were introduced centuries ago not so much as a food source but for the pigeon manure, which was used for fertilising the land.

The bridge is 205m long. Above the bridge's seven arches are small arches through which water can pass when the river is in spate, lowering the risk of flooding.

Accommodation and food

**L'Agora € *9 pl. Nationale, Montauban; tel: 05 63 63 05 74. Closed Sun.* A snack bar handy for shoppers and stallholders in the market.

**Café des Brasseurs € *22 pl. Nationale, Montauban; tel: 05 63 63 54 56.* Good beer and a modestly priced menu.

**Bar Comedy €–€€ *2 r. de la Résistance, Montauban; tel: 05 63 63 24 72.* Good choice of hot and cold food served promptly and with a smile. Pricey bottled beer. As still happens in France, women from abroad may find the toilet arrangements disconcerting – they have to go by men in the urinal to reach their toilet.

**Café Flamand €–€€ *8 r. de la République, Montauban; tel: 05 63 66 12 20. Open daily until 0200. Closed all day Sun and Mon lunchtime.* Call here for the beer – they specialise in Belgian, German and English brews.

**Hôtel du Commerce €–€€ *19 pl. Franklin Roosevelt, Montauban; tel: 05 63 66 31 32; e-mail: info@hotel-commerce.com; www.hotel-commerce-*

Fairs and markets

In spring the countryside around Montauban turns pink and white with fruit tree blossom. The Saturday market teems with townspeople and the farming community from surrounding villages has stalls piled high with local walnuts, cheeses, live chickens, flowers, herbs, pickles, jams and salad crops. In spring bunches of young asparagus are a big attraction, then the first of the strawberries arrive. Apples, peaches, nectarines, dessert grapes, plums, greengages and mushrooms vie for space on the stalls; geese, ducks, *foie gras* and the new crop of walnuts, hazelnuts and chestnuts make an appearance in autumn.

Montauban goes in for markets. As well as the all-day Saturday market there's one on Wednesday mornings at pl. Lalaque, another on Tuesday afternoons and evening markets in July and August. An agricultural show takes place on the first weekend in October. Fairs are held in every season – in March, July, October and December, and in mid-November there's a honey fair.

⬤ **Camping du Lac €** *Vallée des Loisirs, Lafrançaise; tel: 05 63 65 89 69; e-mail: theolor@orange.fr; http://pagesperson-orange.fr/Icampingdulac82. Open mid-Jun–mid-Sep.* Approximately halfway between Montauban and Moissac, 17km northeast of Montauban on the D927, this 3-star, 33-pitch campground offers tennis, a swimming pool, showers, restaurant and bar among its facilities.

Camping Municipal d'Ardus-Plage € *Lamothe-Capdeville; tel: 05 63 31 32 29.* The shady campground 8km north of Montauban has a restaurant and bar, grocery store, electricity, showers and telephone. There are 33 pitches.

montauban.com. There are 27 tastefully decorated rooms in this 1-star hotel near the Cathedral. Bar, garage parking.

Hôtel du Lion d'Or €–€€ *22 av. de Mayenne, Montauban; tel: 05 63 20 04 04; e-mail: liondor@tiscali.fr.* The 21-room hotel, close to the railway station, has a bar and restaurant and parking for guests' cars.

Hôtel Campanile €€ *R. Louis Lepine, Parc Albasud, Montauban; tel: 05 63 23 00 02; e-mail: mario.giardini@laposte.fr; www.montauban. cci.fr/campanile.* Some of the 46 rooms are non-smoking. The 2-star hotel, *open all year*, has a restaurant and enclosed parking.

Hôtel Climat de France €€ *Aussonne (RN20), Montauban; tel: 05 63 66 51 61.* Quiet 38-room, 2-star hotel with restaurant and bar handy for the autoroute A20 north of the town.

Hôtel Ibis €€ *Pont de Chaume, Rocade Est, av. de Montclar, Montauban; tel: 05 63 20 20 88.* The largest of the town's hotels, the Ibis has 62 comfortable air-conditioned rooms, swimming pool, tennis court and garden, restaurant and bar. Easy access to the RN20.

Hotel Kyriad €€ *1461 route du Nord, Montauban; tel: 05 63 66 51 61; e-mail: Kyriad-montauban@wanadoo.fr.* Thirty-seven rooms and the hotel offers a car washing service.

Hôtel d'Orsay €€ *31 av. Roger Salengro, Montauban; tel: 05 63 66 06 66; www.hotel-restaurant-orsay.com. Closed for the two middle weeks in August.* Opposite the railway station, the hotel has 20 soundproofed rooms with air conditioning. There is a restaurant of high repute and a bar. Secure parking.

Cuisine d'Alain €€–€€€ *29 av. Roger Salengro, Montauban; tel: 05 63 66 06 66; e-mail: cuisinedalain@wanadoo.fr.* This is the restaurant at the Hotel d'Orsay, of which Alain Blanc and his wife are the proprietors. Fresh home-grown herbs are used in his innovative dishes. Most of the ingredients are produced locally. Desserts are artistic: if not rushed off

Planning a picnic? Call at **Tartabelle**, 9 r. de la Comédie, Montauban; tel: 05 63 91 10 74. They have good quiches, pizzas, vegetarian tarts, sandwiches and other savouries.

his feet your waiter may create a design on your plate with sauces and cream, such as a seahorse, bird or flower. Alain's cuisine has a devout following – best to book.

Crowne Plaza Montauban €€€ *6–8 Quai de Verdun, Montauban; tel: 05 63 22 00 00; e-mail: contact@cp-montauban.com; www.crowneplaza-montauban.com.* A new hotel in town with a fine restaurant, Les Capucins, run by the respected former Paris chef Hervé Sauton. Eighty elegant en-suite rooms with all modern hotel amenities, set in a building that once was a 17th-century monastery. Spa treatments available.

Suggested tour

Abbaye de Beaulieu €€ Ginals; tel: 05 63 24 50 10; http://beaulieu-en-rouergue. monuments-nationaux.fr. Open Jul & Aug daily 1000–1200, 1400–1800; Apr–Jun, Sep, Oct Wed–Mon 1000–1200, 1400–1800. Closed Nov–Mar & 1 May. Free entry to under-18s and students of art.

Total distance: The main route covers 123km. The detour adds 30km.

Time: Driving time for the main route is about 3 hours, with an extra hour if the detour is followed. Give yourself a full day's outing, however, to get the most out of the varied scenery, towns and villages.

Links: From Caylus the D926 heads northeast to Villefranche-de-Rouergue, from where the D922 travels due north to Villeneuve and Figeac (*see pages 172–6*). At Caussade you can head north to Cahors (*see pages 182–91*) on the N20 or the faster A20, the autoroute that opened in the summer of 1998. From Lafrançaise the D927 takes you west to Moissac (*see pages 212–21*), where the N113 continues to Agen.

Route: From **MONTAUBAN ❶** follow the D115 east. At first the countryside is fairly bland, but at Montricoux, after 20km, the road begins to run alongside the Aveyron river, which is soon twisting and turning through the famed Gorges de l'Aveyron. The road also twists and turns as the terrain becomes more rugged, the river on one side and forested hills on the other. **St-Antonin-Noble-Val ❷**, 26km from Montricoux, is a lovely old riverside town sustaining a medieval ambience. Its town hall, built in 1125, is the oldest civic building in France. Visitors can enjoy canoeing, caving, climbing, cycling, horse riding, rambling, swimming and tennis. The town is named after an early evangelist who brought Christianity to the area.

Detour: Leaving St-Antonin on the undulating D75 brings you in 13km to the D33, where a left turn leads within 2km to the **Abbaye de Beaulieu**, founded in 1144, now restored and housing a collection of modern art. Continue north on the D33 for 8km to reach **Parisot**. Standing 375m above sea level, the village offers a superb panorama of the northeast Quercy and Rouergue. It has a lovely 16th-century covered market. Join the D926, turning left to reach Caylus in 9km.

From St-Antonin, continue on the main route by following the D19 for 12km north to **Caylus ❸**, a small, ancient town with a fortified

Caussade 11 r. de la
République; tel: 05 63
26 04 04; e-mail: caussade.
tourisme@wanadoo.fr.
Open daily.

Montpezat-de-Quercy
Blvd des Fossés; tel: 05 63
02 05 55; e-mail:
ot.montpezat.de.quercy
@wanadoo.fr; www.
montpezat-de-quercy.com.
Open daily (Apr–Oct).

Gothic church and a covered market dating from the 14th century and other medieval buildings. The large village of **Septfonds** ❹, 15km west of Caylus on the D926, has a number of prehistoric standing stones and dolmens. **Caussade** ❺, 7km further on, is a hat-making town: everything from beach caps to creations for the couturiers of Paris, as well as traditional straw boaters. It also has a wealth of 16th- and 17th-century architecture.

Leave Caussade on the N20 north. After 6km head west on the D38 to reach **Montpezat-de-Quercy** ❻ in a further 6km. Highlights here are the 16th-century Flemish tapestries in the Collégiale St-Martin, and the 17th-century cloisters in the old Couvent des Ursulines, now a school. Continue on the D20 for 12km to **Molières** ❼, a 13th-century *bastide*, and a further 15km to Lafrançaise, where a left turn on to the D927 will take you over the confluence of the rivers Aveyron and Tarn to return to Montauban in 17km.

Also worth exploring

From St-Antonin you can continue to follow the Aveyron upstream by taking the D115 east to **Féneyrols**, a village whose remedial mineral waters have been renowned since Roman times, **Varen**, which has an 11th-century church and a 15th-century château, and **Laguépie**, an attractive village standing on a bend in the river. 25km in total.

Below
St-Antonin

Castelnau-
Montratier

Montpezat-
de-Quercy **6**

A20
E9

Belfort-du-Quercy

Puylaroque

D17

3 Caylus

Parisot

23

Ancienne Abbaye
de Beaulieu-
en-Rouergue

azes-
ondenard

14

7

Molières

Monteils

11

D926

13

Verfeil

D958

Caussade **5**

4 Septfonds

9

11

St-Antonin-
Noble-Val

2

10

Mirabel

D115

12

D600

Lafrançaise

L'Honor-
de-Cos

24

N20

Réalville

14

Forêt de la Grésigne

Cazals

△
520

21

Albias

Montricoux

Gorges

18

Nègrepelisse

D115

Penne

Vaour

5

Bruniquel

eauzac

D927

15

D115

24

Vaïssac

0   10km

D958

Montbeton

1 **Montauban**

14

D964

31

Castelnau-de-
Montmiral

Cahuzac-
sur-Vère

12

11

Monclar-de-Quercy

22

10 km

Moissac

Ratings

Ecclesiastical art	●●●●●
History	●●●●●
Arts and crafts	●●●●○
Food	●●●●○
Scenery	●●●●○
Walks	●●●●○
Children	●●●○○
Sport	●●●○○

For many people on a history and culture tour of Southwest France, Moissac is the ultimate site. They marvel at the sheer beauty of the 76 decoratively carved capitals of the cloisters of St-Pierre. This wealth of Romanesque art from the 12th century has a powerful emotional impact. The abbey church's great south doorway is a masterpiece of the same period. Intricately carved in stone are the figures of Christ, St John and figures from the Book of Revelation. Set in fruit-growing country, Moissac is a small town through which the Canal Latéral à la Garonne runs. Nearby is the confluence of the rivers Tarn and Garonne. The area is famous for the golden *Chasselas de Moissac* – the sweet grape served as a dessert. Painters, potters, glass-blowers, stained-glass makers, *objets d'art* restorers and other artists and craftspeople have studios and workshops in r. Jean Moura.

History

ⓘ **Moissac Office de Tourisme** 6 pl. Durand de Bredon, Moissac; tel: 05 63 04 01 85; e-mail: tourisme@moissac.fr; www.moissac.fr. Open daily Jul–Aug 0900–1900; Oct–Mar 1000–1200 and 1400–1700 (weekend pm only); May, Jun & Sep 0900–1200 and 1400–1800 (weekend and public holidays opens 1000). Closed 1 Jan and 25 Dec. Guided walks are organised daily and Fri evenings in Jul and Aug, and by reservation the rest of the year.

Moissac is an attractive little town by any standards, but, as its inhabitants will tell you, it has three things that give it special appeal to the tourist: stone, water and fruit. The first refers to the Romanesque carvings in the abbey cloisters and around the south portal. There is a 10-minute film about the carvings and history of the 76 individually carved capitals of the cloisters available to watch in the video theatre of the town's tourist office, which is conveniently placed within the abbey complex.

The water is in the River Tarn, and its port at Moissac, which joins the Garonne nearby, and the Canal Latéral à la Garonne, which brings boating visitors to the town and flows beneath flower-bedecked bridges. An aqueduct carries the canal over the river.

The fruit has grown in the wide acreages in the surrounding countryside since Roman times. Today, 200,000 tonnes of fruit a year

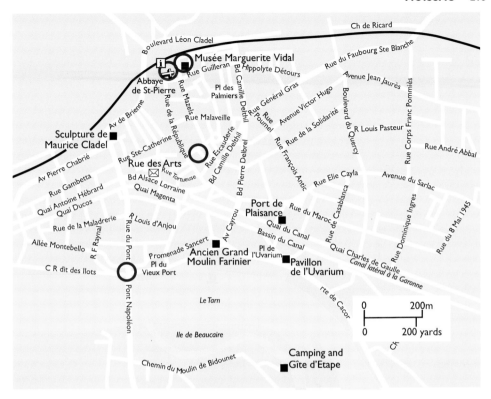

are produced – peaches, pears, nectarines, cherries, plums, greengages, melons, kiwi fruit and soft fruits. Adding another 15,000 tonnes to this figure is the supreme sweet Chasselas table grape. Moissac is also known for its arts and crafts shops. Local people and visitors promenade by the Canal Latéral à la Garonne on summer evenings, admiring the moored boats, or walk in the meadows by the River Tarn.

Sights

Abbaye de St-Pierre €€

Pl. Durand de Bredon; tel: 05 63 04 01 85; cloisters; tel: 05 63 04 05 73. Open daily 0800–1800, services Mon–Fri 1830, Sat 1930 and Sun 1030.

Abbaye de St-Pierre

The Abbey was founded in the 7th century but was subject to a series of attacks by Normans, Arabs and others. The present building was consecrated in 1063. Pilgrims on their way to Compostela stopped in the church.

The south door is a venerated work of art: a Romanesque sculpture illustrating the Apocalypse recorded by St John in the Book of Revelation. The carved stone, said to date between 1100 and 1130, shows Christ sitting in judgement; Matthew, Mark, Luke and John are represented; the Elders sit in a long row, each with individual and expressive faces. A guided tour reveals much of the detail.

Centre d'Art Roman € *blvd Léon Cladel, 82200 Moissac; tel: 05 63 04 41 79; e-mail: infomoissac@frenchcom.com*

Part of the Abbey is Gothic, built of brick, and part is Romanesque. The Cloisters, nearly 1000 years old, cannot fail to impress. Forming archways along each of the four sides of a grassy square, the 76 columns, alternately single and double, present a symphony of light and shade. The capitals and their sculpted marble panels are amazing sculptures, both because of the detail – each one is different – and because of their incredibly fine state of preservation. Many relate to the sculptor; others show birds, flowers, palm leaves and embellishments. At one time there were plans to build a railway line through the site, but sanity prevailed and an act of official vandalism was averted. Four groups of polychrome sculptures are among the restored wall decorations in the church.

A unique collection of 2000 reproduction illuminated manuscripts in the **Centre d'Art Roman** (Romanesque Art Research Centre) in the former seminary is available to researchers and is sometimes on public display.

Musée Marguerite Vidal

Below
The 11th-century Cloisters of the Abbaye de St-Pierre

Housed in 17th-century abbey lodgings, the museum displays important regional collections of furniture, pottery, earthenware, headdresses and religious art.

 **Musée Marguerite Vidal** € *In the Abbaye de St-Pierre; tel: 05 63 04 03 08. Open daily except Mon.*

Espace Montauriol Galerie du Cloître € *Pl. Durand de Bredon, Moissac; tel: 05 63 04 06 81. Open all year.*

Souffleurs de verre (glass-blowers) € *9 r. des Arts, Moissac; tel: 05 63 04 21 46. Open to the public Tue–Sun 1000–1230, 1500–1830.*

 **Le Petit Train de Moissac** provides a useful introduction to the town (€€ *tel: 05 63 04 01 85. Open May–Sept daily*).

Pont Napoléon

Planned by Napoleon I on his return from Spain and inaugurated by Napoleon III, the bridge, of brick and stone, crosses the Tarn and links r. du Pont and av. Marcel Cugat.

Rue des Arts

Spend a few fascinating hours among the art and craft outlets and workshops, the antique and bric-a-brac shops. Rue Jean Moura is the main 'street of arts' but some artists are located in adjacent town-centre streets. There are art and porcelain restoration people, specialists in lace, painters, stained-glass artists, potters, glass-blowers, woodcarvers, jewellers, antique dealers and second-hand dealers. For more information contact the Association Rue des Arts (*9 rue des Arts, 82200 Moissac; tel: 05 63 04 21 46*).

Ceramics, paintings, sculptures and other works by artists living in the region are exhibited at the **Espace Montauriol Galerie du Cloître**.

Activities

Children
The tourist office in Moissac holds discovery visits to the Cloisters and other parts of Moissac especially for children, offering them guided tours to find the hidden treasures of the town. Also for children, the tourist office suggests that a family boat trip on the Tarn towards St-Nicolas-de-la-Grave would be interesting, learning about the locks system and the birds of the river. Another idea is donkey riding at Lauzerte farm, 8km out of town.

Farmers' markets
These are held on *Saturday and Sunday mornings* in Moissac's town centre at pl. des Récollets. A covered market offering fish, meat, cheese, bread and other goods takes place *Tue–Sun*.

Festivals
The first major annual festival in Moissac's calendar is in *late April* when the two-day Arts Festival is held. Arts and crafts are demonstrated in the r. Jean Moura. Street entertainments, music, merrymaking, special events and regional food are enjoyed.

More than 100 attractions are staged for the three-day Feast of Pentecost in late May, with bread blessed and distributed and a parade of decorated boats.

For four days in *mid-July* Moissac holds its Festival of the Voice, with singing, classical music and various events, and *July and August* bring free Saturday-night music events on the square.

September marks the three-day Feast of the *Chasselas* exhibition, with awards for the most beautiful and best-flavoured grapes. The *Chasselas*, with its sweet taste and fine skin, has had the rare distinction for a fruit of being entitled to an *appellation contrôlée*. Its juice and other fruit juices can be sampled at the Uvarium, a 1930s kiosk decorated in art deco style at *2 av. de l'Uvarium, 82200 Moissac, by the River Tarn (closed in winter) (tel: 05 63 04 53 1)*.

Hiking
The waymarked Pilgrims' Route to Compostela in Spain passes through Moissac and two villages in the area, Lauzerte and Auvillar. This is the GR65, now used as a long-distance footpath, considered the most important cultural path in Europe. Hundreds of kilometres of signposted walks and country lanes are available for walkers, mountain bikers and horse-riders. Information is available at local tourist offices.

Historic villages
For the visitor who likes to potter around a town's historic sites and arts scene and do a little gentle motoring to explore old towns and

villages, Moissac makes an agreeable holiday base. You'll find much of interest at some of the places within an easy distance along the Tarn and Garonne valleys.

The two rivers join together near Moissac at **St-Nicolas-de-la-Grave**: pilgrims on their way to Compostela waited for the ferry here. The Base de Loisirs is a watersports centre on a 400-hectare stretch of water with an extensive campsite (*tel: 05 63 95 50 00; fax: 05 63 95 50 01; www.stnicolasdelag.online.fr/loisirs*). A sailing school welcomes learners and individual sailing enthusiasts. If you fancy getting afloat, you also have a choice of canoes and kayaks, pedalos and electric boats. Trip boats take passengers past Bird Island, a stopover for migratory species.

Richard Coeur-de-Lion's castle (12th and 13th centuries) is in the village of St-Nicolas-de-la-Grave: an exhibition of paintings and sculptures is held here in *July and August*.

The birthplace of the man who founded Detroit in the USA, and who had cars named after him nearly two centuries later, is now a museum. Antoine Laumet de Lamothe-Cadillac was born in St-Nicolas-de-la-Grave in 1658. His home became a small museum. A farmers' market is held in the village on *Monday mornings*.

To the northeast of Moissac is medieval **Lauzerte**, a halt for the Compostela pilgrims, fêted as one of the loveliest villages in France. (Several southwestern towns make this claim, usually with some justification.) Lauzerte sits high on a rock, and has narrow streets, old mansions and an art colony whose works blend in with those from past ages. Several studios are open to the public. The market is on *Saturday morning*. Lauzerte Tourist Office is at *pl. des Cornières; tel: 05 63 94 61 94; e-mail: lauzerte.tourisme@quercy-blanc.net; www.quercy-blanc.net*

Lauzerte's **Museum of Archaeology** has exhibits from the palaeolithic age to the 17th century. There are guided tours in French and English. The museum is in *r. de la Gendarmerie; tel: 05 63 94 62 40. Open 1430–1830 weekends and public holidays in May; daily except Tue in Jun and Sept, and daily 1030–1230 and 1400–1700 Jul and Aug.*

Producing quill pens from goose feathers was a major industry in **Auvillar**, southwest of Moissac on the Garonne river, in the 18th century. In the 19th century the local economy was based on earthenware pottery, and some fine examples can be seen in the **Musée d'Art et Traditions Populaires** in *pl. de la Halle; open 1430–1830 daily except Tue from Easter–Sep; 1500–1730 Sat and Sun Oct–Easter*. Auvillar pottery is greatly prized by collectors.

Picturesque houses of the 16th and 17th centuries, the site of a castle destroyed in the Wars of Religion in 1572 – providing a wonderful view of the Garonne Valley – and the 17th-century clock-tower on the site of one of the old wall's gates make this a pleasant place to stroll in. It is a fine example of an old Ocitan market town with its river port. The triangular 'square', in which stands a circular covered market, is unique in France; the medieval grain measures are still in place.

A farmers' market is held on *Sunday mornings*. The tourist office is at *pl. de la Halle, Auvillar; tel: 05 63 39 89 82; e-mail: office.auvillar@ wanadoo.fr; www.auvilla.com/ot.php*

Just north of Auvillar is **Valence d'Agen** where old lavoirs – predecessors of today's launderettes – may be seen.

Leisure afloat

Summer cruises aboard the péniche *Grain d'Or* provide a leisurely way of experiencing the countryside (*Moissac Navigation Plaisance, quai Charles de Gaulle, Port de Plaisance, Moissac; tel: 05 63 04 48 28. Times vary*). Alternatively, you can provide your own paddle power in a canoe or kayak (*tel: 05 63 04 10 42*).

Accommodation and food

Camping Municipal *€ L'Ile du Bidounet, Moissac; tel: 05 63 04 03 08. Open daily except Mon.: l'Ile du Bidounet, Moissac; tel: 05 63 32 52 52; e-mail: camping.bidounet@ wanadoo.fr; http://moissac.fr/ tourisme/camping/camping- bidounet/index_e.htm (English). Open Apr–Sep.* On an island site 2km from Moissac town centre, the campground offers furnished tents sleeping four people, and places for caravans. Hot showers, laundry facilities and a swimming pool are on site. Canoes, pedalos and electric boats can be hired. 100 pitches.

La Ferme de Lamouroux *€ Boudou; tel: 05 63 04 27 32*. Stay on a farm on the Pilgrims' Route to Compostela on a *chambre d'hôte* basis. The farm, 5km from Moissac, is a convenient overnight stop for long-distance walkers and all-terrain cyclists. Pets are allowed and horses and riders can be accommodated by prior arrangement. Breakfast is included in the price. Gastronomic meals can be provided at other times of the day.

Lou Grill *€ 3 r. du Marché; tel: 05 63 04 32 80. Closed Mon.* Meat and fish grilled on a wood fire, buffet of hors d'oeuvres.

Le Luxembourg *€ Av. Pierre Chabrie, Moissac; tel: 05 63 04 00 27; www.hotelluxembourg82.com/Page1.html*. This traditional hotel two minutes from the Abbey was founded in 1883. All 12 rooms are soundproofed. Close to A62 autoroute.

Pub Murrayfield *€ 4 r. de la République, Moissac; tel: 05 63 04 49 12.* Bar with snacks and ice cream, popular with the sporty set.

Hôtel Aube Nouvelle *€–€€ Durfort-Lacapelette; tel: 05 63 04 50 33; www.chez.com/aubenouvelle. Closed Dec–Jan.* Set in *Chasselas* grape country, with a shady garden, the hotel is 12km from Moissac on the road towards Lauzerte. Nine rooms.

Hotel des Crêtes de Pignols *€–€€ 1167 chemin de Pignols, Moissac; tel: 05 63 04 04 04; e-mail: hotel@cretesdepignols.com; www. cretesdepignols.com*. A small, quiet country hotel 4km from Moissac town centre. The comfortable rooms are en suite; regional cuisine is served in the restaurant. Swimming pool.

Restaurant de l'Abbaye *€–€€ Pl. Roger Delthil, Moissac; tel: 05 63 04 81 01; e-mail: j-p.jalin@restaurant-de-labbaye.com; http://restaurant-de-labbaye.com*. The restaurant on the square in front of the abbey is *open daily* for lunch and dinner, serving grills and regional dishes such as breast of duck, duck *confit* and *cassoulet*.

Le Chapon Fin €€ *Pl. des Récollets, Moissac; tel: 05 63 04 04 22; e-mail: info@lechaponfin-moissac.com; www.lechaponfin-moissac.com.* Each room in the 2-star hotel near the market has a bath or shower, TV and direct-dial telephone – and there's a honeymoon suite. Cuisine in the restaurant ranges from traditional regional fare to the innovative.

Hôtel de la Poste €€ *Pl. de la Poste, Moissac; tel: 05 63 04 01 47.* The hotel building is a former convent in the heart of Moissac. Tea dances are sometimes held.

Le Moulin de Moissac €€–€€€ *Esplanade du Moulin, Moissac; tel: 05 63 322 88 88; e-mail: hotel@lemoulindemoissac.com; www. lemoulindemoissac.com.* Thirty-five en-suite rooms with restaurant and piano bar. A grand hotel built on the site of an ancient riverside mill that burnt down in 1916. In World War II it was a refuge for Jewish children and later a school. Internet wifi available.

Le Pont Napoléon €€–€€€ *2 allée Montebello, Moissac; tel: 05 63 04 01 55; e-mail: dussau.lenapoleon@wanadoo.fr; www.pays-de-moissac.com/ pont-napoleon.* Beside the River Tarn and close to the town centre, the 2-star hotel has 12 peaceful and attractive en-suite rooms. Michel Dussau's acclaimed 3-star restaurant (*closed Wed*) is mentioned in several good eating guides.

Right
The Abbaye de St-Pierre

Suggested tour

Total distance: The main route totals 126km. The detour covers 45km, adding 22km to the main route.

Time: Allow 3 hours' driving time for the main route. The detour will take about an hour to drive.

Links: From Lafrançaise you can head south on the D927 to reach Montauban (*see pages 202–11*) in 17km. From Montcuq, the D653, heading northeast, will take you to Cahors (*see pages 182–91*) in about 24km, and from Valence-d'Agen you can take the N113 west for 28km to Agen (*see pages 222–3*).

Route: From **MOISSAC** ❶ head east on the D927 for 14km, turn left on to the D2 and in less than 400m turn right on to the D68.

Detour: Continuing on the D927 towards Montauban for a further 3km brings you to **Lafrançaise**, where you can take the D20 northeast. This road runs more or less parallel with the D68 on the main route, never more than 10km away, but leads to the old *bastide* villages of **Molières** (*see page 146*) and **Montpezat-de-Quercy** (*see page 210*). At Montpezat, noted for its covered arcades, half-timbered houses and 15th-century town gate, head northwest on the D38 for 3.5km, then continue on the D4 for a further 8.5km to rejoin the main route at Castelnau-Montratier.

From the D2 on the main route, follow the D68 for 25km to **Castelnau-Montratier** ❷, passing through typical Quercy Blanc countryside – a narrow, sparsely populated but fertile valley of chalky soil. Castelnau-Montratier, a hilltop *bastide* founded in the 13th century, has a triangular main square and three old windmills, one still working. Leave the village on the D74, which crosses a number of *serres* – rows of long plateaux separated by narrow valleys – and reaches **Montcuq** ❸ in 19km.

Montcuq has a long and violent history. It dates from the 12th century and during the Albigensian Crusade, the Hundred Years War and the Wars of Religion suffered numerous battles. A 12th-century castle keep stands as a reminder of those terrible times. From Montcuq take the D953 to **Lauzerte ❹**, 11.5km to the southwest. Founded as a *bastide* in 1241 and once occupied by the English, Lauzerte is a peaceful village with a mixture of half-timbered, Gothic and Renaissance houses.

Continue on the D953 for a further 25km, following the course of the River Barguelonne to **Valence-d'Agen** on the north bank of the Canal Latéral à la Garonne. Cross the canal to reach the attractive hilltop village of **Auvillar ❺**, overlooking the Garonne river just a few kilometres downstream of its confluence with the Tarn. A promenade at the top of the village has picnic sites and is a good place for a rest and to enjoy the view.

From Auvillar continue east for 11km on the D12, then take the D158 for 3.5km, crossing the Autoroute de Deux Mers to reach **St-Nicolas-de-la-Grave ❻** at the confluence of the Tarn and Garonne. Take the D26 south of St-Nicolas and return to the D12 (3.5km), which leads to the canalside town of Castelsarrasin. From here head north on the N113 for 8km, crossing the Tarn to return to Moissac.

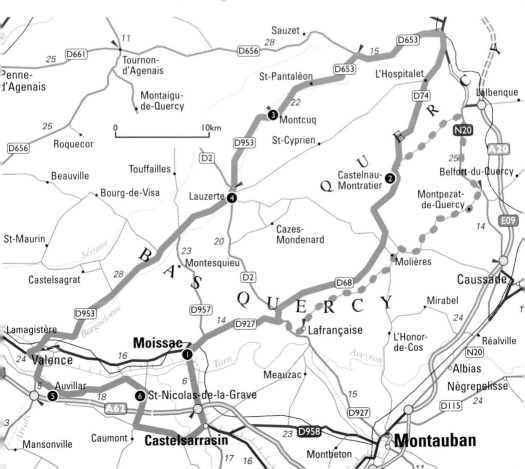

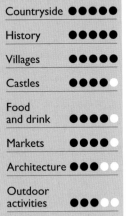

BAS ARMAGNAC

LABASTIDE D'ARMAGNAC

St JUSTIN

Around Agen and Condom

Ratings

Countryside	●●●●●
History	●●●●●
Villages	●●●●●
Castles	●●●●○
Food and drink	●●●●○
Markets	●●●●○
Architecture	●●●○○
Outdoor activities	●●●○○

South of the Garonne river and west of the city of Agen, the *département* of Gers is truly French – even though many of its small towns and villages had their beginnings as English *bastides* in the Middle Ages. It is a rural area, producing more garlic than anywhere else in the country, as well as vast quantities of *foie gras, confit,* chickens, eggs and cereals. It has rolling hills, sweetly running rivers, ancient churches and abbeys and stately châteaux. And as you might expect of the homeland of that dashing Musketeer d'Artagnan, it is peopled with a breed of individuals who are prepared to take direct action when confronted by awkward authority – dumping with great élan a wagonload of dung on the steps of the town hall, for example. They also have spirit in another sense, for this is where that great brandy Armagnac is produced.

AGEN

ⓘ Agen *107 blvd Carnot; tel: 05 53 47 36 09; e-mail: otsi.agen@wanadoo.fr; www.ot-agen.org. Open Jul–Sep Mon–Sat 0900–1900, Sun 0930–1230. Guided tours of the city can be arranged.*

Maybe it's the 35,000 tonnes of prunes they produce each year or the fact that they have one of the best rugby teams in France – whatever the reason, a national poll has decreed that the citizens of Agen are the most contented in the country. Sprawling along the banks of the River Garonne and set on a fertile plain halfway between Toulouse and Bordeaux, Agen is a busy but pleasant city earning its living largely from the surrounding area of market gardens and orchards of peach and plum trees. The old town has some interesting squares and streets with noteworthy houses, shops and public buildings dating from the 14th to 19th centuries.

The Cathédrale St-Caprais, founded as a collegiate church in the 11th century, was granted cathedral status in 1802. Frescoes on the walls inside the building portray the city's patron saints. Esplanade du Gravier, fronting the river, is a pleasant area for a walk, with a pond and lawns in the shade of plane trees.

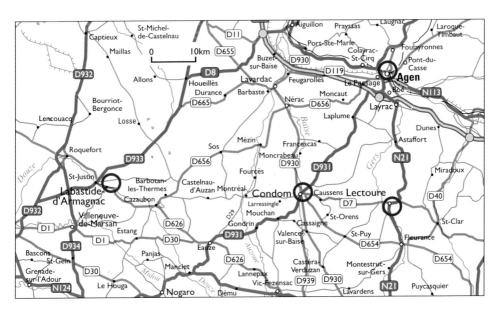

Musée des Beaux-Arts €€ *Pl. du Docteur Esquirol, Agen; tel: 05 53 69 47 23; e-mail: musee@agen.fr; www.agen.fr/musee. Open 1000–1800. Closed Tue.*

The city's pride and joy is the **Musée des Beaux-Arts**, housed in three stately mansions dating from the 16th and 17th centuries, though the cellars of one were once used as a prison and the iron rings to which prisoners were shackled are still fixed to the walls of the museum's prehistoric section. The museum contains a collection of fine paintings, including works by Corot, Goya and Watteau. Its finest possession is the Vénus du Mas d'Agenais, on show in the Gallo-Roman archaeology department. The gracefully proportioned Greek marble statue, dating from the 1st century BC, was found at nearby Mas d'Agenais in 1876.

CONDOM

Condom *Pl. Bossuet; tel: 05 62 28 00 80; e-mail: contact@tourisme-tenareze.com; www.tourisme-tenareze.com/gb/index.php (English). Open all year 0900–1200, 1400–1800.*

Boat trips €€ *Gascogne Navigation, Condom; tel: 05 62 28 46 46; e-mail: gascogne-navigation@club-internet.fr. Cruises Jul–Aug daily.*

The attractive country town of Condom stands on the River Baïse and its fine 17th- and 18th-century mansions speak of its importance as a centre for the trade in Armagnac, Gascony's rival to Cognac brandy. You can take a **boat trip** along the river, which was turned into a canal to ship Armagnac to Bordeaux, and rowing boats and motor boats are available for hire.

The town's focal point is the **Cathédrale de St-Pierre** (*Guided tours, tel: 05 62 28 00 80*), completed in 1531 and battered about a bit over the centuries. In 1569, during the Wars of Religion, the people of Condom paid a ransom of 30,000 francs to prevent the Huguenot army from demolishing it. Inside, there are big gallery windows – some of the stained glass is original, but most dates from the 19th

ⓘ Musée de l'Armagnac €€
*2 r. Jules Ferry, 32100
Condom; tel: 05 62 28 47 17;
www.condom.org/musee_
armagnac.htm. Open daily
except Tue, Apr–Oct 1000–
1200, 1500–1800;
Nov–Mar 1400–1700.*

Abbaye de Flaran €€
*Off the D142, 32310
Valence-sur-Baïse; tel: 05 62
28 50 19; e-mail:
mhue@cg.32.fr. Open daily
1000–1200, 1400–1800,
except Jul and Aug
0930–1900; closed
mid-Jan–mid-Feb.*

**Château du Busca-
Maniban €€** *Off the
D229, 3km south of
Cassaigne, near Condom;
tel: 05 62 28 40 38;
www.buscamaniban.com/
index-en.php. Open (guided
tour) Apr–Nov daily
1400–1800. Closed Sun.*

Château de Cassaigne
*€€ Cassaigne, near
Condom; tel: 05 62
28 04 02; e-mail:
chateaudecassaigne@
teleparc.net; www.
chateaudecassaigne.com.
Open (guided tour) mid-
Feb–late Jan daily
0900–1200, 1400–1900.
Closed Mon mid-Oct–
mid-Mar.*

century – and complex vaulting. Outside, the 16th-century cloisters, restored in the 19th century, now serve as offices for the Mairie.

The **Musée de l'Armagnac** houses a collection of vintage tools and machinery once used in local vineyards and features the history of the region's special spirit. The **Abbaye de Flaran**, 7km south of Condom, was founded by the Cistercians in 1151. Restored and extended over the centuries, it now serves as a regional cultural centre where concerts, dramatic performances and exhibitions are staged, but guided tours are available. Visitors are shown the abbey church, built 1180–1210, the 14th-century cloisters, the living quarters built to accommodate the prior and guests in the 18th century, the monastic buildings, monks' dormitory and dining room and the kitchens. Outside, there is a formal French garden with a herb plot.

Just over 10km southwest of Condom is the grand **Château du Busca-Maniban**, which is fronted by an expansive courtyard and has a terrace from which on a clear day you can see the Pyrénées. A splendid staircase leads from the imposing hall to a gallery supported by columns. Elegant pieces of period furniture are on show. The **Château de Cassaigne**, 7km southwest of the town, was built in the 13th century, though the present façade dates from the 1700s. For many centuries it served as the country residence of the Bishops of Condom. A tour of the castle includes the 16th-century kitchen, with big solid tables and benches, earthenware pots and jars and lots of copper and pewter utensils. For some visitors, however, the highlight will be the store where Armagnac is aged in oak barrels. An audio-

Opposite
Condom

visual presentation features the production of the brandy and there is a tasting session.

LABASTIDE-D'ARMAGNAC

 Labastide-d'Armagnac
Pl. Royale; tel: 05 58 44 67 56; e-mail: tourisme-labastide@wanadoo.fr; www.labastide-d-armagnac.com/eng/index.php3. Open all year.

 Ecomusée de l'Armagnac €€
Château Garreau, 40240 Labastide-d'Armagnac; tel: 05 58 44 88 38. Open Mon–Sat 0900–1200, 1400–1800; Sun and public holidays 1500–1800.

This small town of half-timbered houses built on a typical gridiron of streets probably looks much the same as it did when it was founded as an English *bastide* at the end of the 13th century. Its central square, pl. Royale, with its arcaded buildings, is said to have inspired Henri IV to build the pl. des Vosges in Paris. Henri spent some time in Labastide-d'Armagnac before he was enthroned.

The **Ecomusée de l'Armagnac** focuses on the famous liquor but also deals with the region's ecology, and nature trips into the surrounding terrain can be arranged. Off the D626, 3km southeast of the town, is **Notre-Dame-des-Cyclistes €€** (*off the D626, 3km southeast of Labastide-d'Armagnac. Open Tue–Sun 1430–1800; Jul–Aug 1000–1200 and 1430–1800*), the official chapel for France's racing cyclists. It also houses a small museum of cycling memorabilia. The full story is told on the website of the tourist office (in English).

LECTOURE

 Lectoure Hôtel-de-Ville, pl. du Général de Gaulle, 32700 Lectoure; tel: 05 62 68 70 22; e-mail: infos@lectoure.fr; www.lectoure.fr. Open all year.

 Musée Lapidaire €€ Open Jul and Aug daily 1000–1200, 1400–1900; rest of year 1000–1200, 1400–1700. Visits arranged through the tourist office.

Until the French Revolution Lectoure was always on the centre stage of the nation's history – and frequently suffered for it. It was built on a cliff for reasons of defence, which meant it repeatedly invited attack from invading armies. Its first occupants were the Lactoratii, a Celtic tribe who collaborated with the Romans at a time when other Gauls were at war with them. The Lactoratii were rewarded by being allowed to form a semi-independent republic and the city of Lactora became one of the most important in the region during Roman times.

Later it was knocked about by both the Visigoths and Normans and in the Middle Ages it became the capital of the counts of Armagnac. After the Hundred Years War the army of Louis XI attacked Lectoure and there was a long siege, which ended in an agreement that the Armagnacs would accept the king's authority while their own rights and those of the town would be guaranteed. But when the town gates were opened, the king's troops set fire to the town and murdered the count and most of the citizens.

The **Cathédrale St-Gervais et St-Protais** dates from 1488. On a clear day there is a stupendous view from the top of the bell tower. The **Musée Lapidaire** is in the Mairie, formerly the episcopal palace. It houses a collection of Gallo-Roman funeral monuments in the form of altars decorated with bulls' heads, which were found in the 19th century by workmen excavating under the cathedral. There is also a collection of Roman and Merovingian jewellery.

Accommodation and food

Hôtel de Bordeaux €–€€ *8 pl. Jasmin, Agen; tel: 05 53 68 46 46. Open all year.* The hotel has 22 rooms, but only nine have en-suite facilities. There is a restaurant.

Table des Cordeliers €–€€€ *R. Cordeliers, Condom; tel: 05 62 68 43 82; e-mail: info@latabledescordeliers.fr; www.latabledescordeliers.fr. Closed Oct–mid-Nov, 2–16 Jan, Sun night and Mon.* A comfortable restaurant with a dining terrace and private car park.

Atlantic Hôtel €€ *133 av. Jean Jaurès, Agen; tel: 05 53 96 16 56; www.agen-atlantic-hotel.fr/uk/default.asp. Open 2 Jan–24 Dec.* No restaurant but breakfast is available. Each of the hotel's 44 rooms has direct-dial telephone and television, but three do not have en-suite facilities. There is a swimming pool. Cars may be garaged or left in the private car park.

Chez Simone €€ *Opposite the church, Montréal; tel: 05 62 29 44 40. Closed Sun lunch and all day Mon, except Jul–Aug.* A pleasant restaurant offering good-value food, with a budget meal available at lunchtime.

Ferme de Flaran €€ *Route Condom, Valence-sur-Baïse; tel: 05 62 28 58 22; e-mail: hotel-flaran@wanadoo.fr; www.fermedeflaran.com.* Good accommodation and food (€€–€€€) in rural surroundings. There are 15 rooms with direct-dial telephones and television, a garden, dining terrace and a swimming pool.

Stim'Otel €€ *105 blvd Carnot, Agen; tel: 05 53 47 31 23; e-mail: stimotel@wanadoo.fr; www.stimotel.com or www.citotel.com. Open 2 Jan–24 Dec.* There are 58 en-suite rooms with direct-dial telephones and television. The restaurant (€€) is air conditioned and wine is available by the glass.

La Bohème €€–€€€ *14 r. Emile Sentini, Agen; tel: 05 53 68 31 00. Closed 15–30 Sep.* A simple, inexpensive (€) meal is served at lunchtime in this pleasant establishment, which has a terraced dining area and serves wine by the glass.

Hôtel de Bastard €€–€€€ *R. Lagrange, Lectoure; tel: 05 62 68 82 44; e-mail: hoteldebastard@wanadoo.fr; www.hotel-de-bastard.com. Closed mid-Dec–Jan.* Don't worry about the name – this is a legitimate, friendly hotel with 27 en-suite rooms in a tasteful 18th-century mansion. Each room has a direct-dial telephone and television. There is a swimming pool and garage parking. Traditional Gascon and Italian-inspired dishes appear on the menu in the restaurant (€€–€€€), which has an outside dining area.

Logis des Cordeliers €€–€€€ *R. de la Paix, Condom; tel: 05 62 28 03 68; e-mail: reception@logisdescordeliers.com; www.logisdescordeliers.com. Closed Jan.* The hotel has no restaurant, but breakfast is available. Its 21 en-suite rooms have direct-dial telephones and television. Swimming pool; private parking.

Opposite
Lectoure's early-morning market

● **Camping l'Oasis €**
*1120 av. des Pyrénées,
40190 Villeneuve-de-Marsan;
tel: 05 58 45 36 23. Open
all year.* Here's a rarity – a
campground that's open all
year. It has only 16 pitches
but you can rent a tent,
mobile home or chalet
and there are spaces for
motor homes. The site has
a takeaway food service
and bar.

Château de Fourcès €€€ *Fourcès; tel: 05 62 29 49 53; e-mail: contact
@chateau-fources.com; www.chateau-fources.com/inex.gb.htm (English).
Closed mid-Nov–Mar.* A magnificent castle set in the walled town of
Fourcès, a jewel of Gascony. Each of the 18 rooms is fitted with a bath
or shower room, direct telephone and television. Breakfast can be
taken in the room, in the dining room or on the terrace. The main
dining room inside the castle is lit by candles, and dinner is served
also on the outdoor terrace beside the swimming pool.

Hôtel Château des Jacobins €€€ *1 ter, pl. des Jacobins, Agen; tel: 05 53 47
03 31; e-mail: hotel@chateau-des-jacobins.com; www.chateau-des-
jacobins.com/swfEng/index.htm. Open all year.* The hotel has 15 en-
suite rooms with direct-dial telephones and television and there
is an enclosed car park. Tennis court. No restaurant, but breakfast
is available.

Hôtel Hélène Darroze €€€ *57 Grand Rue, Villeneuve-de-Marsan; tel: 05
58 45 20 07.* Three well-justified stars have been awarded to this hotel-
restaurant, which has 14 well-appointed en suite rooms and a
restaurant (**€€–€€€**) specialising in seafood and regional duck and game
dishes. The hotel has a garden, dining terrace and swimming pool.

Hôtel Hervé Garrapit €€€ *21 av. Armagnac, Villeneuve-de-Marsan; tel: 05
58 45 20 08; e-mail:info@herve-garrapit.com; www.herve-garrapit.com. Open
all year.* Nine en-suite rooms, a restaurant and swimming pool.

Hôtel des Trois Lys €€€ *38 r. Gambetta, Condom; tel: 05 62 28 33 33;
e-mail: hoteltroislys@wanadoo.fr; www.lestroislys.com. Closed Feb.
Restaurant closed Sun and Mon midday.* An elegant 18th-century
mansion, the hotel has 10 en-suite rooms with direct-dial telephones
and television. Wine is available by the glass in the restaurant
(**€€–€€€**). Swimming pool; enclosed parking.

Suggested tour

Total distance: The main route covers a total of 147km. The detour
totals 37km.

Time: Driving time for the main route is about 3 hours. Allow an
hour's driving for the detour.

Links: Agen is on the main route between the Atlantic Ocean and the
Mediterranean, with the A62 – the Autoroute des Deux Mers –
providing a fast link between Bordeaux and Montauban. North of
Agen the N21 travels 28km to Villeneuve-sur-Lot (*see page 197*).

Opposite
Labastide-d'Armagnac

Route: From **AGEN ❶** head south on the N21 for 36km to **LECTOURE**
❷ then take the D7 west for 16km to the village of Caussens.

Château de Monluc €€ *St-Puy; tel: 05 62 28 94 00; e-mail: administration@monluc.fr; www.monluc.fr. Open (guided tours) daily 1000–1200, 1500–1900. Closed Sun am, public holidays and Jan.*

Above
Montréal's Roman villa

Detour: From Caussens take the D204 south for 4km to St-Orens, a hilltop fortified village. Take the D232 west for 2km and turn left on to the D654, which in 4km reaches St-Puy, where you can visit the **Château de Monluc**, home of the cocktail ominously known as *pousse-rapière* – 'the rapier thrust'. It's made by steeping oranges in Armagnac then adding dry sparkling wine. Leave St-Puy by the D42 south and after 1.5km turn right on to the D142, which reaches **Valence-sur-Baïse** in 8km. With a typical gridiron of streets, Valence is a *bastide* founded in 1274. Continue on the D142, passing the **Abbaye de Flaran** to reach **Cassaigne** after 4.5km. Take the D208 west for 3km to **Mouchan**, an attractive village with a church dating in part from the 10th century. From Mouchan head north on the D931 for 10km to CONDOM ❸.

On the main route, from Caussens continue on the D7 west for 5km to Condom and leave on the D15 west. After 5km it's worth straying

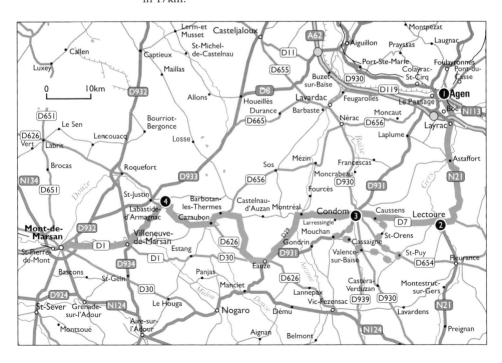

Musée Archéologique €€
Pl. de la Mairie, Montréal;
tel: 05 62 29 42 85. Open
Mar–Nov 1000–1200,
1400–1800.

Gallo-Roman Villa €€
Séviac; tel: 05 62 29 48 57;
www.seviac-villa.com. Open
Mar–mid-Nov daily
1000–1900.

just off the road to visit **Larressingle**, a 13th-century walled village reached by a bridge over a moat. You can take a walk around the ramparts to see the fortified church and a ruined keep. Further west, 10km on, the D15 reaches picturesque **Montréal**, founded as an English *bastide* in 1256. It has arcaded houses surrounding a central square. A collection of Gallo-Roman pottery and metal artefacts and a striking mosaic of trees are displayed in the **Musée Archéologique**. At **Séviac**, just outside Montréal, is the impressive archaeological site of a 4th-century **Gallo-Roman Villa**, with the ruins of the baths and a pool, some fine mosaics and two 7th-century skeletons.

From Montréal, head south on the D29 for 14km to the flourishing market town of Eauze, leaving on the D30 and after 3km heading northwest on the D626. After a further 2.5km bear right on to the D10, which soon becomes the D37. Turn left in 9km on to the D15 then left again after 2.5km on to the D656, reaching in 2km the spa town of **Barbotan-les-Thermes**, known since Roman times for the therapeutic properties of its mud.

Leave the spa town on the D656 and at Cazaubon, 3km away, follow the D626 for 11km to **LABASTIDE-D'ARMAGNAC** ❹. Next, take the D11 southwest for 14km to **Villeneuve-de-Marsan**, noted for its *foie gras* markets. From here, the D1 west reaches Mont-de-Marsan in 17km.

Northern Gascony and the Landes Regional Nature Park

Ratings

Museums	●●●●●
Nature	●●●●●
Outdoor activities	●●●●●
Children	●●●●○
Food and drink	●●●●○
Art and craft	●●●○○
Villages	●●●○○
Historic sites	●●○○○

The Landes has two distinctions based on size: it is the second largest *département* in France and it contains the largest forest in Europe – 600,000 hectares of cultivated trees, mostly maritime pines. And within that forest is the massive Parc Naturel Régional des Landes de Gascogne – 290,000 hectares set aside for the protection of wildlife and the environment and for humans to enjoy. Within its boundaries are waymarked tracks, footpaths, bridle paths and cycle routes and there are opportunities galore for canoeing, cycling, fishing, hiking and riding. It's all very green and very healthy, but until the second half of the 19th century the Landes was a region to avoid, where a few permanent inhabitants struggled to make a living as they went about on stilts tending miserable flocks of sheep in a desert of marshy moorland. Few landscapes have undergone a more dramatic transformation.

BELIN-BELIET

ⓘ Parc Naturel Régional des Landes de Gascogne *Maison du Parc, 33 route de Bayonne, Belin-Béliet; tel: 05 57 71 99 99; e-mail: info@parc-landes-de-gascogne.fr; www.parc-landes-de-gascogne.fr*

Belin-Béliet *Office de Tourisme, 6 av. Aliénor; tel: 05 56 88 06 14. Open Jul and Aug.*

Until the 11th century Belin was the capital of Gascony and a serious rival to Bordeaux. In 1122 the powerful Eleanor of Aquitaine, mother of Richard Coeur-de-Lion, was born here. In one sense, at least, this modest village on the banks of the Leyre river is a capital once again, for here is the headquarters of the **Parc Naturel Régional des Landes de Gascogne**. Today, a plaque on a low mound near the village centre identifies all that is left of the castle in which Eleanor was born. One survivor of her time, though, is the Eglise St-Pierre-de-Mons, on the edge of Belin, a stop for pilgrims on the road to Santiago de Compostela. Its bell tower was fortified during the Hundred Years War. Inside the church itself are four elaborately carved capitals.

About 3km out of the village, off the D110 west, is **Vieux-Lugo**, an ancient village that was abandoned in 1869 when the inhabitants decided to relocate on to a healthier site to the west. Its fortified,

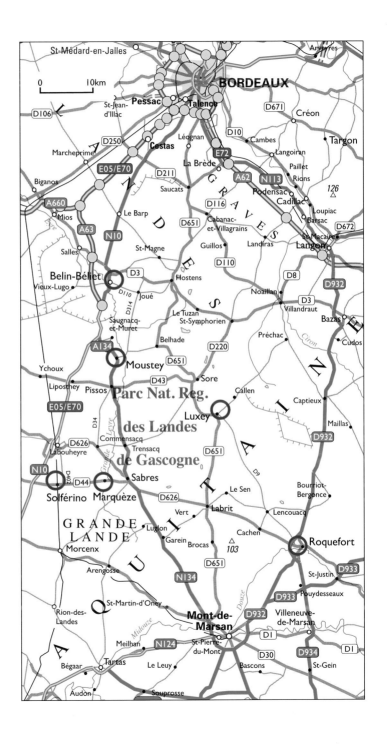

Centre d'Animation du Graoux *31 r. du Graoux, Belin-Béliet; tel: 05 57 71 99 29; e-mail: centre-graoux@parc-landes-de-gascogne.fr; www.parc-landes-de-gascogne.fr. Open all year.*

Romanesque church of St-Michel contains 16th-century frescoes illustrating the Seven Deadly Sins and the Works of Mercy. The **Centre d'Animation du Graoux**, just north of Belin-Béliet, offers courses in environmental studies and such outdoor activities as archery, canoeing, cycling and rambling.

Right
Belin-Béliet

LUXEY

Ecomusée de la Grande Lande €€ *Sabres (administration); tel: 05 58 08 31 31; e-mail: ecomusee-marqueze@parc-landes-de-gascogne.fr. The museum has sections at Luxey, Marquèze and Moustey, each illustrating a different aspect of daily life in the region during the 18th and 19th centuries. It was the first open-air folk museum in France when it opened in 1968. You can buy a discounted combination ticket for the three sections, even if you plan to visit them on different days.*

This attractive little village illustrates the dramatic changes that occurred as the ancient moorlands of the Landes gave way to the vast pine forest of today. The shepherds who had traditionally followed their flocks for centuries adapted to their new environment by becoming *gemmeurs* – resin tappers. The sticky discharge from the pine trees is the raw material for turpentine and rosin oil and was very much in demand from the beginning of the Industrial Revolution until the introduction of synthetic products after World War II.

The story of the *gemmeurs* and their way of life is told at the **Atelier des produits résineux Jacques et Louis Vidal**, part of the **Ecomusée de la Grande Lande** (*Luxey; tel: 05 58 07 56 85. Open Jun–Sept daily 1000–1200 and 1400–1900; Apr–May Mon–Fri 1000–1200, Sat 1400–1900, Sun 1000–1200 and 1400–1900; Oct Sun only 1000–1200 and 1400–1900. Closed Nov–Mar and public holidays*). Located in an old resin distillery founded in 1859 and in operation until 1954, the workshop demonstrates the various stages in the traditional production of turpentine and other products. The industry's heyday was during the American Civil War (1861–5) when imports from the United States were cut off and the price of resin rose by more than 600 per cent. Today, there are about 50 *gemmeurs* still working in the forest, compared with an estimated 30,000 at the beginning of the 20th century.

MARQUEZE

Le Quartier de Marquèze €€

Sabres; tel: 05 58 08 31 31; www.parcs-landes-de-gascogne.fr. Jun–Sep train departures from Sabres daily every 40 minutes 1010–1210, 1400–1720 (last train returns from Marquèze 1900); Apr–May Mon–Fri 1500, returning 1730, Sat 1400–1720, Sun as Jun–Sep; Oct Mon–Fri 1500–1640, Sat 1400–1640, Sun 1010–1210, 1400–1640. Closed Nov–Mar.

There's only one way you can get to Marquèze, and that is by special steam train from Sabres. The 5km journey takes 10 minutes. This section of the folk museum is called **Le Quartier de Marquèze**.

In the past, *communes* in the Landes were divided into *quartiers*. One would contain the church, school, local government offices and shops, and others would contain farm workers' cottages, agricultural buildings and particular areas of farmland. Marquèze covers 70 hectares and is a reconstruction of an abandoned *quartier* of Sabres.

Most of the 30 or so traditional buildings date from the late 19th century, and a few were recovered from *quartiers* elsewhere. They are spaced around an *airial*, a clearing in the forest, with the *Maison du Maître* – the landowner's house – taking the central position. In addition to houses for the tenant farmer and labourers, there are pig-sties, barns, beehives and hen houses built on stilts to keep foxes out. A waymarked trail leads through woodland to the miller's house and the mill itself and ends where the charcoal burners work.

There are daily demonstrations of baking, the miller grinds grains Mon, Wed and Fri, and resin-tapping is demonstrated on Tue. Exhibits on the Landes, documents, maps and models are on show in an information centre. In a separate area there is a model orchard with more than 1600 varieties of apple, cherry, medlar, plum, quince and other fruit trees native to the region. A snack bar and restaurant are on the site.

MOUSTEY

Syndicat d'Initiative *Pl. de la Mairie; tel: 05 58 07 70 00.*

Standing at the confluence of the Grande and Petite Leyre rivers, the village of Moustey has two 13th-century churches in its central square: St-Martin was built as the parish church; Notre-Dame, a stop for the Santiago de Compostela pilgrims, now houses the **Musée du Patrimoine**

Right
Moustey's Museum of Religion and Popular Beliefs

Eglise Notre-Dame
*Tel: 05 58 08 01 39.
Open Jul and Aug daily
1000–1200, 1400–1900;
Jun, Sep at weekends.*

**Musée du Patrimoine
Religieux et des
Croyances Populaires**
*€€ Moustey; tel: 05 58 07
70 01. Open Jun–Sep daily
1000–1200, 1400–1900,
Sat 1400–1800, Sun
1000–1200, 1400–1800;
rest of year visits by
appointment.*

Right
Moustey's Notre-Dame

Opposite
Detail of flying buttress,
Eglise Ste-Marie, Roquefort

Religieux et des Croyances Populaires, the third part of the Grande Lande folk museum. There are regularly changing exhibitions illustrating local religious beliefs and superstitions and the conflicts that sometimes arose between local churchgoers and the pilgrims.

ROQUEFORT

**Syndicat
d'Initiative** *Pl. du
Soleil d'Or, Roquefort; tel: 05
58 45 50 46; e-mail: ville-
roquefort@wanadoo.fr*

**Maison de la
Chasse** *€€ 149
chemin Faisans,
Pouydesseaux, on the D934,
8km south of Roquefort;
tel: 05 58 93 92 33; e-mail:
contact@fedechasseurslandes.
asso.fr. Open daily 0900–
1200, 1400–1700.*

This is **not** the place where they make the famous cheese. This Roquefort is in the Landes, about 22km northeast of Mont-de-Marsan, and its towers and ramparts, dating from the 12th and 14th centuries, testify that it was once a fortified town. Its Gothic church, with a square tower and arrow slits, was founded in the 11th century by the Benedictine monks of St-Sever. The church was later used by a hospitaller order of Antonites who looked after people suffering from 'St Anthony's Fire' or ergotism, a type of food poisoning caused by eating diseased cereal.

The tiny hamlet of Pouydesseaux, 8km to the south, is noted for its **Maison de la Chasse**, a museum dedicated to pigeon shooting, a popular pastime in the Landes and a major contributor to the region's dining tables.

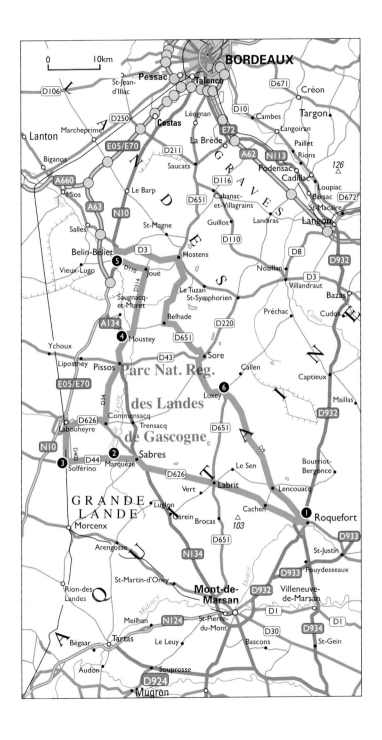

Dax–Biarritz

Ratings

Art	●●●●●
Pelota	●●●●●
Surfing	●●●●●
Beaches	●●●●○
Nightlife	●●●●○
Spa treatments	●●●●○
History	●●●○○
Architecture	●●○○○

Biarritz, originally a small whaling port, has developed into the foremost seaside resort of Southwest France. It has good bathing and surfing, a couple of casinos, a Museum of the Sea and about a dozen golf courses. Drive northeast from Biarritz, at the threshold of the Basque Country, to the urban sprawl of the French Basque capital, Bayonne, on to the Landes spa city of Dax, with its hot springs, to the bullfighting centre of Mont-de-Marsan. Bayonne, an administrative and industrial centre, is a major port on the wide River Adour. One of its famous products is Bayonne ham. The Musée Bonnat is a mecca for art lovers, displaying works by some of the world's greatest painters. The *Fontaine Chaude* in Dax gushes 2400 cubic metres of water daily, and its constant temperature is 64°C: several hotels offer thermal treatments.

BIARRITZ

 **Comité Départemental du Tourisme Béarn Pays Basque** 2 allée des Platanes, 64100 Bayonne; tel: 05 59 46 52 52; www.bearn-basquecountry.com. Open all year.

Office de Tourisme 1 square d'Ixelles, 64200 Biarritz; tel: 05 59 22 37 00; www.biarritz.fr. Open daily Jul and Aug 0800–2000; Sep–Jun Mon–Sat 0900–1800, Sun 1000–1700.

History

This great playground of the Southwest was a small whaling port until sea bathing became popular in the 19th century. It was Eugénie de Montijo, the future wife of Napoleon III, who launched the fashion for sea bathing, and Biarritz – with its fine sandy beaches, its setting between the ocean and the foothills of the Pyrenees and its gentle climate – soon developed as a glittering holiday resort. In 1854 Napoleon and Eugénie had a summer villa built there (where the Hôtel du Palais is today), and many followed their example.

Today much of the coast is lined with smart villas and homes and about a quarter of the population are retired residents. Biarritz has become an important conference venue. A buzzing nightlife centred on the gaming tables, and other late-night spots, attracts holiday-makers all year. As well as family beaches there are some of the

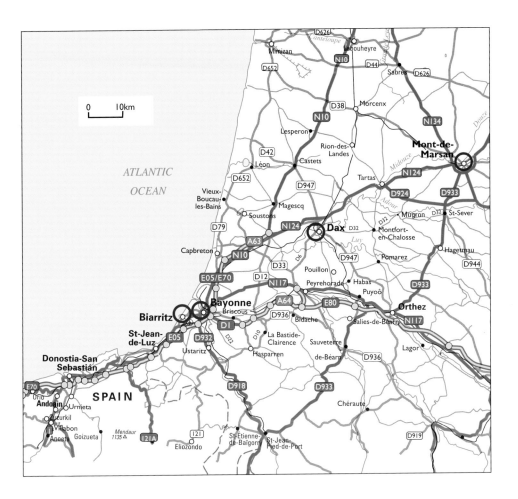

Le Phare/
Lighthouse € *Pointe*
St-Martin, Biarritz. Open Jul
and Aug daily 1000–1200,
1500–1900. Closed Mon.
For a view of Biarritz and
beyond it to the Basque
Pyrenees climb the steps up
to the top of the
lighthouse, which stands
73m above sea level.

Fast play

Every Basque town and village has its *fronton* where *pelota*, involving a wall
and a ball – it's described as the world's fastest ball game – is played. There
are various forms of the game, the most spectacular being one in which
wicker 'gloves' are worn. Guides to the big matches can be obtained from
the Agence Touristique du Pays Basque. Children learn to play from a
young age. The very fast version of *pelota* that has become popular in the
USA and Central America in the past 35 years, Cesta Punta (or jai alai), is
played in summer contests in Biarritz.

Hippodrome des Fleurs €€ *Av. du Lac Marion, Biarritz. For information on events and race days, tel: 05 59 41 27 34 or contact the tourist office; e-mail hippodrome-biarritz@wanadoo.fr; www.hippodrome-biarritz.com.* This is where competitive riding events take place and trotting races are held regularly.

Musée de la Mer €€ *Esplanade du Rocher de la Vierge, Biarritz; tel: 05 59 22 33 34; www.museedelamer.com. Open daily all year, mid-Jun–mid-Sep 0930–1900 (to midnight mid-Jul and all of Aug), rest of year 0930–1230, 1400–1800. (Feeding time 1030 and 1700.)*

Musée Historique de Biarritz €€ *R. Broquedis, Biarritz; tel: 05 59 24 86 28; e-mail: avb.mhb @laposte.net. Open Tue–Sat 1000–1200, 1430–1830.*

The surf also rises

Surfing in the waves on the Biarritz beaches was popularised by film scriptwriter Peter Viertel during the shooting of *The Sun Also Rises* in the 1950s. Viertel, husband of actress and film star Deborah Kerr, introduced some of surfing's pioneers to Biarritz, and they found it an ideal location for the sport. The pounding Atlantic waves have made Biarritz a world-class surfing centre ever since.

world's best surfing beaches and rocky headlands on which Atlantic rollers crash dramatically.

Surfing is just one of the sports at which the Basques excel. They are passionate about rugby and have a great reputation for ball games such as *pelota*, bred into them by a pedigree of generations of *pelota* players. Golf is an obsession, with a good choice of courses for visitors and locals: the first course in Biarritz was opened in 1888. Sea-water treatments (thalassotherapy) are a speciality in Biarritz, recommended for good health and mental stability.

Musée de la Mer

This is a combined museum, aquarium and scientific research centre, which was founded in 1835. A display on whaling, a study of the ocean in the Biarritz area, conservation matters, boat models, navigational aids and fishing methods, many fish species in a series of aquaria, and seals and sharks in an underwater tank – these are just some of the exhibits that make this an interesting place to visit. Shore birds and sea birds of the area, and birds of the Pyrenees may be seen in the ornithology gallery, where recordings of their calls are played. From a terrace visitors can watch seals having their twice-daily feed and get a great view along the coast.

Musée Historique de Biarritz

In the early days when sea bathing first became fashionable in the 19th century, Biarritz grew from a small whaling port into a resort favoured by the crowned heads of Europe, the rich and the famous. This was before the days of the railway. Some made the journey across country. A wicker seat was mounted on the back of a donkey or mule, enabling ladies in elaborate gowns to lounge gracefully aboard while a young maiden led the animal. Between the two World Wars dinner parties and casinos were attended by such celebrated visitors as Winston Churchill, Charlie Chaplin and Ernest Hemingway. Later visitors included the Duke and Duchess of Windsor, Frank Sinatra and Rita Hayworth. All these times and other aspects of old Biarritz are recalled through pictures and paraphernalia at the small museum.

Plateau de l'Atalaye *(for more information, contact the tourist office)*

The last of the Biarritz watchtowers is here. From it, centuries ago, smoke signals were sent to announce that a school of whales had been sighted, and the men would take to the boats in pursuit. The area can be explored by a series of reefs, causeways and tunnels between rocky islands. A footpath leads to the Virgin's Rock landmark. The Plateau provides a view of the Port des Pêcheurs – now used by pleasure craft rather than fishing boats.

A marble statue of the Virgin Mary stands on the largest rock on the Plateau de l'Atalaye. Choose a calm day to walk to it – in windy weather great waves crash aggressively over the footbridge leading to Virgin's Rock.

Institut Louison Bobet (Thalassotherapy) €€€
11 av. Louison Bobet; tel: 05 59 24 20 80. One of the many Thalassotherapy centres in Biarritz.

Below
Biarritz seafront

Thalassotherapy

Sea-water baths and allied treatments were introduced in the Hôtel Miramar in 1979 by champion cyclist Louison Bobet. There are other centres along the Basque coast. Warm sea-water baths, mud and seaweed baths are administered with advanced techniques for the treatment of stress, rheumatism and back problems, poor circulation, excess weight and tobacco dependency. New mothers are said to benefit from postnatal treatments.

BAYONNE

ⓘ Bayonne *Pl. des Basques, Bayonne; tel: 08 20 42 64 64; e-mail: infos@ bayonne-tourisme.com. Open daily in high season 0900–1900, Sun 1000–1300; off-peak Mon–Fri 0900–1800 and Sat 1000–1800, closed Sun. Guided tours take place in July and Aug for individuals and groups, in French, English, German and Spanish. Information from the tourist office.*

ⓗ Cathédrale de Ste-Marie € *Grand Bayonne; tel: 05 59 59 17 82. Open Mon–Sat 0700–1230, 1500–1900, Sun 1500–1745.*
Cloisters €€ *Open Jun–Sep 0930–1230, 1400–1800, rest of year to 1700.*

Musée Bonnat €€ *5 r. Jacques Laffitte, Bayonne; tel: 05 59 59 08 52. Open daily 1000–1830, Wed to 2130.*

ⓐ Markets take place in Bayonne every morning except Sun (all day on Fri) in modern covered market premises along the quai de Cdt Roquebert.

ⓑ River cruises €€ *Tel: 05 59 59 21 93. Half-day cruises are from 1400–1800 and full-day excursions are from 1030–1630.*

River boat cruises are available in the season on the River Adour, departing from allée Boufflers.

Opposite
The port of Bayonne

History

The capital of the French Pays Basque is a sprawling commercial and administrative centre and an important port. It is worth a visit for the old quarters of Grand Bayonne, with its pedestrianised shopping streets, and Petit Bayonne. To the east of Petit Bayonne is the Château Neuf, a great fortification built around 1460 at the end of three centuries of English rule: it is not open to the public. Adjacent to the Château Neuf, outside the walls built by Vauban, is the Parc de Mousserolles, a pleasant place to walk or relax, which has a lake and a children's playground.

Between the old quarters flows the River Nive, at right angles to the River Adour. Big cargo ships berth on the Adour, and visitors are also catered for, with half- and full-day river cruises. The front of Bayonne's Gothic cathedral, dating from the 13th century, is reminiscent of the Cathedral of Reims. The town is known for its Bayonne ham and its bullfights. In the festival at the beginning of August, bullfights take place and there's dancing in the street.

Cathédrale de Ste-Marie

The majestic Gothic-style cathedral in the old town was built between the 13th and 16th centuries; its twin steeples are 19th-century additions. The cathedral was one of the stopping places on the pilgrimage route to Compostela. There is some fine Renaissance stained glass in the nave and the Chapelle St-Jerôme. The remaining cloisters are from the 14th century.

Izarra Distillery (€ *9 Quai Bergeret, Quartier St-Esprit, Bayonne. Open Mon–Fri 0900–1130 and 1400–1830, also Sat in peak season*). Visitors can learn about the history and production of Bayonne's sweet liqueur, from the gathering of Pyrénéan herbs to the final alcoholic delight with its hint of brandy and spices.

Maison du Jambon de Bayonne (€ *route de Samadet, Arzacq; tel: 05 59 04 49 35; www.jambon-de-bayonne.com*). *Open Tue–Sat 1000–1300 and 1430–1830.* Learn about the curing process and other aspects of the celebrated local ham, and enjoy a sample.

Musée Bonnat

Léon Bonnat, the portraitist, was born in Bayonne in 1833. He was an ardent collector of paintings and sculptures and when he died in 1922 he left his priceless collection to Bayonne. Musée Bonnat is regarded by many as the most important art museum of Southwest France, with works by Botticelli, Degas, Delacroix, El Greco, Goya, Rembrandt, Rubens, Van Dyck and other all-time greats. The basement is devoted to archaeology, the nucleus of the exhibits having come from Bonnat's collection, which included Greek statuettes, amphorae and Italian glass.

DAX

ⓘ Dax *11 cours Foch, Dax; tel: 05 58 56 86 86; e-mail: info @dax-tourisme.com; www.dax-tourisme.com. Open all year, Jul and Aug daily 0930–1900; Apr–Jun, Sep & Oct 0930–1230, 1400–1830, Sun 1000–1200, 1500–1700; Nov–Mar 0930–1230, 1400–1800 but closed Sat pm and all day Sun.*

ⓜ Musée de l'Aviation € *Base Navelet, 58 av. de l'Aérodrome, 40104 Dax; tel: 05 58 74 66 19. Open Feb–Nov.*

Les Arènes €€ *Parc Théodore Denis, Dax. The cow fights calendar is available from the Departmental Tourist Board of the Landes; tel: 05 58 90 99 09.*

Cathédrale Notre-Dame € *(donations welcome) R. St-Pierre, Dax. Open daily.*

Musée de Borda and Crypte Archéologique €€ *R. Cazade, Dax; tel: 05 58 74 12 91. Open Mar–Nov daily except Tue, Sun and public holidays.*

ⓡ River cruises €€ *Adour Plaisance, quai du 28ème Bataillon de Chasseurs; tel: 05 58 74 87 07.*

A four-hour boat trip on the Adour embarks from Dax at 1400.

Upstream of Bayonne, the River Adour graces Dax, just over the Pyrenees-Atlantique border in Landes. Dax is one of France's premier thermal spa towns, a centre for bullfighting and an attractive place to visit, with its hot water fountain, riverside walks and its 17th-century buildings in the r. Neuve. It has **museums** of *foie gras* and **aviation**, and another displaying curiosities from Roman times to the 20th century.

Many people go to Dax to take the cure for a range of conditions. This usually means a three-week stay, but you can take a week-long 'get into shape' fitness course. One-day stress relief treatments are another option. The hot mud treatments are said to be particularly beneficial for rheumatism sufferers. A dozen hotels in Dax are connected to thermal establishments.

Les Arènes

This grand building from the early 1900s is where bullfights and cow fights are staged between March and October. In cow fights the *escarteur* (from *'faire un écart'* – 'to swerve') has to pit his last-minute swerving skills against the brute strength of the cow, or leap over its horns as it charges. Portuguese-style *corridas* – bullfighting on horseback – take place here. A festival week of celebration centred on bulls and cows is held in August.

Bois de Boulogne

This old oak forest in the west of Dax has been put to good use as a leisure park. It stretches for 6km and contains a golf driving range, jogging circuit, riding school, lake, woodland paths and a restaurant.

Cathédrale Notre-Dame

This is the third cathedral to have been built on the same site: one was destroyed in 1295 by the English; another collapsed in the 17th century. Some of the material was used in the present building. Choir stalls and a fine doorway in the north transept are among treasures retrieved from earlier centuries.

Fontaine Chaude

Dax is worth visiting for this wonder alone. The natural hot spring was known to the Romans; now, channelled through a trio of ornate 'taps' in the town centre, it dispenses 2400 cubic metres of 64°C water a day into a vast basin.

Musée de Borda

This fascinating museum of curiosities, coins and collectables from diverse times and places is named after a seaman who was also a great marine engineer, mathematician and maker of navigational instruments,

Jean-Charles de Borda. He was born in Dax in 1733. A statue of him stands in pl. Thiers. Opposite the museum is the **Crypte Archéologique** – the foundations of a Gallo-Roman temple discovered in the 1970s.

Below
Market day in Dax

MONT-DE-MARSAN

ⓘ Mont-de-Marsan 6
*pl. du Général Leclerc,
Mont-de-Marsan;
tel: 05 58 05 87 37;
www.mont-de-marsan.org.
Open in high season Mon–Sat
0900–1830; off-peak
0900–1230, 1330–1800.
Guided tours available by
appointment.*

**ⓜ Musée Despiau-
Wlérick** €€ *Pl.
Marguerite de Navarre,
Mont-de-Marsan;
tel: 05 58 75 00 45.
Open all year Wed–Mon
1000–1200, 1400–1800.
Free entry Mon.*

Below
Mont-de-Marsan

As well as being an administrative centre for the southeast region of the Landes, Mont-de-Marsan is a noted bullfighting centre and also a famous horse-racing venue. There are 12 events a year at the racecourse – steeplechase meetings, flat racing or trotting races. The foremost bullfighters of Spain and the French Basque country compete in bull and cow events in Mont-de-Marsan, and visitors are assured that the animals are not killed. In July these human-versus-bovine events and other activities and entertainments are presented in the **Fêtes de la Madeleine**, in which the whole town celebrates.

Mont-de-Marsan lies at the confluence of the rivers Douze and Midou, known as Midouze, and has some lovely old riverside houses. Information on guided tours of the town is available at the tourist office.

Named after two sculptors who were born in Mont-de-Marsan within eight years of one another and who died in the mid-1940s, the **Musée Despiau-Wlérick** is in two sections; linking them is a central gallery where temporary exhibitions are staged. Charles Despiau and Robert Wlérick each have a floor devoted to their works. Two other floors present sculptures by their contemporaries.

Accommodation and food

Biarritz Camping
€ *28 route d'Harcet,
Biarritz; tel: 05 59 23 00
12; e-mail:
Biarritz.Camping@wanadoo.
fr; www.biarritz-camping.fr.
Open May–Sep.* Waterside
setting with 196 pitches,
grocery store, takeaway
food and bar. Mobile
homes and chalets can be
rented.

Camping Les Chênes €
*Bois de Boulogne, Dax;
tel: 05 58 90 05 53;
e-mail: camping-chenes@
orange.fr; www.camping-les-
chenes.fr. Open late
Mar–early Nov.* Well-
equipped site with chalets
and mobile homes.
Amenities include grocery
store, takeaway food, bar,
swimming pool and
launderette.

Club Hippique € *Bois de Boulogne, Dax; tel: 05 58 74 09 14. Open Mar–Oct.* Gîte sleeping 20 in the spacious recreational woodland park, offering riding on site or long distance. Individuals or groups.

Hôtel Peyroux € *8 av. Victor Hugo, Dax; tel: 05 58 90 49 49. Open Mar–Nov.* The hotel has 19 en-suite rooms.

Chez Albert €–€€ *Port des Pêcheurs, Biarritz; tel: 05 59 24 43 84; www.chezalbert.fr. Open all year.* Locals and visitors go here for the good seafood and value for money.

Best Western Calicéo €€ *R. du Centre Aéré, St-Paul-les-Dax (across the river from Dax); tel: 05 58 90 66 00; e-mail: caliceo@thermesdous.com. Open all year.* A modern hotel and spa resort overlooking a lake.

Grand Hôtel-Thermes Adour €€ *R. de la Source, Dax; tel: 05 58 90 53 00; e-mail: grandhotel@thermesadour.com; www.thermes-dax.com. Open all year.* The 3-star hotel has 129 en-suite rooms in different styles.

Hôtel Climat de France €€ *N10, Aéroport de Parme, Biarritz; tel: 05 59 23 40 41. Open all year.* All 74 rooms are en suite. The restaurant is gratifyingly easy on the pocket in this 2-star hotel.

Hôtel Ibis Miradour €€ *Av. Milliés-Lacroix, Dax; tel: 05 58 56 77 77; e-mail: H5002@accor.com. Open all year.* The Miradour has 120 en-suite rooms and a restaurant.

Hôtel Monbar €€ *24 r. Pannecau, Bayonne; tel: 05 59 59 26 80. Closed mid-Sep–mid-Oct.* Small 1-star hotel with 10 rooms, all with facilities.

Hôtel Tulip Inn Louisiane €€ *R. Guy Petit, Biarritz; tel: 05 59 22 20 20; e-mail: hotel.louisiane.biarritz@wanadoo.fr; www.louisiane-biarritz.com. Open all year.* Seventy-seven rooms in a modern hotel close to the city centre with easy access to the motorway system, rail station and airport. Excellent restaurant, **Le Baton Rouge €€**.

Restaurant du Bois de Boulogne €€ *Allée du Bois de Boulogne, Dax; tel: 05 58 74 23 32. Open all year.* Regional fare and good seafood give this restaurant much repeat business.

Hôtel Frantour Loustau €€–€€€ *Pl. de la République, Bayonne; tel: 05 59 55 08 08. Open all year.* A 3-star hotel with 44 en-suite rooms and a restaurant.

Hôtel Le Renaissance €€–€€€ *225 av. Villeneuve, Mont-de-Marsan; tel: 05 58 51 51 51; e-mail: lerenaissance@wanadoo.fr; www.hotel-restaurant-renaissance.com. Open all year.* The 3-star hotel has 29 en-suite rooms, with wifi internet access. There is a restaurant (**€€**) and a swimming pool.

Sofitel Thalassa Miramar €€€ *13 r. Louison Bobet, Biarritz; tel: 05 59 41 30 00. Open all year.* Modern 4-star hotel with 126 en-suite rooms, a

good restaurant (€€–€€€), swimming pool and a thalassotherapy centre.

Suggested tour

Total distance: The main route covers 125km. The detour totals 47km.

Time: Allow at least 3 hours for driving the main route, but give yourself a whole day to make the most of it – or take in an overnight stop.

Links: From Mont-de-Marsan you can head northeast towards Agen (*see pages 222–3*) on the D933, north towards Bordeaux (*see pages 42–53*) on the D932 or northwest through the Parc Régional des Landes de Gascogne towards Arcachon (*see pages 262–4*) or Bordeaux.

Musée de la Chalosse €€
Domaine de Carcher, Montfort-en-Chalosse; tel: 05 58 98 69 27; e-mail: musee.chalosse@libertysurf.fr; www.museedelachalosse.fr/ musee. Open Apr–Oct 1000–1200, 1400–1830; Nov–Mar Tue–Fri 1400–1800.

Abbaye d'Arthous €€
Peyrehorade; tel: 05 58 73 03 89; e-mail: arthous@cg40.fr. Open Wed–Mon 0930–1200, 1400–1700. Closed Nov and public holidays.

Route: From **MONT-DE-MARSAN ❶** take the D933 southwest for 14km to St-Sever, which looks out over the Adour river and the huge expanse of the Landes pine forests to the north. The Benedictine abbey church here, founded in 988, has marble columns that originally graced the palace of a Roman governor.

Head west from the town on the D32, which rolls through some lovely countryside, reaching Mugron after 17km and Montfort-en-Chalosse after a further 9km. Founded as an English *bastide* in the 13th century, Montfort is a small hill town where the **Musée de la Chalosse** features country life in the 19th century. Continue on the D32 for 18km to reach the outskirts of **DAX ❷**. Follow the D106 west for 2km, then head south on the D6 for 16km, joining the D33 for 5km into Peyrehorade, once a major river port and now enjoying a new life as a centre for leisure boating.

On the south side of the river, off the D19, is the restored **Abbaye d'Arthous**, founded in 1167, a staging post on the road to Santiago de Compostela and used as farm buildings after the Revolution. Take the D19 south for 10km to Bidache then head west on the D936.

Above
Scenic coastline

Detour: Leave Bidache on the D936 and after 10km, just beyond the hamlet of Nogues, turn left on to the D10: a winding, hilly road reaches La Bastide-Clairence, founded by the king of Navarre in 1314, in 5km and Hasparren in a further 5km. Workaday Hasparren is on the Route Impériale des Cimes, a military road constructed on the orders of Napoleon I to link Bayonne and St-Jean-Pied-de-Port. It is a lovely road with views of the Pyrenees and of the Basque coastline. From Hasparren to St-Pierre-d'Irube, along the Route Impériale (now the D22), is 24km. The D936 covers the final 3km into Bayonne.

Continuing the main route from Bidache, follow the D936 east for 17km to Briscous, then the D312 for 14km to **BAYONNE ❸**. There are a number of routes you can take from Bayonne to **BIARRITZ ❹**, which are less than 8km apart as the crow flies, but you can follow the Adour for 6km to its mouth on the D309, south of the river, then follow the road along the coast for 7km into Biarritz.

Also worth exploring

Continuing south along the coast from Biarritz brings you to **St-Jean-de-Luz**, a whaling port from as early as the 11th century, but a popular resort since the 1840s.

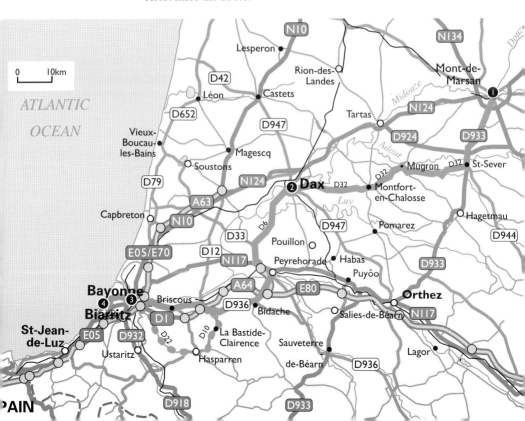

The Southern Côte d'Argent

Ratings

Beaches	●●●●●
Children	●●●●●
Outdoor activities	●●●●●
Food and drink	●●●●○
Villages	●●●●○
Architecture	●●●○○
Boat trips	●●●○○
Museums	●●●○○

The southern half of the Côte d'Argent – between Biarritz and Arcachon – is a paradise for watersports enthusiasts, especially surfers. Those who feel the rolling waters of the Atlantic Ocean might be a bit too much, however, will still be able to enjoy themselves in the cool, clear – and tranquil – waters of the lakes and lagoons a short distance inshore. On lake or sea you can join in a host of waterborne activities – sailing, surfboarding, canoeing – or simply relax in the sun. There are sandy beaches on the lake shores as well as at the seaside. There are splendid seaside resorts and quaint old villages of traditional houses and ancient churches to be discovered, and for cyclists and ramblers a network of trails and paths crisscrosses the pine woods fringing the coast. Campers will find no shortage of places to pitch a tent, or set up their caravan or motor home.

BISCARROSSE

**Office de Tourisme**
55 pl. G. Dufau; tel: 05 58 78 20 96; e-mail: biscarrosse@biscarrosse.com; www.biscarrosse.com. Open Jul and Aug daily 0900–2000; off-peak 1000–1200, 1400–1700.

About 10km inland, Biscarrosse nonetheless has a waterfront setting, located as it is between two lakes – the Petit Etang de Biscarrosse and the very much larger Etang de Biscarrosse et de Parentis. A 2km canal at the northern end of the town forms a link with another large lake, the Etang de Cazaux et de Sanguinet. Before World War II Biscarrosse was an important seaplane base and its story is told in the **Musée Historique de l'Hydraviation**. The museum exhibits models, documents and parts of original aircraft, both civil and military. There is a section on the early days of France's airmail service, and seaplanes and flying boats can be viewed in a giant glass hangar. The pioneer airmail pilot and writer Antoine de Saint-Exupéry used to enjoy sitting in the shade of the ancient elm tree standing in the town's main square. In the past, unfaithful wives were brought to the tree to be shamed, but legend has it that when an innocent woman was brought forward the tree formed a crown of white leaves over her head – a

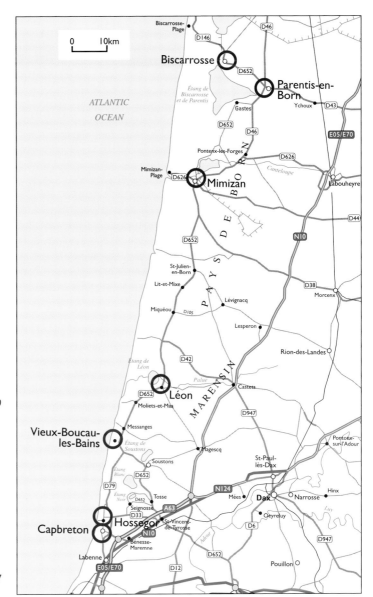

Musée Historique de l'Hydraviation
€€ 332 ave. Louis Breguet, Biscarrosse; tel: 05 58 78 00 65; e-mail: musee.hydraviation@ville-biscarrosse.fr; www.latecoere.com/expos/hydra.htm. Open Jul and Aug daily 1000–1900; Apr–Jun and Sep 1500–1900; rest of year daily 1400–1800. Adapted for disabled and blind people.

Bisca Surf Club €–€€
197 chemin de Mathiou, Biscarrosse; tel: 05 58 78 27 29. Open Apr–Oct, daily in Jul and Aug. A lively club for surfing and body-boarding in the Atlantic breakers on the beaches south of Biscarrosse, with a surf school and qualified instructors.

phenomenon it now displays each year. **Biscarrosse-Plage**, on the coast as you might guess, is a modern seaside resort offering the usual beach and watersports. The advantage here is that if the Atlantic rollers are coming in too fiercely you can move inland to enjoy the calm of the sandy beaches around the lakes.

CAPBRETON

ℹ **Office de Tourisme**
Av. Georges Pompidou,
Capbreton; tel: 05 58 72 12
11; e-mail: capbreton.
tourisme@wanadoo.fr; www.
capbreton-tourisme.com/
ang-44.htm. Open all year.

🏛 **Ecomusée de la
Pêche et de la Mer**
€€ Maison du Port, av.
Georges Pompidou, Capbreton;
tel: 05 58 72 40 50; e-mail:
contact@
ecopeche.fr; www.ecopeche.fr.
Open Jul–Aug 1000–2230,
rest of year 1400–1830
(Oct–Mar Wed & weekends
only). Closed Jan.

Until the 14th century Capbreton was an important whaling and fishing port, then the River Adour changed course and left the place high and dry. It got a new lease of life in the 19th century when Napoléon III began to farm oysters, but the real boost came in the 1930s when property developers started to move in and Capbreton achieved popularity as a resort. Today, it is very much a modern seaside town, separated from neighbouring Hossegor (*see below*) by the Boudigau canal. Bathers are warned to swim only from those designated areas of beach which are protected by lifeguards. Elsewhere there are dangers from the pounding Atlantic rollers. Capbreton's main shore-based attraction is the **Ecomusée de la Pêche et de la Mer**, which features the history of the local fishing industry and marine geology with an aquarium, fossils, shells and model ships. From the museum's terrace you can enjoy a panoramic view of the coast. Offshore, just outside the harbour, lies the **Fosse de Capbreton**, an underwater chasm more than 60km long, up to 10km wide and some 3000m deep.

HOSSEGOR

ℹ Pl. des Halles,
Hossegor; tel: 05 58
41 79 00; e-mail: hossegor.
tourisme@wanadoo.fr;
www.hossegor.fr. Open all
year.

Capbreton's next-door neighbour became a colony for writers and artists in the early 1900s and has since benefited from careful development which has preserved its natural wooded setting of pines and cork oak. Today there are gardens, hotels, a casino, parks and a golf course. Thanks to the powerful groundswell produced by the Fosse de Capbreton (*see above*), the town has become a mecca for surfers, especially during the second half of August each year when the Hossegor Rip Curl championship for professional surfers is staged. For those who prefer calmer conditions, especially toddlers, the tidal salt-water Lac d'Hossegor is ideal. There are sandy beaches, and canoeing, sailing and windsurfing are available.

LEON

ℹ **Office de
Tourisme** 65 pl.
Jean-Baptiste Courtiau; tel:
05 58 48 76 03; e-mail:
ot.leon@ wanadoo.fr;
www.ot-leon.fr. Open all
year.

Tranquil Léon, with its traditional Landes houses faced with diagonal brickwork, stands 6km inland at the southern end of the **Etang de Léon**. Picturesquely set among peaceful countryside, the lake attracts watersports enthusiasts to the village. The area between the lake and the sea is a nature reserve. But the chief attraction in the area is the **Courant d'Huchet**, a meandering river that winds its way for 14km from the lake to the sea through trees garlanded with ivy, water lilies, wild hibiscus and other lush vegetation that give the terrain a sub-

Les Bateliers du Courant d'Huchet
€€€ *Léon; tel: 05 58 48 75 39; www.batelier.com. Departures Apr–Oct daily.*

tropical appearance. There are **boat trips** along the river from Léon to Huchet beach on the coast, but they are very popular and reservations are essential, especially in August when you may have to book two weeks ahead.

MIMIZAN-LES-BAINS

Office de Tourisme Intercommunal *38 av. Maurice Martin, Mimizan-Plage; tel: 05 58 09 11 20; e-mail: contact@mimizan-tourisme.com; www.mimizan-tourism.com. Mimizan-Plage Pavillon de Tourisme open summer 0900–1900.*

Musée d'Histoire de Mimizan €€ *R. de l'Abbaye, Mimizan; tel: 05 58 09 00 61; www.musee.mimizan.com. Open mid-Jun–mid-Sep 1030–1900, closed Sun; rest of year by appointment. Closed on Sundays.*

Woolsack Manor *Not open to the public, but can be seen from the lake.*

Thanks to the planting of grasses, rushes and pine trees, Mimizan's footing is much more secure now than in the past when the town was repeatedly engulfed by shifting sands. In Roman times it was a port named Ségosa, which the sands buried in the 6th century. Rebuilt in the 10th century, it was inundated again in 1342, along with a 12th-century Benedictine abbey of which only the belfry and sculpted Gothic portal survived. The ruins are still standing and can be seen beside the D626, on the way to Mimizan-Plage. Nearby is the **Musée d'Histoire de Mimizan** which has exhibits on the area's ancient and medieval history. On the northwest shore of the picturesque Etang d'Aureilhan, which provides Mimizan with an inshore waterfront, are the ruins of **Woolsack**, a Tudor-style manor built in 1910 by the then Duke of Westminster. Winston Churchill, Coco Chanel and King Gustav II of Sweden were among the celebrities who stayed there before World War II. The mouth of the Courant de Ste-Eulalie divides the long wide beach of **Mimizan-Plage**, but a bridge across the river provides access to both sides. There are four bathing areas, each with lifeguards. The resort is 6km from the main town.

Right
Mimizan-les-Bains

PARENTIS-EN-BORN

Musée du Pétrole €€ *Route des Lacs, Parentis-en-Born; tel: 05 58 78 54 20; www.parentis.com/en/Museum.htm (English). Open for 1-hour guided tours Jul–early Sep daily 1000–1230, 1500–1900.*

The pre-war philosopher, writer and pioneer pilot, Antoine de Saint-Exupéry, described Parentis as a place 'where life flows like honey'. Today, he might be tempted to substitute the word 'oil' for 'honey', for the Etang de Biscarrosse et de Parentis, on which the town stands, is dotted with platforms exploiting the biggest oilfield in France. The story of oil, from prospecting to processing, is told in the **Musée du Pétrole**.

Vieux-Boucau-les-Bains

Until the 16th century this coastal town was known as Port d'Albret. In 1578 the Adour river changed course, shifting its mouth from Port d'Albret to Bayonne, some 30km to the south. As the ancient harbour town sank into decline, its pragmatic citizens sadly renamed it Vieux-Boucau – Old Mouth. Happily, however, the town's fortunes have been revived along with its old name, now applied to a purpose-built tourist resort developed around a 50-hectare lagoon. The old and new parts of the town are connected by an attractive esplanade. Just inland from Vieux-Boucau, **Tropica Parc** is an open-air tropical garden with aviaries and a small zoo. There are lots of exotic Asian plants and trees and spices are grown in glasshouses. It's a pleasant, restful place.

Accommodation and food

Hôtel Aquitaine €–€€ *66 av. de Lattre de Tassigny, Capbreton; tel: 05 58 72 38 11; e-mail: hotelaquitaine@wanadoo.fr; www.hotelaquitaine-capbreton.com. Open throughout the year.* The hotel has a swimming pool and restaurant. Its 24 guest rooms are all en suite.

Hôtel Barbary-Lane €–€€€ *Av. de la Côte d'Argent, Hossegor; tel: 05 58 43 52 19; e-mail: barbary-lane@wanadoo.fr; www.touradour.com/ towns/hossegor/barbarylane/gb/default.htm. Open Apr–mid-Oct.* No more than 1km from the beach, this friendly, family-run establishment has 17 rooms, 14 of them with en-suite facilities. There is a swimming pool but no restaurant. However, breakfast is available.

Hôtel St-Hubert €–€€€ *588 av. G. Latécoère, Biscarrosse; tel: 05 58 78 09 99; e-mail: hotel.saint-hubert@orange.fr; www.vf-online.com/hotelsthubert. Open year round.* There are 16 en-suite rooms, each with television and direct-dial telephone. No restaurant, but breakfast is available.

Aliénor €€ *R. Madrid, Capbreton; tel: 05 58 41 00 18. Open all year.* There are 20 en-suite rooms. No restaurant, but breakfast is available.

Hôtel Côte d'Argent €€ *R. Principale, Vieux Boucau; tel: 05 58 48 13 17; e-mail: hotel-cotedargent@wanadoo.fr; www.lacotedargent-vieuxboucau.fr. Open mid-Nov–Sep.* The hotel has 36 en-suite rooms with television and direct-dial telephones. The restaurant (**€€–€€€**) has an outdoor dining terrace.

Hôtel de la Plage €€ *94 pl. des Landes, Hossegor; tel: 05 58 41 76 41; www.hotel-hossegor.fr.* Superb central location on the beach. Twelve rooms. Restaurant serving regional dishes and a terrace bistro.

Hôtel Atlantide €€–€€€ *Pl. Marsan, Biscarrosse; tel: 05 58 78 08 86. Open all year.* No restaurant, but breakfast is available. The hotel's 33 rooms are all en suite.

Hôtel Emeraude des Bois €€–€€€ *68 av. Courant, Mimizan; tel: 05 58 09 05 28; e-mail: reservation@emeraudedesbois.com. Open*

Apr–Sep (hotel). There are 15 en-suite rooms with television and direct-dial telephones. There is a dining terrace, but the restaurant (**€–€€**) does not serve lunch.

Hôtel Mercedes €€–€€€ *Av. du Tour du Lac, Hossegor; tel: 05 58 41 98 00; e-mail: hotel.mercedes@wanadoo.fr; www.hotel-mercedes.com. Open all year.* Ideally situated for the salt-water lake, the forest and the sea, and just a few steps across the bridge from the town centre. Forty en-suite rooms, equipped with kitchenette so you can bring in your own food; consequently there is no restaurant, but there are many locally.

Au Bon Coin du Lac €€€ *34 av. du Lac, Mimizan; tel: 05 58 09 01 55; e-mail: info@auboncoindulac.com; www.auboncoindulac.com. Open all year.* Nine luxurious en-suite rooms overlook the Etang d'Aureilhan. The restaurant (**€€€**) is noted for its seafood and beef dishes.

Les Hortensias du Lac €€€ *1578 av. du Tour du Lac, Hossegor; tel: 05 58 43 99 00; e-mail: reception@hortensias-du-lac.com; www.hortensias-du-lac.com. Open all year.* Highly regarded luxury hotel set among pine trees. Twenty-three rooms en suite with TV. Swimming pool. Golf course nearby.

Camping

There are a great many campgrounds along the coast between Biscarrosse and Capbreton, some with hundreds of pitches and full facilities, including tent, mobile home and chalet hire, bars, restaurants, grocery stores, launderettes, discos and sports amenities. Here are a few suggestions.

Camping Club Marina € *Plage Sud, Mimizan; tel: 05 58 09 12 66; e-mail: campargent@wanadoo.fr; www.marina-club.net/campsite-france. html. Open mid-May–mid-Sep.* This site has 580 pitches and tents, caravans, mobile homes and chalets for hire. It offers the full range of amenities and sports facilities.

Camping Les Grands Pins € *Av. de Losa (route du Lac), Sanguinet; tel: 05 58 78 61 74; e-mail: info@campinglesgrandspins.com; www. campinglesgrandspins.com. Open all year.* Tents, caravans, mobile homes and chalets may be hired on this 260-pitch site which has all amenities, except a disco.

Camping Municipal les Sablères € *Blvd du Marensin, Vieux Boucau; tel: 05 58 48 12 29; e-mail: lessableres@wanadoo.fr; www.les-sableres. com/index-gb.htm. Open Apr–mid-Oct.* A simple but huge campground with 591 pitches. Launderette.

Camping La Pointe € *Quartier de la Pointe off the D652, Capbreton; tel: 05 58 72 14 98; e-mail: campinglapointe@club-internet.fr; www. camping-lapointe.com. Open Jun–Sep.* The site has 283 pitches, with facilities for motor homes. Tents, caravans, mobile homes and chalets may be rented. Amenities include a shop, takeaway food, bar and launderette.

Camping de la Rive € *Lac de Sanguinet, Biscarrosse; tel: 05 58 78 12 33; e-mail: info@camping-de-la-rive.fr; www.larive.fr. Open Apr–Oct.* A massive site with 640 pitches, facilities for renting tents, caravans, mobile homes and chalets, hook-ups for motor homes, shop, takeaway food, bar, nursery, launderette, swimming, tennis and mini-golf.

Suggested tour

Total distance: Without side trips to the beach resorts associated with some inland places – never more than half a dozen kilometres each way – the main route covers 134km. The detour totals 28km.

Time: The main route can be driven comfortably in under 3 hours. Allow an hour for the detour.

Links: From Capbreton the D652 south leads in 5.5km to Labenne, where it joins the N10, the main route into Bayonne and Biarritz to the south and Dax to the northeast. From Biscarrosse-Plage you can continue north along the D218 through the Forêt de la Teste and past the Dune du Pilat to reach Arcachon (*see pages 262–4*) in 30km.

Route: From **CAPBRETON** ❶ travel north for 3km to **HOSSEGOR** ❷, then turn east on to the D33. After 2km take a left turn on to the D652 for 3.5km to reach the quiet old village of **Seignosse**, nestled at the southern end of the Etang Noir, so-called because of its black mud. Follow the road around the west side of the lake, then turn right after 1km to pass between Etang Noir and Etang Blanc, named for the colour of its sandy bottom. Another 3km and you reach the village of **Tosse** with its 11th-century church. Next, head north on the D652, which reaches **Soustons** after 9km. Soustons, a major market town, makes corks that go into bottles of Bordeaux wine. Follow the D652 west for 8km to **VIEUX-BOUCAU** ❸ and on for a further 4km to **Messanges**, where vines planted among the sand dunes produce *vin des sables*, a rare red wine with an aroma of violets. Another 4km along the D652 brings you to **Moliets-et-Maa**, which has a challenging golf course. Continue along the D652 for a further 5km and you will reach **LEON** ❹. From here keep on the D652 for a further 15km then turn right at the hamlet of **Miquéou** on to the D105 for 10km to **Lévignacq**, a delightful village, typically Landais with timber-framed houses, an old water mill and a 13th-century fortified church. The church has frescoes from the 15th century and a wooden ceiling covered with 18th-century paintings of the Nativity, the Ascension and the Holy Trinity. Leave Lévignacq by the D41 north, rejoining the D652 at **St-Julien-en-Born** after 8km. Follow the D652 north for 16km to **MIMIZAN** ❺, where you

Musée des Sites Lacustres €€ *Pl. de la Mairie, Sanguinet; tel: 05 58 78 54 20; www.musee-de-sanguinet.com. Open July and Aug daily 1000–1200, 1430–1900.*

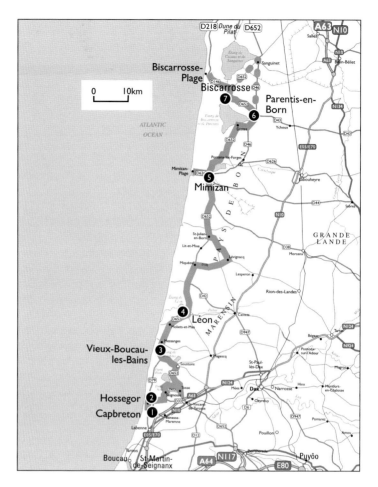

can visit **Mimizan-Plage** by heading west for 6km on the D626. **PARENTIS-EN-BORN** ❻ is reached 24km beyond Mimizan, but before that you can enjoy a good view of the Etang de Biscarrosse et de Parentis from Gastes.

Detour: From Parentis head north on the D46 for 15km to **Sanguinet**, where Iron Age dugout canoes and other finds from excavations in the area are displayed in the **Musée des Sites Lacustres.** Sanguinet stands on the site of a Gallo-Roman village and a stone temple can be seen submerged 4m below the lake's surface. From Sanguinet the D652 heads south for 13km to **BISCARROSSE** ❼.

On the main route, from Parentis the D652 skirts the eastern shore of the lake, reaching Biscarrosse in 9km. From here follow the D146 for 9.5km to **Biscarrosse-Plage**.

Arcachon

Ratings

Beaches	●●●●●
Seafood	●●●●●
Sports facilities	●●●●●
Children	●●●●○
Coastal villages	●●●●○
Ornithology	●●●●○
Architecture	●●●○○
Walks	●●●○○

Developed in the 19th century, Arcachon, with its pine woods, its sandy beaches, its carefully nurtured architecture and its almost landlocked triangular bay, is not just a pretty face. The resort, on Aquitaine's lovely Côte d'Argent, presents a range of activities for the many thousands of people who swarm into Arcachon (resident population 12,000) from Easter to autumn and beyond. Golf, gambling, surfing, hang-gliding, climbing Europe's biggest sand dune and eating oysters are some of the options. Arcachon is one of the most popular yachting centres in Europe, with 2500 boats in its harbour and a 10-year waiting list for moorings. The town, less than an hour's drive or a pleasant train ride from Bordeaux, has four quarters, each named after a season of the year. Oyster parks, which can be visited by boat or on foot, produce 15,000 tons of oysters a year.

ARCACHON

ℹ Office de Tourisme d'Arcachon *Esplanade Georges Pompidou, Arcachon; tel: 05 57 52 97 97; e-mail: tourisme@arcachon.com; www.arcachon.com. Information kiosks also at the railway station and Arcachon harbour. Open all year. Bookings taken for guided walking tours of Winter Town.*

Arcachon has four main quarters, each named after a season of the year. La Ville de Printemps ('Spring Town') includes Péreire Park and Péreire Beach. Tennis, bowling, golf, swimming, jai alai and horse riding are among the pursuits enjoyed in the park. The stretch of seafront, with its pavement cafés and boating events, is in La Ville d'Eté ('Summer Town'). La Ville d'Automne ('Autumn Town') takes in the fishing port, fish market and marina. A large sculpture here, by Claude Dousceau, appears as an anchor from the side and as a cross from the front. The sculpture is a memorial to fishermen who died at sea.

La Ville d'Hiver ('Winter Town'), on a higher level, with fine views of the ocean, is where grand houses in an amazing range of architectural styles were built in the 19th and early 20th centuries for the rich and famous. This development was started by the two Péreire brothers

Apart from a pharmacy and a newspaper outlet, Winter Town has no shops. Residents use a lift in the Parc Mauresque above Summer Town for easy access to and from the business and social area of Arcachon.

Office de Tourisme *19 av. de Lattre de Tassigny, Gujan-Mestras; tel: 05 56 66 12 65; e-mail: otgujan@ wanadoo.fr; www.ville-gujanmestras.fr*

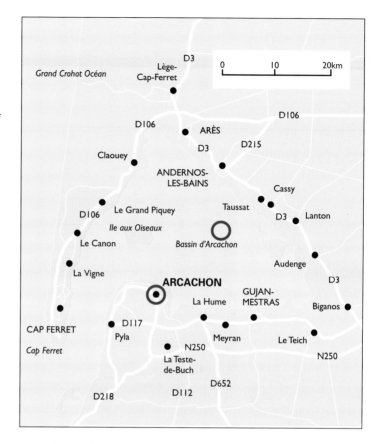

when the Bordeaux–La Teste railway line was extended to Arcachon in the 1840s. The sea air and the scent of pine trees planted around the homes enhanced the town's reputation as being beneficial to people suffering from lung diseases. Guided walks around Winter Town from mid-June to mid-September can be booked at the tourist office.

Les Abatilles € *La Source, Ste-Anne-des-Abatilles, Société des Eaux Minérales d'Arcachon, 157 blvd de la Côte d'Argent, Arcachon; tel: 05 56 22 38 50. Open for visits to the mineral water production centre Jul and Aug at 10.30.*

Les Abatilles

A search for oil in Arcachon was unsuccessful. Instead a mineral water spring was discovered. Visitors can taste the water and learn from guides about its history, production and qualities.

Aqualand

(€€€ *Gujan-Mestras, Bassin d'Arcachon, La Hume; tel: 05 56 66 39 39; e-mail: aqualand.gujanmestras@aqualand.fr; www.aqualand.fr. Open daily mid-Jun–mid-Sept.*) A place to splash around and cool off, with water chutes and attractions for all the family in a 10-hectare park. You can have a restaurant meal or enjoy a picnic in the shade of pine trees.

Aquarium Tropical

(€ *Maison des Jeunes, 8 allée José-María de Hérédia, Arcachon; tel: 05 56 83 19 52; e-mail: aquarium.tropical@free.fr; http://aquarium.tropical. free.fr. Open daily 1400–1800.*) Fascinating displays of tiny and not-so-tiny fish in glorious colours and shapes, from various tropical parts. Information in French and English, and video presentation.

Right
Arcachon oyster boat

BASSIN D'ARCACHON

La Teste-de-Buch Office de Tourisme
Pl. Jean Hameau; tel: 05 56 54 63 14; e-mail: ot.la.teste. de.buch@wanadoo.fr; www.latestedebuch.com. Open all year Mon–Fri 0900–1230, 1400–1800, Sat to 1700. Closed Sun and public holidays. Summer season Pavillon du Marché open 1000–1300 (not Mon am).

Fishing trawlers' catches are unloaded at the dockside. Lying at their moorings are 2500 yachts representing millions of pounds. In summer boat trips go to l'Ile aux Oiseaux (Bird Island), the only island in the bay. At low tide it is 15 times as big as at high tide. Oyster parks are revealed at low tide and can be visited by boat or on foot (*see page 269*). Guided **sea kayak trips** to places of interest are also available, along with other watersports (*Centre Nautique du Port d'Arcachon, quai de Goslar, Arcachon; tel: 05 56 22 36 83. Open all year*).

Fashionable Cap Ferret is at the tip of a narrow peninsula opposite Arcachon, and the two towns are connected by a boat service. You can explore villages, oyster parks and nature study sites along the road around the bay, where there is also a 54km cycle path running alongside between Cap Ferret and Le Teich.

The salt marshes of the **Parc Ornithologique** at Le Teich, which has 260 bird species, are used by huge numbers of migratory birds as a

Parc Ornithologique du Teich € and other natural history venues and activities around the bay: Maison de la Nature; tel: 05 56 22 80 93; e-mail: contact@parc-ornithologique-du-teich.com. Open all year 1000–1800 (2000 in Jul–Aug); www.parc-ornithologique-du-teich.com

Boat trips €–€€ Catamaran, Arcachon Croisière Océan; tel: 05 57 52 24 77. Pinasses, Les Bateliers Arcachonais; tel: 05 57 72 28 28. Atlantic Princess restaurant boat; tel: 05 56 83 39 39.

Pavillon de la Grande Dune Tel: 05 56 22 12 85. Open in high season daily 1000–1300, 1430–1830; rest of year Mon–Fri 0830–1330, 1400–1700.

VSM L'Oceana Diving School €€€ 14 quai du Capitaine Allègre, Arcachon; tel: 05 56 83 98 95; e-mail: contact@oceana.fr; http://oceana.fr. Open all year. Qualified instructors offer dive training in a pool or the natural settings of Caraux lake, Arcachon Bay or the open sea.

stopping place. Guided birdwatching visits with an expert ornithologist are offered, using a series of hides in the park.

Boat trips

From Arcachon public boat services go across the bay to Cap Ferret, l'Ile aux Oiseaux, Andernos and Banc d'Arguin. There is also a service between Le Moulleau and Cap Ferret. Information: **Union des Bateliers Arcachonais** (tel: 05 56 54 60 32; e-mail: contact@bateliers-arcachon.com; www.bateliers-arcachon.com).

In summer you have a choice of boat trips, by catamaran or the traditional Bassin d'Arcachon flat-bottomed 'pinasse', to the Dune de Pyla, the oyster parks or to do a 35km circuit of the Ile aux Oiseaux. A smart restaurant boat more than 30m long, the *Atlantic Princess*, offers popular luncheon and dinner cruises.

Casino de la Plage

(*163 blvd de la Plage, Arcachon; tel: 05 56 83 41 44. Open 1000–0400.*) The chips are down every day as roulette, blackjack and 80 slots go into action at the casino in the Château Deganne. Bowls, a disco, restaurant and bars are added attractions on the premises.

Deep-sea diving

(*€€€ Club de Plongée Arcachonais (CPA), Centre Nautique du Bassin d'Arcachon; tel: 05 56 22 36 83.*) This is available in the bay for novices and people of various levels of ability. Equipment is provided. Exploration dives are an option.

La Dune du Pilat

Europe's largest sand dune was listed as a national site in 1978. A century ago it was 60m high. Today it is almost twice that height, more than 2.5km long and 1km wide. It has been formed over a period of about 6000 years from layers of dune systems. The dune is constantly on the march, moving 6m or more a year.

It can be approached from a few kilometres out of town via Pyla-sur-Mer and Pilat-Plage. People like to get there for the sunset view from the top – well worth the climb – or by narrated boat trip from the Bassin d'Arcachon (*see Boat trips above*). There are campsites and places to eat around the edge of the dune.

Galleries

Arcachon has more than half a dozen art galleries, most of which are on the blvd de la Plage. Some others include the **Galerie St-Martin Côté Océan** (*€€ 253 blvd de la Côte d'Argent, Le Moulleau, Arcachon; tel: 05 56 54 19 91; e-mail: sumart@wanadoo.fr; www.galerie-saint-martin.com; open daily 1100–1300 and 1600–2000, to midnight in summer season*) and the **Galerie Thomas Dubarry** (*€€€ 282 blvd de la Plage, Les Tamaris, Arcachon; tel: 05 56 83 43 82*).

ⓘ Jardin des Papillons/Labiland Park €€€ *Le Teich; tel: 05 57 52 33 52; e-mail: info@ lejardindespapillons.com; http://lejardindespapillons. free.fr/labiland.htm. Open daily Jul and Aug 1030–2000.*

Musée Aquarium €€ *2 r. Jolyet, Arcachon; tel: 05 56 83 33 32. Open daily 0945–1215, 1345–1900.*

ⓐ Bicycles can be hired for a small daily fee, plus a returnable deposit. One of the outlets, *open daily from Mar–Sep*, with telephone bookings available rest of year, is **Locabeach**, *326 blvd de la Plage, Arcachon; tel: 05 56 83 39 64; e-mail: locabeach-33@wanadoo.fr; www.locabeach.com/ index_anglais.htm*

ⓕ Sports fishing €€ *Contact Arcachon Croisière Océan (ACO); tel: 05 56 54 36 70, or Association des Pêcheurs Plaisanciers du Bassin d'Arcachon (APPBA), 53 blvd de la Plage, Arcachon; tel: 05 56 83 82 29.*

Hang-gliding

Take a course at the **Ecole Pyla Parapente** (*€€€ 1 r. Aurelien, Daisson, Gujan-Mestras; tel: 05 56 22 15 02*), or experience hang-gliding in tandem with a professional pilot.

Le Jardin des Papillons (*€€ Le Teich (15km from Arcachon on the RN 250 road to Bordeaux); tel: 05 57 52 32 32; e-mail: info@ jardindespapillons.com. Open daily mid-Apr–1 Nov*). Visitors can wander in exotic gardens, seeing hundreds of butterflies of numerous species flying freely among tropical vegetation and trees. The 2000sq m of the park includes an orchid garden, a butterfly boutique and a shady picnic area.

Labiland Park

As well as a great maze and a children's mini-maze set in the 5-hectare park, a large area is devoted to games: mini-golf, volleyball, basket ball, badminton, mini-tennis, water fun and other pursuits are provided. Costumed entertainers keep youngsters amused with fairy tales and legends of the Middle Ages.

Musée Aquarium

Many species of marine life from the Bassin d'Arcachon and the open sea beyond the bay are displayed in large glass tanks. The museum also has sections showing discoveries from archaeological excavations in the area, aspects of oyster farming and local natural history collections.

Parc Animalier 'La Coccinelle' (*€€€ La Hume; tel: 05 56 66 30 41; e-mail: contact@la-coccinelle.fr; www.la-coccinelle.fr/rep/multi-langue.html. Open daily late May–late Aug. Children under 90cm free*). A delight for the little ones – and grown-ups, too. The 'Ladybird Park' has 800 domestic pets and small farm animals: you can watch some of them being bottle-fed. Amusements include a little train, water to play in and a carousel.

Sports fishing

Mar–May there is migration of several species of fish, notably mackerel and whiting, across the Gasgogne Gulf. *Jun–Sep* shark fishing is possible in larger boats with professional fishermen based in Arcachon. All gear is provided for people going on sea-fishing trips by boat. Jul and Aug are the peak months. Night-time trips can be arranged.

Village Médiéval de la Hume (*€€ 33470 Gujan-Mestras; tel: 05 56 66 16 76. Open 1000–1930 mid-Jun–early Sep*). A back-in-time experience, seeing costumed craftspeople making farm implements, jewellery and various artefacts and crafts. Knights, jugglers and torture at the pillory add to the medieval atmosphere. Arts and crafts are on display.

Right
Grand villa in Arcachon

Accommodation and food

☾ More than 80 hotels – small by international standards – and a generous assortment of house rentals and guesthouses welcome visitors in Arcachon and its environs. But if you plan a holiday here in July or August, it's wise to book your accommodation months in advance.

Les Baguettes d'Or € *43 bis, r. Maréchal de Lattre de Tassigny, Arcachon; tel: 05 56 83 84 79. Open all year, closed Mon lunchtime.* Asian food, including Vietnamese specialities, at remarkably good prices.

Le Bistrot € *3 av. du Général de Gaulle, La Teste; tel: 05 57 15 11 11. Open all year.* Traditional bistro fare with *prix fixe* menus at modest levels and a children's menu.

La Coquille € *55 cours de Verdun, Gujan-Mestras; tel: 05 56 66 08 60. Open all year.* 1km from the beach, the 23-room hotel has its own restaurant.

Pizzeria Azzurra € *13 r. du Professeur Jolyet, Arcachon; tel: 05 56 83 58 97. Open all year.* Good pizzas with Italian wine, and a children's menu. Close to the beach.

Camping Club d'Arcachon €–€€ *Allée de la Galaxie, Abatilles, Arcachon; tel: 05 56 83 24 15; e-mail: info@camping-arcachon.com; www.camping-arcachon.com. Open all year. Open all year.* One of well over a dozen campsites in Arcachon and around the bay: it has well-maintained sites within 2km of the town and beach. 250 pitches.

Thinking of renting accommodation for a week, fortnight or month? Local renting agencies include **Dazens Immobilier**, 43 av. des Violettes, Pyla-sur-Mer; tel: 05 56 54 54 26, **Agence du Littoral**, 151 blvd de la République, Andernos; tel: 05 56 82 02 68; e-mail: contact @agencedulittoral.com; www.agencedulittoral.com and **Agence Reichert**, 29 av. du Vieux Bourg, Audenge; tel: 05 56 26 84 81.

Opposite
Oyster boat in the Bassin d'Arcachon

Below
An oyster farmer at work

Camping de la Dune €–€€ *Route de Biscarrosse, Pyla-sur-Mer; tel: 05 56 22 72 17; www.campingdeladune.fr/fra1.htm. Open all year.* One of the campsites around the Dune du Pilat.

Hôtel Marinette €€ *15 allée José-María de Hérédia, Arcachon; tel: 05 56 83 06 67; e-mail: contact@hotel-marinette.com; www.hotel-marinette.com. Open mid-Mar–Oct.* In Winter Town, the hotel is within 1km of the beach and the town. Each room has its own breakfast terrace.

Chez Yvette €€–€€€ *59 blvd Général Leclerc, Arcachon; tel: 05 56 83 05 11. Open daily all year.* The restaurant specialises in oysters, *fruits de mer* and fish and offers a good choice of Bordeaux Blanc wines.

Arc Hôtel sur Mer €€€ *89 blvd de la Plage, Arcachon; tel: 05 56 83 06 85; e-mail: reservation@arc-hotel-sur-mer.com; www.arc-hotel-sur-mer.com. Open all year.* The 4-star hotel, right on the beach, has a large swimming pool, solarium and sauna. Most of the 30 rooms have a balcony. There is no restaurant, but a brasserie is *open Mar–Oct.* There is private enclosed parking.

Cap Péreire €€€ *1 av. du Parc Péreire, Arcachon; tel: 05 56 83 24 01. Open all year.* Seafood specialities in a colonial-style building by the ocean.

Hôtel du Parc €€€ *5–7 av. du Parc, Arcachon, tel: 05 56 83 10 58; e-mail: b.dronne@wanadoo.fr; www.hotelduparc-arcachon.com. Open May–Sept.* Each of the 30 en-suite rooms has its own spacious covered terrace. The 3-star hotel, set among pine trees, has private parking.

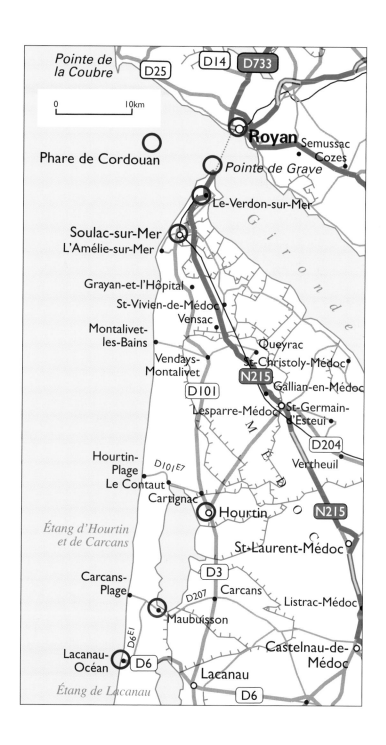

on the lake as well as on the coast. Surrounded by moorland, forest and massive dunes and fringed by marshes, the lake covers an area of more than 6000 hectares and has plenty of room for those who like seclusion. Opposite Hourtin, on the lake's northwestern shore, is Le Contaut, a training centre for the French navy, where visitors can join a tour through protected wetlands (*details from the tourism office*).

LACANAU-OCEAN

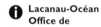 **Lacanau-Océan Office de Tourisme** *Pl. de l'Europe; tel: 05 56 03 21 01; e-mail: lacanau@lacanau.com; www.lacanau.com. Open all year except 1 Jan and 25 Dec. Tourist office at rail station open Jun–Sep.*

A surfer's paradise, with the Atlantic Ocean pounding onto wide beaches of fine sand, the resort is in an idyllic setting of sand dunes and plantations of sea pines. Lac de Lacanau, a lovely stretch of fresh water, offers an extensive range of water activities and is popular with families. Boat rentals are available. Its great shoals of fish – especially eels, perch and pike – make it a favourite with anglers. Cycle trails and footpaths circle the lake.

MAUBUISSON

Musée des Arts et Traditions Populaires €€ *Maubuisson; tel: 05 56 03 33 69. Open May–Sep Sun–Fri 1500–1900.*

Etang de Cousseau *Tel: SEPANSO (Society for the protection of nature in the southwest) 05 56 91 33 65, or tourist office Lacanau-Ocean 05 56 03 21 01; e-mail: rnn-cousseau@ wanadoo.fr*

Maubuisson, at the southwestern end of Lac d'Hourtin-Carcans, lies on the edge of the extensive pine forest that fringes the coast, and the forest's influence on local life is featured in the **Musée des Arts et Traditions Populaires**. A little over 2km north of the village is **Bombannes** (*tel: 05 56 03 95 95*), an open-air leisure centre covering 200 hectares. Visitors can take part in archery, boating, swimming, tennis and a host of other activities. There are attractive picnic areas among the pines and overlooking the lake.

A fascinating nature trail follows the western shore of the 2km-long **Etang de Cousseau**, a nature reserve just south of Maubuisson and about halfway between Lac d'Hourtin-Carcans and Lac de Lacanau. You can access the reserve only by a footpath through the Forêt de Lacanau or on paved cycle trails. Bikes are not allowed into the reserve, and must be left in designated areas. The area surrounding the lake – the eastern shore is marshy and inaccessible – has an interesting range of flora and fauna, including wild boar. There are guided tours *daily mid-Jun–mid-Sept*, when you can see demonstrations of resin-tapping. Reservations for the tours must be made at the Lacanau tourist office (*see above*).

PHARE DE CORDOUAN

There has been a lighthouse of sorts guarding the Gironde estuary since the 14th century. When the Black Prince ordered a fire to be kept going

Phare de Cordouan
€€ *The lighthouse is accessible by boat from the Pointe de Grave (Jul–Aug), Royan and Le Verdon-sur-Mer (weather permitting). Guided tours of the lighthouse and its museum in high season 1030–1200, 1400–1800; off-peak at weekends 1400–1800, by appointment only, tel: 05 56 09 62 93; www.littoral33.com/cordouan/visite_cordouan.htm*

24 hours a day on an octagonal tower, the rocks on which it stood were part of the mainland at the Pointe de Grave, but by the 17th century they had become separated. The lighthouse now stands some 8km offshore. The Black Prince's tower was replaced by an ornate wedding-cake structure designed by Louis de Foix, the engineer who diverted the River Adour. In 1788 the upper levels were remodelled to a more practical shape, but the lighthouse today retains some of its old extravagant style. Reaching a height of 66m, it contains a King's Apartment and a chapel. Reaching the lamp involves a climb up 301 steps.

POINTE DE GRAVE

ⓘ *A tourist information booth opposite the Pointe de Grave landing stage is open Jul and Aug daily. Tel: 05 56 73 37 73.*

Boat trips
€€–€€€ *La Bohême II, landing stage, Pointe de Grave; tel: 05 56 09 62 93; e-mail: vedettelaboheme@aol.com; www.vedette-laboheme.com. Trips to Cordouan lighthouse and along the Gironde estuary.*

Scenic railway €€€
Departure times and other information from the tourist offices at Le Verdon, tel: 05 56 09 61 78 and Soulac, tel: 05 56 09 86 61. This little train runs between the Pointe de Grave and Soulac, with splendid views of the coastline and the forests. Journey time about 1 hour.

The most northerly point of the Côte d'Argent, overlooking the mouth of the Gironde, has been of strategic importance in World Wars I and II. It is marked by a monument commemorating the landing of American troops in 1917 – the original, a 75m pyramid, was destroyed by the Germans in 1942. Allied forces landed in France in June 1944, but it took them nearly a year to shake the Germans from Pointe de Grave.

It's a peaceful enough spot today, however, with magnificent views of the Phare de Cordouan, the Gironde estuary and Le Verdon-sur-Mer. A lighthouse on the point serves as the **Musée du Phare de Courdouan** (*Rue François Lebreton; tel: 05 56 09 61 78; http://pagesperso-orange.fr/cordouan/cordouan.htm*), featuring the old structure's history and the life of a lighthouse keeper. There is also an aquarium. **Boat trips** may be taken from Pointe de Grave, which is also a terminus for a 10km **scenic railway** trip along the pine-fringed shore to Soulac-sur-Mer.

Right
Sunrise at Pointe de Grave

ROYAN

ⓘ **Office de Tourisme**
Av. des Congrès, Royan;
tel: 05 46 23 00 00; e-mail:
info@royan-tourisme.com;
www.royan-tourisme.com
Open Jul and Aug Mon–Sat
0900–1930, Sun 1000–
1300, 1500–1800; Sep–Jun
Mon–Sat 0900–1800.

🐾 **Zoo de la Palmyre**
€€€ Les Mathes; tel:
05 46 22 46 06; e-mail:
info@zoo-palmyre.fr;
www.zoo-palmyre.fr. Open
Apr–Sep daily 0900–1900;
Oct–Mar daily 0900–1200,
1400–1800.

Five kilometres across the mouth of the Gironde from the Pointe de Grave – a 30-minute ferryboat trip – Royan, in Charente-Maritime *département*, is a popular coastal holiday centre. Almost flattened by bombing during the closing months of World War II, the town, which had been the archetypal Victorian French resort, had to be rebuilt after losing many of its overblown villas and grand hotels. Despite its post-war architecture, Royan is a lively and fitting capital for the Côte de Beauté, as the coastline that runs north from here is known.

The town is graced with 2km of crescent-shaped beach – the **Front de Mer** – fringing the large cove which holds the main harbour. This is where ferryboats depart for the Pointe de Grave. Four smaller coves also on the west side of the harbour have fine sandy beaches. The town's main church, the **Eglise Notre-Dame**, was completed after three years in 1958 and is strikingly built of reinforced concrete coated with resin to protect it from wind and weather. It is noted for its glass walls and 65m belfry.

The coast on the Atlantic side of Royan invites exploration. **St-Palais-sur-Mer**, only 5km away, is a small, elegant resort. The **Zoo de la Palmyre**, in a forest of pines and oaks 15km from Royan, is an extended nature trail through 14 hectares of lakes and hills where some 1500 animals from all parts of the world live in habitats as near-natural as possible. Among the zoo's stars are families of gorillas, flying foxes and lion cubs. Just beyond La Palmyre is the **Forêt de la Coubre** where deer roam – and you can enjoy a guided tour – among 8000 hectares of pine and ilex trees. Enquire at tourist office.

SOULAC-SUR-MER

ⓘ **Office de Tourisme**
68 r. de la Plage,
Soulac-sur-Mer;
tel: 05 56 09 86 61; e-mail:
tourismesoulac@wanadoo.fr;
www.soulac.com. Open daily
in high season 0900–1900;
off-peak Mon–Sat 0900–
1230, 1400–1730.

🏛 **Fondation Soulac-
Médoc** €€ Soulac-
sur-Mer; tel: 05 56 09 83
99. Open Jul–mid-Sep daily
1700–1930.

Right
Pine forest at dawn,
Soulac-sur-Mer

The town has had at least three incarnations. Until the 6th century it was the ancient city of Noviomagus, then the sea swept over it. Next, it was an important port with a large natural harbour where pilgrims would disembark before setting off overland on the road to Santiago de Compostela. This time, in the 17th century, the fickle sea ran out and the harbour became marshland. Now it's a popular seaside resort at the

southern end of the scenic railway to the Pointe de Grave (*see page 275*).

A survivor from Soulac's second life is the **Basilique Notre-Dame-de-la-Fin-des-Terres** (Our Lady of Land's End), which was uncovered and restored in the 19th century after being almost totally buried in sand. There are traces of 12th-century Romanesque architecture and its belfry dates from the 14th century. Among the decorated capitals

Musée d'Art et d'Archéologie €
Av. El Burgo de Osma, Soulac-sur-Mer; tel: 05 56 09 83 99. Open Jul and Aug daily 1500–1900; rest of year daily 1500–1800. Closed Wed.

inside the church is one depicting the tomb and shrine of St Veronica, who died in Soulac. Another portrays Daniel in the lions' den and a third shows St Peter in prison.

Paintings and sculptures by contemporary artists from the area are displayed in the **Fondation Soulac-Médoc**. A collection of tools and weapons from the Neolithic and Bronze Ages and artefacts from the Gallo-Roman period – including ceramics and glassware – is on show in the **Musée d'Archéologie**.

LE VERDON-SUR-MER

Office de Tourisme 2 r. des Frères Tard, Le Verdon-sur-Mer; tel: 05 56 09 61 78; e-mail: tourismeleverdon-sur-mer@wanadoo.fr; www.littoral33.com/Le_Verdon.htm. Open Mon–Sat 1000–1200, 1500–1900.

Apart from being a departure point for boat trips along the estuary and to the Phare de Cordouan, Le Verdon-sur-Mer is a deep-water port and container terminal handling huge container vessels and oil tankers on their way to and from various parts of the world.

Accommodation and food

La Biche aux Bois €–€€ *141 blvd Côte de Beauté, route de St-Palais, Vaux-sur-Mer; tel: 05 46 39 01 52; e-mail: hotel.biche-au-bois@ wanadoo.fr. Closed Oct–Nov.* The restaurant offers very reasonably priced meals and wine is available by the glass. Accommodation (€€) is in 12 en-suite rooms with direct-dial telephones and television. Garden; enclosed parking.

Hôtel La Dame de Cœur €–€€ *103 r. de la Plage, Soulac-sur-Mer; tel: 05 56 09 80 80; e-mail: la.dame.de.coeur@wanadoo.fr; www.hotel-ladamedecoeur. com. Open all year.* The hotel has 12 en-suite rooms and a restaurant.

Hôtel Le Dauphin €€ *17 pl. de l'Eglise, Hourtin; tel: 05 56 09 11 15. Open all year.* The hotel has 20 en-suite rooms and a restaurant.

Hôtel Michelet €€–€€€ *1 r. Bernard Baguenard, Soulac-sur-Mer; tel: 05 56 09 84 18; www.hotelmichelet33.com. Closed Nov–Feb.* No restaurant, but breakfast is available at this hotel with 20 en-suite rooms.

Hôtel des Pins €€–€€€ *92 blvd de L'Amélie, Soulac-sur-Mer; tel: 05 56 73 27 27; e-mail: info@hotel-des-pins.com; www.hotel-des-pins.com. Closed Jan–mid-Mar.* The restaurant (€€) here offers terraced dining and wine by the glass. The hotel's 31 en-suite rooms have direct-dial telephones and television. Private parking for guests.

Océan Hôtel Amélie €€–€€€ *L'Amélie, Soulac-sur-Mer; tel: 05 56 09 78 05; e-mail: mail@oceanhotelamelie.com; www.oceanhotelamelie. com/index_en.html. Open early Jun–mid-Sep.* The hotel has 21 en-suite rooms, a swimming pool and restaurant.

Le Pavillon Bleu €€–€€€ *Allée des Algues, Pontaillac, Royan; tel: 05 46 39 00 00; e-mail: le.pavillon.bleu@wanadoo.fr; www.le-pavillon-bleu.com.*

Open Apr–Sep. House wine by the carafe is available at the hotel's restaurant, Pavillon Bleu (€–€€). There are 40 en-suite rooms with direct-dial telephones and television; private parking.

Family Golf Hôtel €€€ *28 blvd Garnier, Royan; tel: 05 46 05 14 66; e-mail: family-golf-hotel@wanadoo.fr; www.hotel-family-golf.com. Open mid-Mar–Oct.* No restaurant, but breakfast is available. The hotel has 33 en-suite rooms with direct-dial telephones and television. Private parking.

Hôtel du Golf €€€ *Domaine de l'Ardilouse, Lacanau-Océan; tel: 05 56 03 92 92; e-mail: info@golf-hotel-lacanau.fr; www.golf-hotel-lacanau.fr. Open all year.* Adjoining an 18-hole golf course, the hotel has 50 en-suite rooms, each with direct-dial telephone and television, and a restaurant (€€–€€€). There is a terraced dining area, a swimming pool and garden.

Résidence de Rohan €€€ *Parc des Fées, Vaux-sur-Mer; tel: 05 46 39 00 75; e-mail: info@residence-rohan.com; www.residence-rohan.com. Open Apr–mid-Nov.* Situated in a park setting overlooking the beach, the hotel has 41 en-suite rooms with direct-dial telephones and television. Swimming pool, tennis and private parking. No restaurant, but breakfast is available.

Vitalparc €€€ *Route de Baganais, Lacanau-Océan; tel: 05 56 03 91 00; e-mail: info@vitalparc.com; www.vitalparc.com. Open mid-Feb–mid-Nov.* There are two swimming pools – one indoors, one outside – at this hotel, which also has a restaurant (€€€) with terraced dining area. There are tennis courts and a fitness room, and 59 en-suite rooms with direct-dial telephones and television.

Camping

Airotel de l'Océan € *R. du Repos, Lacanau-Océan; tel: 05 56 03 24 45; e-mail: airotel.lacanau@wanadoo.fr; www.lacanau-airotel.com. Open Apr–Sep.* A disco and swimming pool are among the amenities at this 550-pitch site which has tents, caravans, chalets and mobile homes for rent and facilities for motor homes.

Camping de la Côte d'Argent € *Hourtin-Plage; tel: 05 56 09 10 25; e-mail: info@cca33.com; www.cca33.com. Open mid-May–mid-Sep.* A massive campground with 750 pitches. Caravans, tents, mobile homes and chalets are available. Launderette; pool.

Les Genêts € *Blvd de l'Amélie, Soulac-sur-Mer; tel: 05 56 09 85 79; e-mail: camping.lesgenets@wanadoo.fr. Open Apr–Sep.* The site has a launderette and swimming pool and there are 250 pitches, with spaces for motor homes. Caravans, chalets, mobile homes and tents for hire.

Les Grands Pins € *Lacanau-Océan; tel: 05 56 03 20 77; e-mail: reception@lesgrandspins.com; www.lesgrandspins.com. Open mid-Apr–late*

Sep. Spaces for motor homes are among the 560 pitches, and mobile homes and chalets may be rented. Launderette; pool, bicycle rental.

Le Lilhan € *8 allée Michel de Montaigne, Soulac-sur-Mer; tel: 05 56 09 77 63; e-mail: contact@lellilhan.com. Open Jun–mid-Sep.* Caravans, chalets, mobile homes and tents may be hired at this site, where there are 170 pitches including spaces for motor homes. Launderette; pool.

La Mariflaude € *Off the D4, Hourtin; tel: 05 56 09 11 97; e-mail: mariflaude@camping-la-mariflaude.com; www.camping-la-mariflaude.com/ uk/index_uk.html (English). Open mid-May–mid-Sep.* Mobile homes and chalets may be rented at this 166-pitch site, which has places for motor homes. Launderette; swimming pool.

Les Sables d'Argent Camping Club de Soulac € *Blvd de l'Amélie, Soulac-sur-Mer; tel: 05 56 09 82 87; www.sables-d-argent.com. Open Apr–Sep.* The site has spaces for motor homes on its 152 pitches. Caravans, tents, chalets and mobile homes are available for hire. Launderette.

Talaris Vacances € *Route de l'Océan, Lacanau-Océan; tel: 05 56 03 04 15; e-mail: talarisvacances@free.fr; www.talaris-vacances.fr. Open Jun–mid-Sep.* The site has 200 pitches, including spaces for motor homes. Caravans, tents, chalets and mobile homes for hire. Launderette; pool.

Below
Atlantic breakers

Suggested tour

Moulin de Vensac
€€ Tel: 05 56 09 45
00; e-mail: infos@
moulindevensac.fr;
www.moulindevensac.fr.
Guided tours (30 mins) Jul
and Aug daily 1000–1230,
1430–1830; Jun and Sept
Sat and Sun same times;
Mar–May, Oct & Nov Sun
1430–1830. Closed
Dec–Feb.

Total distance: The round trip covers 192km. From Soulac to Lacanau the distance is 89.5km.

Time: Driving time for the total route is about 4 hours.

Links: The N215 from the outskirts of Soulac is the main route to Bordeaux (*see pages 42–53*). From Lacanau the D3 south reaches the northern part of the Bassin d'Arcachon (*see page 264*) in 24km.

Route: The route begins, as it did for many pilgrims setting out on the road to Santiago de Compostela, at **SOULAC-SUR-MER ❶**. The route took those pilgrims right down to Spain, but we're following the 'English Way' only as far as Lacanau, then returning through the Médoc with a chance perhaps to try some of the region's splendid wines. From Soulac take the D101, which runs behind the dunes, and follow the road for 4.5km towards L'Amélie-sur-Mer. From here, those on foot or bicycle can continue along a coastal path to Hourtin-Plage. In a car, continue on the D101, turning away from the sea for 2.5km.

Turn left and continue for 6.5km to Grayan-et-l'Hôpital, where a hospital, which no longer exists, was founded in the 12th century to receive pilgrims coming from Soulac. The D101 continues south for 11km to Vendays-Montalivet, where there are a number of hotels and campgrounds. Montalivet-les-Bains, a seaside resort, is 8km west on the D102. From Vendays-Montalivet continue south along the D101 for 17km, through the hamlet of Cartignac and across the Marais-dit-Palu, an area of marshland. Continue through **Le Contaut** to reach **Hourtin-Plage** in 8.5km. The small town of **HOURTIN ❷**, a focal point of campgrounds, is 3km south of Cartignac.

From Hourtin, continue south on the D3 for a further 12km and at Carcans turn right on to the D207, skirting the southern end of Lac d'Hourtin-Carcans to reach **MAUBUISSON ❸** in 8.5km. Carcans-Plage is a further 4.5km along the D207, but 3.5km out of Maubuisson the D6e1 leads off to the south to form a very scenic route through the Forêt de Lacanau. After 9km it rejoins the D6 on the edge of **LACANAU-OCEAN ❹**. Head inland on the D6, which follows the northern shore of Lac de Lacanau, reaching the town of **Lacanau** in 12km.

Continue east on the D6 for 16km to Ste-Hélène, then follow the D5 northeast for 10km to Castelnau-de-Médoc, where the D105 heads east for 7km to Margaux, home of the noted wine château. The D2 goes north for 21km, following the Gironde to Pauillac (*see pages 57–8*), then continues for another 8km to Vertheuil, passing the great châteaux of Mouton-Rothschild and Lafite-Rothschild on the way. From Vertheuil take the D204 for 10.5km to Lesparre-Médoc, where it joins the N215, which continues north, returning you to Soulac in 30km. On the way, stop off at the village of **Vensac**, where you can watch corn being ground in the traditional way in an 18th-century stone-built mill.

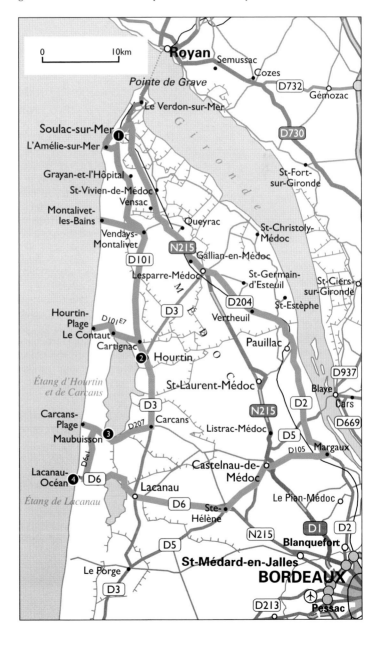

Language

Although English is spoken in most tourist locations it is courteous to attempt to speak some French. The effort is generally appreciated, and may even elicit a reply in perfect English! The following is a very brief list of some useful words and phrases, with approximate pronunciation guides. For driver's vocabulary, see page 28. The *Thomas Cook European 12-Language Phrasebook* (£4.99) lists more than 350 travel phrases in French (and in 11 other European languages).

- **Hello/Goodbye**
  Bonjour/Au revoir *Bawngzhoor/Ohrevwahr*
- **Good evening/Goodnight**
  Bonsoir/Bonne nuit *Bawnswahr/Bon nwee*
- **Yes/No**
  Oui/Non *Wee/Nawn*
- **Please/Thank you (very much)**
  S'il vous plaît/Merci (beaucoup) *Seelvooplay/Mehrsee (bohkoo)*
- **Excuse me, can you help me please?**
  Excusez-moi, pouvez vous m'aider, s'il vous plaît? *Ekskewzehmwah, pooveh voo mehydeh seelvooplay?*
- **Do you speak English?**
  Parlez-vous anglais? *Pahrleh voo ahnglay?*
- **I'm sorry, I don't understand.**
  Pardon, je ne comprends pas. *Pahrdawn, jer ner kawnprawn pah.*
- **I am looking for the tourist information office.**
  Je cherche l'office de tourisme. *Jer shaersh lohfeece de tooreesm.*
- **Do you have a map of the town/area?**
  Avez-vous une carte de la ville/région? *Ahveh-voo ewn cart der lah veel/rehjeeawn?*
- **Do you have a list of hotels?**
  Avez-vous une liste d'hôtels? *Ahveh voo ewn leesst dohtehl?*
- **Do you have any rooms free?**
  Avez vous des chambres disponibles? *Ahveh voo day shahngbr deesspohneebl?*
- **I would like to reserve a single/double room with/without bath/shower.**
  Je voudrais réserver une chambre pour une personne/pour deux personnes avec/sans salle de bain/douche. *Jer voodray rehsehrveh ewn shahngbr poor ewn pehrson/poor der pehrson avek/sawns sal der banne/doosh.*

- **I would like bed and breakfast/(room and) half board/(room and) full board.**
  Je voudrais le petit-déjeuner/la demi-pension/la pension complète. *Jer voodray ler pewtee-dehjerneh/lah dermee-pahngsyawng/lah pahngsyawng kawngplait.*
- **How much is it per night?**
  Quel est le prix pour une nuit? *Khel eh ler pree poor ewn nwee?*
- **I would like to stay for . . . nights.**
  Je voudrais rester . . . nuits. *Jer voodray resteh . . . nwee.*
- **Do you accept traveller's cheques/credit cards?**
  Acceptez-vous les chèques de voyages/les cartes de crédit? *Aksepteh voo leh sheck der vwoyaj/leh kart der krehdee?*
- **I would like a table for two.**
  Je voudrais une table pour deux personnes. *Jer voodray ewn tabl poor der pehrson.*
- **I would like a cup of/two cups of/another coffee/tea.**
  Je voudrais une tasse de/deux tasses de/encore une tasse de café/thé. *Jer voodray ewn tahss der/der tahss der/oncaw ewn tahss der kafeh/teh.*
- **I would like a bottle/glass/two glasses of mineral water/red wine/white wine, please.**
  Je voudrais une bouteille/un verre/deux verres d'eau minérale/de vin rouge/de vin blanc, s'il vous plaît. *Jer voodray ewn bootayy/ang vair/der vair doh mynehral/der vang roozh/der vang blahng, seelvooplay.*
- **Could I have it well cooked/medium/rare, please?**
  Je le voudrais bien cuit/à point/saignant, s'il vous plaît. *Jer ler voodray beeang kwee/ah pwahng/saynyang, seelvooplay.*
- **May I have the bill, please?**
  L'addition, s'il vous plaît? *Laddyssyawng, seelvooplay?*
- **Where is the toilet (restroom), please?**
  Où sont les toilettes, s'il vous plaît? *Oo sawng leh twahlaitt, seelvooplay?*
- **How much does it/this cost?**
  Quel est le prix? *Kehl eh ler pree?*
- **A (half-) kilo of . . . please.**
  Un (demi-) kilo de . . . s'il vous plaît. *Ang (dermee) keelo der . . . seelvooplay.*

Index

Acknowledgements

Project management: Cambridge Publishing Management Limited
Project editor: Karen Beaulah
Series design: Fox Design
Cover design: Liz Lyons Design
Layout and map work: Concept 5D/Cambridge Publishing Management Ltd
Repro and image setting: PDQ Digital Media Solutions Ltd/
                                Cambridge Publishing Management Ltd

We would like to thank Image Select International/Chris Fairclough Colour Library for the photographs used in this book, to whom the copyright in the photographs belongs, with the exception of the following:

David Browne (page 47); **J Allan Cash** (pages 102, 104, 122, 212, 214, 219 and 257); **Dreamstime.com** (page 27 Spectrumoflight); **Les Eyzies-de-Tayac Sireuil** (page 35); **John Heseltine** (page 18); **Spectrum Colour Library** (pages 98, 100, 108, 110, 114, 118, 121, 125, 126, 128 and 220); **Pictures Colour Library** (pages 59, 126 and 137); **Wikimedia Commons** (pages 112 Iwan van Rienen and 195 Sébastien Crêteur); **World Pictures** (pages 13, 40, 56, 67, 145, 268 and 270).

Picture research: Image Select International

Feedback form

We're committed to providing the very best up-to-date information in our travel guides and constantly strive to make them as useful as they can be. You can help us to improve future editions by letting us have your feedback. Just take a few minutes to complete and return this form to us.

When did you buy this book? ....
....

Where did you buy it? (Please give town/city and, if possible, name of retailer)
....
....

When did you/do you intend to travel in Dordogne? ....
....

For how long (approx)? ....

How many people in your party? ....

Which cities, national parks and other locations did you/do you intend mainly to visit?
....
....
....
....

Did you/will you:
❏ Make all your travel arrangements independently?
❏ Travel on a fly-drive package?
Please give brief details: ....
....

Did you/do you intend to use this book:
❏ For planning your trip?   ❏ Both?
❏ During the trip itself?

Did you/do you intend also to purchase any of the following travel publications for your trip?
A road map/atlas (please specify) ....
Other guidebooks (please specify) ....

Have you used any other Thomas Cook guidebooks in the past? If so, which?

....

....

Please rate the following features of *Drive Around Dordogne and Western France* for their value to you (circle VU for 'very useful', U for 'useful', NU for 'little or no use'):

The Travel Facts section on pages 14–22	VU	U	NU
The Driver's Guide section on pages 23–29	VU	U	NU
The Touring itineraries on pages 40–41	VU	U	NU
The recommended driving routes throughout the book	VU	U	NU
Information on towns and cities, National Parks, etc	VU	U	NU
The maps of towns and cities, parks, etc	VU	U	NU

Please use this space to tell us about any features that in your opinion could be changed, improved, or added in future editions of the book, or any other comments you would like to make concerning the book:

....

....

....

....

....

....

....

Your age category: ❑ 21–30 ❑ 31–40 ❑ 41–50 ❑ over 50

Your name: Mr/Mrs/Miss/Ms ....

(First name or initials) ....

(Last name) ....

Your full address: (Please include postal or zip code)

....

....

....

....

....

....

Your daytime telephone number: ....

Please detach this page and send it to: Drive Around Series Editor, Thomas Cook Publishing, PO Box 227, The Thomas Cook Business Park, 9 Coningsby Road, Peterborough PE3 8SB.

Alternatively, you can e-mail us at: *books@thomascook.com*